DATE DUE

Critical Essays on
Melville's
Billy Budd, Sailor

Critical Essays on Melville's Billy Budd, Sailor

Robert Milder

G. K. Hall & Co. • Boston, Massachusetts

Library of Congress Cataloging in Publication Data

Critical essays on Melville's Billy Budd, Sailor.
      p. cm. — (Critical essays on American literature)
    Includes index.
    1. Melville, Herman, 1819-1891. Billy Budd.
I. Milder, Robert. II. Series.
PS2384.B7C75 1989   813'.3   88-35784
ISBN 0-8161-8889-0   (alk. paper)

CRITICAL ESSAYS ON AMERICAN LITERATURE

This series seeks to anthologize the most important criticism on a wide variety of topics and writers in American literature. Our readers will find in various volumes not only a generous selection of reprinted articles and reviews but original essays, bibliographies, manuscript sections, and other materials brought to public attention for the first time. *Critical Essays on Melville's "Billy Budd, Sailor"* contains a balanced historical record of critical reaction to Herman Melville's famous novel. The book contains both early reviews and comments and a broad selection of more modern scholarship. Included are an essay on the growth of the manuscript by Harrison Hayford and Merton M. Sealts, Jr., and early estimates by John Middleton Murry, John Freeman, Raymond Weaver, and Lewis Mumford. Among the authors of reprinted articles are E. L. Grant Watson, Joseph Schiffman, Richard Harter Fogle, Warner Berthoff, Paul Brodtkorb, Jr., Joyce Sparer Adler, and Barbara Johnson. In addition to an extensive introduction by Robert Milder, tracing the history of *Billy Budd* and critical reactions to it, an essay commissioned specifically for publication in this volume by James McIntosh explores the novel as a romance, and a revised essay by James R. Hurtgen discusses the political implications of Melville's narrative. We are confident that this book will make a permanent and significant contribution to American literary study.

Northeastern University   JAMES NAGEL, GENERAL EDITOR

CONTENTS

Contents

INTRODUCTION

Published posthumously in 1924, *Billy Budd, Sailor* has become Melville's second most widely read book, and his most divisive. While interpreters may dispute the symbolism of *Moby-Dick* or the treatment of race in "Benito Cereno," nothing in Melville studies approaches the antagonism with which rival camps have regarded one another since positions began to harden in the 1950s. Quite simply, *Billy Budd*, a masterwork of ambiguity, taps commitments of ethical, political, and philosophical value that make its criticism peculiarly confessional and urgent. Like "Platonist or Aristotelian," "conservative or radical," the tale separates its readers into timeless parties of the mind, though not without allowing them their distinct temporal coloring of method and ideology. Indeed, the development of the critical debate comprises an unusually manifest record of English studies from the waning of literary / biographical humanism in the late 1940s through the rise and triumph of New Criticism to the battles between varieties of traditionalism and poststructuralism waged to define the criticism of the 1980s and beyond.

GENESIS AND HISTORY OF THE TEXT

When Melville resigned his position in the New York Custom House on 31 December 1885 after nineteen years of service, it is doubtful his plans included a sustained venture in fiction. Since the late 1850s Melville had devoted his literary energies almost exclusively to poetry, publishing two important but little-noticed volumes, *Battle-Pieces and Aspects of the War* (1866) and *Clarel* (1876), and drafting numerous other poems he would revise in the leisure of his retirement. From this older work and a significant body of new poems written after 1885, Melville assembled three late verse collections: *John Marr and Other Sailors* (1888) and *Timoleon* (1891), each published privately in an edition of twenty-five copies, and *Weeds and Wildings Chiefly: With a Rose or Two*, left unfinished at his death on 28 September 1891.

Billy Budd, Sailor grew out of the prose headnote to an early version of the poem "Billy in the Darbies," apparently intended for *John Marr*. As the reverie of a sailor facing execution, the original prose/verse composition outwardly resembles the deathbed monologue "Tom Deadlight," but its evocation of the simpler, more colorful world of wooden ship days links it as well to other poems in the collection: to "John Marr" itself, an aging ex-sailor's reminiscence of former shipmates; to "Jack Roy," Melville's elegy for his old messmate from the *United States*, Jack Chase, to whom he would dedicate *Billy Budd*; and to "Bridegroom Dick," an *ubi sunt* tribute to martial gallantry that passingly alludes to Melville's naval cousin Guert Gansevoort ("Tom Tight"), "lieutenant in the brig-o'-war famed / When an officer was hung for an arch-mutineer," a reference to the *Somers* incident of 1842, long considered a source for *Billy Budd*, in which Gansevoort joined in sentencing three alleged conspirators to death.

Melville's initial Billy was "an older man, condemned for fomenting mutiny and apparently guilty as charged."[1] At some point during the writing, however, Billy's situation came to dramatic life, and by November 1888 Melville had transformed his ballad into what he then considered a complete narrative of more than 150 manuscript leaves (well under half the final number) in which Billy, now the upright barbarian of later versions, is sentenced to hang for striking and killing his false accuser, Master-at-arms John Claggart. The focus of this second-phase *Billy Budd* seems to have been the fate of good-natured innocence amid the mantraps of the world, a theme in Melville's mid-century fiction and again in *John Marr* but one that began to assume theological overtones as Melville retouched his portrait of Claggart. Questions of law and political morality were well in the background at this stage of composition, and "So minor was the commander's part . . . that only a few leaves stood between the killing of Claggart and the beginning of the ballad."[2] Melville's action was firmly in place, that is to say, before he returned to *Billy Budd* during the last years of his life to develop the characterization of Captain Vere and add the chapters between Claggart's death and Billy's that have long claimed the bulk of critical attention. Melville was still revising the language and emphasis of his story when he died, leaving behind a chronologically complete manuscript dotted with inconsistencies and in such physical disarray that an authoritative text of *Billy Budd* would not appear until the Hayford-Sealts edition of 1962, long after the critical debate, founded on the flawed texts of Raymond Weaver and F. Barron Freeman, had taken shape.[3]

The composition and textual history of *Billy Budd* are discussed in detail by Harrison Hayford and Merton M. Sealts, Jr., in the editors' introduction to their Reading Text, a portion of which is reprinted here as a prologue to the criticism, and in their commentary on their accompanying Genetic Text, a literal transcription of the surviving manuscript leaves. Aside from differences of wording and punctuation, the Hayford-Sealts Reading Text departs from earlier editions in four important particulars: 1) it omits two paragraphs on the background of the age erroneously regarded as Melville's preface to the story and invoked by various critics as key evidence for their readings; 2) it omits two apparently superseded leaves on Claggart's depravity headed "Lawyers, Experts, Clergy" that Weaver included in chapter 11 and Freeman printed as chapter 12; 3) it titles the story *Billy Budd, Sailor (An Inside Narrative)* rather than *Billy Budd, Foretopman,* lending prominence to Melville's cryptic parenthesis; and 4) it rechristens (and de-Christens) Vere's warship the truculently martial *Bellipotent,* Melville's later choice, in place of the more honorific *Indomitable.*[4] Not all critics have been pleased by these changes, and a few have chosen to found their readings on Milton R. Stern's 1975 re-editing of the Hayford-Sealts Genetic Text, which, adopting a principle of inclusiveness toward "questionable material," restores Melville's comments on "the Spirit of the Age" (repositioned as paragraphs 4 and 5 of the trial scene) and joins Freeman in assigning "Lawyers, Experts, Clergy" to a separate chapter 12.[5] The forthcoming Northwestern-Newberry edition of *Billy Budd* is expected to follow the Hayford-Sealts Reading Text on all significant matters of content while pursuing a more conservative policy toward regularizing Melville's spelling and punctuation.

THE DEVELOPMENT OF *BILLY BUDD* CRITICISM

The discovery of a deathbed manuscript is a natural invitation for critics to fashion a myth of closure for an author's career, especially a career like Melville's so turbulent in its metaphysical and social rebellion and so enigmatic in its thirty-five years of prose silence. The archetypal plot and characterization of *Billy Budd* spoke directly to this presumption of a "final word," and responding to the exalted serenity of the hanging scene, early commentators unhesitatingly pronounced the book (in E. L. Grant Watson's phrase) a "testament of acceptance."[6] Like Shakespeare in *The Winter's Tale* or Milton in *Samson Agonistes,* Melville, it appeared, had surmounted his anger and reconciled himself to . . . what? Much of the confusion, wrangling, and downright ill will of *Billy Budd* criticism stems from the failure of early readers to specify what Melville's testament was an acceptance *of.* To Raymond Weaver, for example, *Billy Budd* was an effort to "justify the ways of God to man," yet Weaver's neat Miltonic formulation was almost directly contradicted by his appeal to the celebration of human greatness that marks high tragedy. With "no friends among the living or dead, no help in God, only calamity everywhere," Weaver wrote, the tragic hero may yet find "in the very intensity of his affliction . . . the splendour undiscoverable in any gentler fate. . . . Only when worldly disaster has worked its utmost can we realize that there remains something in man's soul which is for ever beyond the grasp of the accidents of existence, with power in its own right to make life beautiful. Only through tragedy of this type could Melville affirm his everlasting yea."[7]

The difficulty that vexed interpreters like Weaver was translating the tonal sublimity of the hanging scene into thematic meaning. Did *Billy Budd* justify the ways of God to man, or did it deify the ways of extraordinary men in a world abandoned by God? Intoxicated by the prose of the hanging scene, Weaver was elusive about whether the "affirmation" it seemed to bespeak was Christian or humanistic, preferring (like most of his contemporaries) to dissolve the issue in rhetoric about the tragic vision.

It is ironic that the testament of acceptance theory should have become identified with Christian reconciliation, for its leading proponent, Watson, clearly adopted a humanistic line. Where early admirers commonly patronized *Billy Budd* as "the simplest of stories,"[8] a parable of good and evil whose meaning was "so obvious that one shrinks from underlining it,"[9] Watson found the tale unfathomably deep in human content and marked by a density of poetic implication that resisted any univocal statement of theme. An acquiescence to tragic necessity lay at the heart of Watson's reading, yet when Watson described Melville as "no longer a rebel"[10] he did not mean that Melville had accepted God's ways or society's but simply that he had ceased to torment himself about either; he had turned to the mystery of human behavior and, in the execution scene, had rendered, not an otherworldly redemption, but rather the wondrous secular "communion between personality at its purest, most-God-given form" — Billy — "and character, hard-hammered from the imperfect material of life on the battleship *Indomitable*" — Vere.[11]

As articulated by Watson and later by William Ellery Sedgwick in *Herman Melville: The Tragedy of Mind* (1944), the humanistic version of the acceptance theory sought to enclose the tragic sacrifice of Billy within the radiant vision of private apotheosis evoked by the hanging scene and the closeted interview between Billy and Vere. In one form or another, the argument has been a constant in *Billy Budd* criticism, and it receives its most eloquent expression in Warner Berthoff's " 'Certain Phenomenal Men': The Example of *Billy Budd*" (1960), which rejects systematic Christian and mythic interpretations and identifies Melville's theme as "the motions of magnanimity under the most agonizing worldly duress."[12]

Surveying the body of acceptance theories, Christian and humanistic alike, one is struck by how few of them contend for an implausible volteface reconciliation with God and Creation. Their greater weakness is their insistence on the eternal and immutable in *Billy Budd* to the near exclusion of the social, as if to allow the exigencies of time and place were to diminish the grandeur of the tale. Temperament is a factor here, but so for early readers was literary training. Berthoff aside, acceptance critics belonged to a pre-New Critical generation keenly sensitive to *Billy Budd* as spiritual drama yet lax in its attention to the nuances of language and technique through which the particularities of history were made to modify the enclosing structure of exemplary action. Nothing in the logic of their position required acceptance critics to focus narrowly upon the hanging and interview scenes, to identify Melville's judgment with Vere's, to sever the tragic from the political, and to write with a generalist's disdain for evidence, but almost universally they did so, leaving themselves vulnerable to a later generation of ironists who would challenge both the substance of their reading and their critical naiveté.

The essay that inaugurated the debate, "Melville's Final Stage, Irony: A Re–examination of *Billy Budd* Criticism" (1950) by Joseph Schiffman (on the suggestion of Gay Wilson Allen), had few of the virtues of the New Criticism and none of the old, but its point was sufficiently well-taken to disrupt a dull consensus. Schiffman's Melville was the social rebel of midcentury whose commitments remained constant through forty years and "who, late in life, turned to irony for his final attack upon evil."[13] Irony is more easily asserted than proved, yet rather than comb the text for evidence Schiffman chose to appeal to Melville's early work, chiding Watson and others for their neglect of literary context yet conspicuously ignoring the politically charged poetry of Melville's last twenty-five years. By any standard, Schiffman's case for Billy as an unwitting prophet of bluejacket solidarity and naval reform, though not without merit, was poorly made; his most telling insight was into the latent ideological bias that colored Watson's language, an insight that extended the ground of discussion to the interpreter's implied politics and anticipated two points that partisan critics like Brook Thomas would argue with greater sophistication years later: that no readings of literature are ideologically innocent and that to commend Melville's supposed acceptance of Billy's execution is to confess one's own conservative bias and align oneself with the repressive society of the book.[14]

Following Schiffman's lead, critics of the 1950s reversed the judgment of their predecessors and pronounced *Billy Budd* ironic in mode, social or antireligious in content, and rebellious in posture. Indicative of the new counterorthodoxy was Phil Withim's "*Billy Budd*: Testament of Resistance" (1959), which distanced Melville from the "narrow, literal, prejudiced" Vere and evolved the lesson that "Man should not resign himself to the presence of evil but must always strive against it."[15] Pursuing his thesis of Melville's lifelong "quarrel with God," Lawrance Thompson (1952) took a more radical position by detaching Melville not only from Vere ("an emblem of divine depravity") but from the narrator, a believing Christian whom Melville "arranges to let us see" is "just a wee bit stupid."[16] Variations on Thompson's approach, some religious in theme, some political, appear in later readings by Stanton Garner (1978), Lyon Evans, Jr. (1982), and James Duban (1983), but most ironists have tended to find their evidence in language, allusion, symbol, and structure, not in point of view.[17]

Though written at a time of New Critical ascendance and nominally au courant, the ironist readings of the 1950s were seldom more close-grained than those they attacked. The outstanding New Critical interpretation was in fact an anti-ironist one: Richard Harter Fogle's "*Billy Budd*: The Order of the Fall" (1960), which, together with Fogle's "*Billy Budd*—

Acceptance or Irony" (1958), tried to refound the acceptance theory on the more technical understanding of irony advanced by the New Critics. In two influential works of the late 1940s, *The Well-Wrought Urn* and "Irony as a Principle of Structure," Cleanth Brooks had offered a modernist defense of poetry as a unique and valuable form of knowledge by defining what he deemed its essential characteristic, irony, as 1) a special use of language in which all statements are warped by "the pressure of the context" in ways antithetical to the straightforward discourse of philosophy and science; and 2) a complexity of attitude that "does not leave out what is apparently hostile to its dominant tone" but preserves and "triumphs over the apparently contradictory and conflicting elements of experience by unifying them into a new pattern."[18] Applying Brooksian principles to *Billy Budd*, Fogle was able to incorporate the "ironies and ambiguities" that resistance critics had uncovered by contending that these elements "do not reverse the direct statements upon which our sense of the meaning rests, but modify, enrich, and complete them."[19] So, too, he could recognize crucial ambivalences on the part of the narrator and still affirm a "Melville-the-man-and-the-artist . . . quite complex enough to encompass both assertion and negation, the hope and the fear, the generality and its completion by the particular."[20]

Had Fogle been more open-minded in considering the resistance argument, his essay might have effected the brilliant synthesis of opposites we still await. Fogle's concessions were only tactical and minor, however, and his avowed purpose (more orthodox, religiously, than most resistance critics') was "to emphasize the large affirmative elements of *Billy Budd*, which make of it a celebration rather than a condemnation of reality and its mysterious Master."[21] Beyond the claims of ideology or even of religion, Fogle's essay seems premised on the root fact of metaphysical taste. A tragic *Billy Budd*, Fogle argues, "portrays men as better than they are" and is dignified and sublime,[22] while a subversively ironic *Billy Budd* demeans its author and humanity both and "would if it existed be cheap, puerile, and perverse."[23] Whole areas of inquiry are thus foreclosed a priori by Fogle, to whom any suggestion that Melville treats Vere with psychological irony or locates his narrative against a backdrop of cosmic or social injustice threatens to reduce the tale to ugly mockery.

As accomplished as they are, Fogle's essays are symptomatic of the hostility that has divided acceptance and resistance critics beyond any legitimate interpretive differences. In "The Problem of *Billy Budd* " (1965) Edward H. Rosenberry addressed this situation directly, proposing to "end the war" between straight readers and ironists but on terms that demanded nothing less than unconditional surrender by the latter.[24] Rosenberry's keenest points were directed at the underpinnings and methodological lapses of the resistance argument, in his view a form of modish irony-hunting (of the non-New Critical variety) prompted by its advocates' belief that the Melville they admired "could not possibly have written" an obeisance to social evil.[25] A critique of shoddy reasoning was much in order by that time, yet chiding the ironists for their failings also meant, for Rosenberry, dismissing their claims about a political or antireligious *Billy Budd*. The issue, as Rosenberry saw it, was simple: "are we to take Melville at his word and read *Billy Budd* as a parable of the plight of innocence in a 'man-of-war world,' or are we to find beneath its tragic benediction a satiric attack on the complacency of earthly and heavenly authority?"[26] Like Fogle, Rosenberry sided unequivocally with the straight readers and tragedians (synonymous in his mind), and it did not occur to him that his either/or question might be factitious insofar as the plight of innocence in *Billy Budd* derived tragically from earthly misgovernment and heavenly silence.

Reductive and crudely argued, ironist readings were easy game for an incisive critic like Rosenberry, yet at the core of the ironist position was an emotional truth that could not easily be denied: a feeling of outrage at Billy's execution as visceral and overwhelming as the acceptance critics' feeling of exaltation. Nearly every reader shares both emotions to some degree, opposite though they are and resistant though they seem to thematic reconciliation. The preference for a straight or an ironic reading of *Billy Budd* depends partly on whether one responds primarily to the serenity of Melville's prose or to the horror of his action — and beyond that, perhaps, on the moral susceptibility that causes one reader to shiver at Billy's "God bless Captain Vere!" and another (as Schiffman said) to "gag."[27] The humbling reality, in any case, is that Melville seems to contain both emotions not simply at once but *as one*, and that the history of the acceptance/resistance debate is the disheartening spectacle of two parties almost constitutionally unable to appreciate each other's hold on the truth and thereby rise to the fullness of Melville's.

The conflict between acceptance and resistance critics raged most visibly from 1950 to 1965, after which it did not so much abate as assume a different set of terms. Questions of Melville's reconciliation with God and the universe were shunted to the margins, save as the story was taken to illustrate what Wendell Glick had previously called "the eternal conflict between absolute morality and social expediency."[28] The newer interest was in politics, defined inclusively by Milton R. Stern as "deep attitudes and visions, often unspoken and even unformulated, concerning the nature of human possibility and, therefore, the nature and possibility and desirability of liberation and, therefore again, the nature and function of the state, the very concept of government."[29]

The development of political criticism from the early 1960s to the mid-1980s is difficult to summarize, partly because there was so little "development" at all. Despite the ferment in literary theory, New Critical readings of *Billy Budd* continued to prevail, "New Criticism" having come to stand for the classes of questions — scholarly, biographical, historical, methodological — one didn't ask. Solid contextual studies like Stern's "The Politics of

Melville's Poetry" (1975) were a rarity among arguments for a conservative Melville, while up-to-date Marxist readings like Brook Thomas's "*Billy Budd* and the Judgment of Silence" (1982) found strange allies in the naive polemics that sometimes succeeded them. Several of the more important contributions came from professors of law and political science and from literary critics who wrote in an interdisciplinary idiom. The most pronounced thematic tendency was an increased skepticism toward the character and motives of Captain Vere, though few later analyses were as subtle and judicious as Merlin Bowen's in *The Long Encounter* (1960).

The controversy over Vere might never have flourished as it did if the surgeon's doubts concerning Vere's procedures and even his sanity (the primary internal evidence against Vere) had not been reinforced by legal arguments based on eighteenth-century naval practice. In their "Notes and Commentary" to the Chicago edition of 1962, Hayford and Sealts demonstrated that Vere was not empowered to try and execute Billy under the laws governing the case, a conclusion reached independently by C. B. Ives (1962), who added that Vere "could undoubtedly find support in the British naval customs that allowed latitude to a captain's authority in defiance of statute."[30] Within this ambiguous legal context, issues of politics and character leaped to prominence and beckoned critics to read between the lines. Ives's own conjecture was psychological: "the Captain's sudden decision to hang Billy was a sacrificial gesture, born out of a kind of self-punishment that had become habitual in Vere's life" and aimed at denying the affective, feminine side of his nature, which Billy provoked.[31] A 1982 reading by Richard I. Weisberg, a professor of literature turned professor of law, supplemented Ives's evidence (with fewer qualifications about usage) but offered a contrasting portrait of Vere as an able but unheroic commander who chafed at his deficiencies and revenged himself upon Billy as a stand-in for his real love/hate object, "the envied, magnificently overt Admiral Nelson."[32]

Ives's and Weisberg's arguments depend not only on Melville's knowledge of British naval law (which seems to have been acquired after he determined his plot) but on his communication of that knowledge to the reader through the surgeon, a figure of uncertain authority whose opinions introduce more ambiguities than they resolve. The legal facts of the time have no bearing on *Billy Budd* if Melville, for fictive purposes, chose not to invoke them. In that case, the text would create a purely internal legal world, one response to which, as Charles A. Reich suggested in 1967, would be to accept Vere's statement of the necessities that bind him and consider the nature of law itself as Melville depicts it, logical in its forms and necessary for social order yet desperately in need of "the imagination and the insight of art" if it is not to "imprison the human spirit" it was meant to serve.[33] In retrospect, Reich's argument points toward the revitalization of institutional forms from within, or revolution by consciousness, that he would later prophesy in his critique of the modern corporate state, *The Greening of America* (1970). A signpost of a more recent academic radicalism — revisionary Marxist historicism rather than neo-Emersonian millennialism — is Brook Thomas's "The Legal Fictions of Herman Melville and Lemuel Shaw" (1984), which, drawing its inspiration from critical legal studies, traces Vere's "forms, measured forms" to their roots in institutional and class interest and presents the law as an instrument by which a ruling group legitimates the status quo.

Despite the scholarship and intellectual vigor they have frequently brought to the criticism, legal approaches to *Billy Budd* tend to founder on the indeterminacy of the text, which forces interpreters either to rely on external evidence or to exchange the role of legal historian for that of social philosopher or political advocate. In this respect, legal readings, too, are "confessional" and belong to a larger group of political/philosophical interpretations (most of them latently, and some openly, ideological) that evolved concurrently and dealt with the nature of man and his relationship to social institutions. The parable of good and evil that early readers found "so obvious" in *Billy Budd* became, for critics in this tradition, an ambiguous drama of the fall from natural simplicity into the labyrinths of politics and history. Exploring this theme, interpreters frequently secularized the Adamic imagery of the tale's opening chapters and likened Billy to Melville's sensuous, good-natured but fundamentally preconscious Polynesians doomed to extinction by the advance of technological civilization, which Melville identified with war, the conquest of nature, social oppression, and psychological and sexual repression. To some readers like Christopher W. Sten (1975), *Billy Budd* posed the philosophical question of whether "the end of civilization justif[ied] the inevitable sacrifice of the natural man";[34] to others like John B. Noone, Jr. (1957), it dramatized the iron logic of history that seemed to require the sacrifice, which Melville had first described in *Typee* and subsequently come to ponder in the opposing terms of Paine and Burke, Rousseau and Hobbes.

In light of the developing but needless division between social critics and tragedians that marked the writings of the 1950s, Noone's essay was notable in conceiving the story as tragic *because* social; it was also one of the first efforts to draw historical optimism from the ending of the tale, for while Noone found Melville agreeing with Hobbes on the necessity of rational order, he tried to mitigate the sacrifice of Billy by inferring from Melville's portrait of the dessicated Vere the hope that "a judicious combination of instinct and reason can meliorate the crueler aspects of formalism, eventually producing a new set of conditions which require less repressive forms."[35] The impulse behind Noone's reading, and behind others that would express a similar hope, was a visible reluctance to leave Melville's narrative as bleakly resigned to the rule of authority at its action might suggest. So long as the problem of social injustice was absorbed in a more inclusive affirmation, as it was for acceptance critics, "the redemptive sacrifice of Billy [in Thomas J. Scorza's words] both indicated and justified Melville's tragic acceptance of convention, law, expediency, and authority."[36] Not so for secular-minded but nonironist readers like Noone or Scorza himself (1979) who, skeptical of both the acceptance critics' everlasting yea and the resistance critics' "NO! in thunder," saw *Billy Budd* as a complex and agonized political meditation and sought to define the precise character of its vision. If Melville was committed to resting society not on the laws of nature or the will of God but on man's "creative capacity, operating in the light of his own history" and without the assurance that temporal wrongs will be rectified in a divine accounting,[37] what type of society did his commitment imply and what philosophical conviction guided it?

For readers who posed these questions, the issue was not whether *Billy Budd* was tragic or social in content, grave or ironic in tone, but whether its gravely ironic social tragedy testified to a conservative or a progressive Melville of some particular philosophical stripe. Milton R. Stern (1975) and James R. Hurtgen (1982) both presented a conservative Melville who affirmed "the regularities of custom and law,"[38] yet Stern's Melville was a protoexistentialist who viewed man as the beleaguered but heroic architect of his world, while Hurtgen's was a post-Machiavellian realist who adopted a *"Rhetoric of Concealment"* to disguise the unsettling truth that political life took place in an unsanctified mid-world "not only separate from the divine and the demonic . . . but *opposed* to the divine *no less* than to the demonic."[39] By contrast, Joyce Sparer Adler in *"Billy Budd* and Melville's Philosophy of War" (1976) argued strenuously for the tale's indictment of the ruling militaristic order and (developing Schiffman's point of 1950) for its vision of a more peaceful and humane society augured by Billy's legacy to the crew. Less overtly political, John W. Rathbun's *"Billy Budd* and the Limits of Perception" (1965) balanced the elements of protest, irony, wintry acquiescence, and regret that comprise Melville's tone and found in the tale a sober acknowledgement of human fallenness that resisted ideological categories. "Our insight . . . clogged by forms and conventions," Rathbun summarized, "we fail to properly understand our saints," though "occasionally [as in the execution scene] we can be stirred to a muted awareness of our humanity," if never quite to a true comprehension of our condition.[40]

Among critics who focused more restrictively on the judgment, behavior, and motives of Captain Vere, a courtroom atmosphere came to pervade much of the discussion, with two lines of argument prevailing—the first, ethical and political: what Vere ought to have done (an inquiry into Melville's politics, which, pursued in a scholarly vacuum, commonly resolved itself into what the critic would have done);[41] the second, psychological and dramatic: why Vere, as characterized by Melville, acted as he did and could scarcely have acted otherwise. Seldom have the political readings been adequately psychological or the psychological readings astutely political. Among interpreters critical of Vere (by far the larger party), Merlin Bowen (1960) most successfully joined understanding with moral judgment in his portrait of an "overcivilized" Vere, sincere but wrongheaded, and eliciting our sympathy in his tortured situation but by no means our assent. The limitation of Bowen's reading, from a political standpoint, is its focus on Vere's Burkean conservatism as an essentially temperamental phenomenon (a need for stable forms and fixed opinions that issued from a deep fear of "patternless life"[42]) and its corresponding neglect of the ways in which "Melville's narrative *accounts* for what Billy's captain is and does in terms of his class and military vocation."[43] Narrowly conceived, efforts at such "accounting" have sometimes made for splenetic distortions of Vere's character and motives,[44] but at their best, as in Adler's "*Billy Budd* and Melville's Philosophy of War," they have gone far toward illuminating Vere as a roundly human but representative product of his sociohistorical world.

Though ironic readings of Vere have generally been vehicles for evolving a specific political lesson from *Billy Budd*, it is also possible, as Ralph W. Willett (1967) showed, to understand Vere's failings metapolitically not as Melville's attacks upon a particular society or even upon social repression in general but as his reflection on the circumstanced nature of all political judgment — in Willett's words, on the tragically ironic fact "that man, at any level below that of the hero, is the victim of his own ambiguities and inconsistencies, and of history."[45] In readings like Willett's, *Billy Budd* achieves a tragic universality not by scanting the politics and psychology of governance (as Fogle and Rosenberry had insisted) but by dramatizing their inevitable presence.

The persistent division among *Billy Budd*'s interpreters, repeated on every plane of critical sophistication and infused subtly or crudely with many of the same passions, has suggested to some readers that *Billy Budd* is an indeterminate work, not only because it is unfinished (and therefore might have been brought to clarity had Melville lived[46]) but by design. Indeed, as Paul Brodtkorb, Jr., argued in 1967, indeterminacy, together with the strategies it evokes for fixing "the always problematic nature of the *other*,"[47] is finally what *Billy Budd* is about. And just as the book's characters try to negotiate experience by subsuming the mysterious "other" (notably Billy) to their own particular mode of being, or phenomenological "language," so the warring factions of acceptance and resistance critics, straight readers and ironists, conservatives and progressives, subsume an ambiguous text to their characteristic ways of ordering the world and assigning value. "[W]e stake ourselves on what we see in books," Brodtkorb commented, "just as on what we see in life."[48]

It is a measure of the distance between late 1960s activism and late 1970s deconstruction that where Brodtkorb, while insisting on indeterminacy, acknowledged both our disposition toward ethical choice and the pressures in the text impelling us to choose, Barbara Johnson (1979) saw a paralyzing skepticism as the very essence and mode of the tale. Recasting elements of Brodtkorb's argument in Derridean terms, Johnson offered *Billy Budd* as a parable of "reading," or interpreting the problematic relationship between the signifier and the signified, that operated both within the text and among its various construers. Billy himself (like acceptance critics) was a "literal" reader who took experience at face value; Claggart (like resistance critics), an "ironic" reader who reversed the outward meaning of the sign; and Vere (like would-be adjudicators of the criticism), a reader of readings who needed first to decide between rival versions of the truth and later to establish a suitable context for judging Billy's act. By invoking a narrow and rigid construction of the law rather than other contexts available to him, Vere predetermined the verdict of the court (much as critics predetermine their reading of the story by the frame of reference they bring to it). The issue for Johnson, however, was not whether Vere was right or wrong, for what Melville was dramatizing in *Billy Budd* was not a political conviction but an epistemological one: the dependence of "every act of judgment" upon "the position of the judge within a structure of value," for which there could ultimately be no extra-systemic justification.[49]

Johnson's skepticism toward all grounds of authority would seem to exempt her argument from political advocacy, but, in fact, countered Brook Thomas in *"Billy Budd* and the Judgment of Silence" (1982), a direct attack upon Johnson and deconstruction, all readings have ideological bearings and Johnson's refusal to judge Vere involved her in a silent acquiescence to social tyranny that revealed "a conservative ideology."[50] Variations on "judge" and "judgment" figure heavily in Thomas's "with me/agin' me" argument, which makes small distinction between literary judgment (the interpretation of textual meaning) and ethical judgment (the bestowal of praise or blame upon fictive characters as if they were engaged in a life situation). Thomas does not dispute Johnson's claim of textual indeterminacy; rather, in an effort to preempt deconstruction, he makes indeterminacy the basis for appealing beyond the text to the explanatory framework of Marxism — itself an ungrounded "text," as Johnson might reply, but a text of such methodological utility and moral valor, Thomas contends, that one is pragmatically justified in invoking it.

Marxism provides Thomas with what Frank Lentricchia calls one of the basic tools of the "activist intellectual," "a theory of reading that will instigate a culturally suspicious, trouble-making readership."[51] The approach works in Thomas's hands largely because in using literature to reorient an audience toward political life, Thomas is insightful about and reasonably faithful to the literary "facts" of *Billy Budd*, though some may feel that his Manichaean divisiveness misrepresents the tragic complexity of experience on which Melville understood a humane democracy to rest. Thomas's attention, in any case, is not matched by overtly partisan critics like H. Bruce Franklin (1984), who calls the story "fundamentally unambiguous" and blames "the confusion (or worse) of some academics" for "depriv[ing] us of its guiding light";[52] nor is it equaled by more ingenious, covertly partisan critics like James Duban (1983), who (with barely a nod to textual evidence) dismisses the story's "arch-conservative"[53] narrator as utterly unreliable and posits a backstage Melville curiously "like a self-portrait of a modern academic."[54]

The flourishing of partisan and hortatory readings of *Billy Budd* is ground for reconsidering E. D. Hirsch's simplistic but useful distinction between interpretation, which concerns itself with the "objective" (or authorial) meaning of a work, and criticism, which places the work in an extra-literary context of value.[55] "Objective interpretation" is a mirage on historical and psychological counts both, but the fact that we can never fully possess ourselves of the author's consciousness or escape from our own is no basis for denying that there are degrees of objectivity and a greater or lesser responsibility to a text and respect for the conditions under which it was produced. Restoring a work so far as possible to an authorial context is only one of many legitimate critical enterprises, but with a text like *Billy Budd*, rife with uncertainties and almost uniquely susceptible to inkblot projections, it seems particularly well-suited both for advancing new lines of interpretation and for weighing the probability of established ones.

As a first step, "Scholars and critics wishing to minimize the subjective element in their approach to *Billy Budd, Sailor*," as Merton M. Sealts, Jr., observed, "will need to devote more attention than their predecessors to the story as the work of an older Melville"[56] and as a book at once continuous and discontinuous with his mid-century fiction. The similarities of setting and theme are obvious and tend to lure readers unacquainted with Melville's later writings into an ill-founded assurance of familiarity. Ironists, especially, find the nostalgic, apparently conservative narrator of *Billy Budd* inconsistent with the Melville of 1850, although a reading of *Battle-Pieces*, *Clarel*, and *John Marr* would demonstrate that Melville's ideas about history, progress, and egalitarian democracy underwent a major reorientation in the decade beginning with his journey to the Holy Land (1856–57) and ending with the Civil War.

Except for Richard Harter Fogle's brief but excellent discussion of Melville's poetry in "*Billy Budd*: The Order of the Fall," Milton R. Stern's "The Politics of Melville's Poetry," a section from Stern's 1975 introduction to *Billy Budd*, was the first important effort to bring the pressure of literary context to bear on the dispute between straight readers and ironists. In Stern's view, the "general conservatism . . . unmistakable in all the poetry which was the genesis of the narrative" makes it "clear that if one is to take into account the mind of the writer when evaluating the written product, the conservative tone of the tale is to be taken not ironically but at face value."[57] Critics may use the narrative for whatever didactic purpose they wish, Stern implies, but to speak responsibly of

"Melville" in *Billy Budd* means submitting oneself to the probabilities of authorial context, whether or not their political tendencies accord with one's own.

Methodologically, of course, Stern is right, and the thoroughness of his argument for a conservative Melville may be one reason why progressive-minded critics have almost universally chosen to neglect the poetry. Yet one can agree with Stern's advocacy of contextualism and still take issue with his interpretation and application of the relevant contexts. For example, one might question, as Thomas J. Scorza did, whether Melville is "conservative in the same sense as Captain Vere is conservative,"[58] a correspondence Stern tends to assume without sufficiently examining the ambiguities in Melville's portrait of the captain. One might further ask whether categories like "conservative" and "progressive" are adequate to define the politics of a man who combined a Calvinistic distrust of the *nature* of man and a consequent belief in the necessity of social forms with a romantic conviction of the *rights* of man and a loathing for injustice wherever he found it. The common opinion, largely accepted by Stern, is that Melville was egalitarian in his youth, conservative in his middle and old age; yet Melville's social thought had always been an uneasy mixture of what he described to Hawthorne in 1851 as "an unconditional democracy in all things, and yet . . . a dislike to all mankind — in the mass."[59] Only the balance shifted as he aged, and even then his "conservatism" was less a Burkean defense of the ruling order (which he detested) than a nostalgia for an age of philosopher-kings such as he imagined in his poem "The Age of the Antonines." Inevitably there will be disagreements about the nature and emphasis of Melville's later thought, so that to invoke the context of his poetry, letters, or reading marginalia is by no means to accede to a conservative, nonironic *Billy Budd*. Contextualism is a method of no definite ideological character save as its impulse toward the fullness of authorial meaning frustrates the partisan's effort to put literature to immediate use. And finally, perhaps, the greatest political "use" of *Billy Budd* may not be its availability for latter-day purposes of indicting or defending established order but its illumination of how social thought is a function of history — specifically, of how so double-minded a vision of political life emerged from the consciousness of a late-nineteenth century writer brooding on experience through the ideological cul-de-sacs of his age.

Nonpolitical concerns from Melville's later life and poetry also bear significantly on *Billy Budd*. For example, critics arguing for Melville's Christian acceptance need to contend with the metaphysical bleakness of *John Marr*, whose presentation of the ocean (Melville's image of the Creation, silent and implacable) anticipates the indifference of "the blank sea" in *Billy Budd*. Nostalgia for a romantic past is an equally prominent theme in *John Marr*, casting doubt on those readings of *Billy Budd* that separate Melville from his narrator on the basis of the latter's alleged sentimentality. *Timoleon* is less directly pertinent to Melville's story, yet its interest in worldly reputation and the trials and rewards of truth's votaries — evidence of Melville's bitterness about his public career — is reflected in the ironic reversal of guilt and innocence that occurs when Billy strikes Claggart and becomes known to the naval world as a killer of "extreme depravity," with the "respectable and discreet" Claggart his blameless victim. In "Melville's Late Poetry and *Billy Budd*: From Nostalgia to Transcendence" (1987), Robert Milder tried to relate the governing themes of *John Marr* and *Timoleon* to those of *Billy Budd* as the story evolved through its successive phases.[60] More needs to be done with these late verse collections and with the posthumous *Weeds and Wildings*, which to acceptance critics like Newton Arvin has seemed (from afar) "an extraordinarily peaceful and pastoral coda to a body of work that had been predominantly stormy."[61]

Other contextual studies have looked beyond the immediate period of Melville's retirement and speculated broadly on the biographical roots of *Billy Budd*. For psychobiographer Edwin Haviland Miller (1975), "The power of the drama" — its source in Melville's experience and "enormous pull on readers, particularly on 'sons' " — derived from "the affective reverberations caused by a father's betrayal which no son can perhaps ever forgive."[62] Where Miller cast Melville as the wounded son, Peter L. Hays and Richard Dilworth Rust (1979) identified him with the wounding father "striv[ing] to make amends through some form of expiation" for the suicide of his older son, Malcolm, in 1866, and the failure and premature death of his younger son, Stanwix, in 1886, the year of *Billy Budd*'s probable inception.[63] Still more recently, Michael Paul Rogin (1980) synthesized biography and politics and presented *Billy Budd* as "reimagin-[ing] the familially based conflicts [of the Melvill[e]s, Gansevoorts, and Shaws] which the *Somers* mutiny had first brought into Melville's fiction forty years before" in *White-Jacket*.[64]

Among the areas most promising for future investigation are Melville's late reading, his response to contemporary social and political developments, his interest in the arts and in myth,[65] and the relationship of *Billy Budd* to the unpublished prose/verse compositions that will appear in a forthcoming volume of the Northwestern-Newberry Edition. Surprising discoveries are also to be made on matters of fact, as Stanton Garner (1982) showed when he unearthed a Civil War incident involving a drumhead court and an execution within the Army of the Potomac regiment Melville visited in 1864.[66] Altogether, contextual studies are a major recent addition to *Billy Budd* criticism, and as the focus of Melville scholarship shifts toward the later writings, and thereby toward a reinterpretation of the entire career, they will become increasingly important not only in breaking the logjam of ideological readings but in establishing *Billy Budd* as the final product of a continuous forty-five-year intellectual and imaginative development.

By far the most crucial questions yet to be explored are those raised by the Genetic Text. Much may be learned about *Billy Budd*'s artistry and themes from studying Melville at work;[67] much may also need to be unlearned, for not only does the compositional evidence subvert particular readings of the story, but it challenges the premise of aesthetic unity on which nearly all readings are based. "Because the book was left in [an] unfinished and contradictory state," Hershel Parker stated flatly in 1975, "any New Critical reading which takes a published text . . . as that of a final, unified work of art, is a waste of time."[68]

There is truth to Parker's claim, but it is much overstated, for several reasons. Except among literalists, New Critical "unity" within the pre-Jamesian novel has generally been understood as a heuristic principle that allowed the interpreter to search for patterns of coherence, not (as with lyric poetry) an assumption of absolute organic harmony. With American fiction, particularly, New Critics have been forced to tolerate an unusual degree of inward contradiction even in polished works like *The Scarlet Letter*, whose narrative attitude toward Hester is scarcely more consistent than *Billy Budd*'s toward Vere. Above all, it is uncertain how much revision — and what kinds of revision — Melville might have made had he lived. Melville's longer fictions were rarely ever "finished" in the sense of being carried to a highly wrought unity; they were simply ended due to external pressures or authorial exhaustion and were published with large structural flaws indicating shifts of interest and attitude as well as with many smaller inconsistencies of fact and presentation. The situation is more complicated with *Billy Budd*, which was painstakingly revised to the last but which was nonetheless the work of an author whose conception of unity was less spatial (a simultaneous grasp of one's materials in their complex interrelationship, the New Critical idea of unity) than temporal (a disposition to allow one subject or theme to evolve from another, so that the coherence of the work came to reside in the process of thought that guided its unfolding and was visible in the fault lines of the final product). Nothing in the late revisions of *Billy Budd* shows Melville dissatisfied either with the broad thematic disjunctions of his narrative or with its subtler inconsistencies of attitude and tone; on the contrary, the penciled revisions Hayford and Sealts assign to the latest substage of composition were limited in extent and (most notably with the surgeon's role) aimed in the direction of greater, not lesser, ambiguity. Possibly Melville intended to reconcile the surgeon's opinion with the narrator's basic (but equivocal) support of Vere, but it is at least equally possible that in expanding the role of the surgeon he was deliberately giving his involuted story one more turn of the screw.

It is true, then, that *Billy Budd* lacks unity in the strict New Critical sense, but not necessarily for the reason that it is unfinished. The absence of New Critical unity, moreover, does not imply the absence of any unity; it simply directs the search elsewhere to Melville's characteristic practice of "sailing on." And here we are fortunate (as we are not with *Moby-Dick* or

Pierre, where compositional interpretations must be highly speculative) to have the wealth of evidence contained in the Genetic Text. The main lesson this material appears to teach is that the critics of *Billy Budd* have often been like blind men touching the elephant, feeling a tusk or a leg and taking it for all. Thus an intention operative at one or another stage of composition and surviving in the published text as a major regional emphasis is identified with Melville's governing idea and allowed to control the reading of the entire story to the distortion or neglect of other regionally dominant emphases. To be specific, we know from the Genetic Text that the manuscript of November 1888 that Melville apparently considered complete passed quickly from Claggart's death to Billy's without the trial scene, Vere's interview with Billy, or the execution scene; that the idiom of this book was significantly theological, with echoes of *Paradise Lost*; that the narrative concluded with the report of events from "News from the Mediterranean" and the moralizing remark, "Here ends a story not unwarranted by what sometimes happens in this [one undeciphered word] world of ours";[69] that the tone of the book was ironic and its inferable theme a protest against God (held responsible for Claggart's evil) and society; and that despite considerable growth and revision of the manuscript, these early emphases were not so much altered as *succeeded* by others more political and psychological in nature and more dramatically ambiguous in presentation. If we attend to this evidence, some of the major interpretations of *Billy Budd* would seem to rest on conflicts with fact: 1) The testament of acceptance theory in its Christian form pointedly ignores the anti-Christian emphasis of the Claggart sections and uses the imagery and mood of the post–November 1888 hanging scene as a lens through which to view the entire narrative. 2) Politically oriented critics routinely do violence to the metaphysical themes that dominated the 1888 *Billy Budd*, either ignoring them wholly or fitting them to the procrustean bed of social analysis. On their part, universalist critics habitually slight the sociopolitical themes of the book, which were urgent enough to return Melville to a manuscript he thought complete. 3) Readings that focus on the transfiguring gestures of Billy and Vere to the prejudice of both social *and* metaphysical themes are responses to a powerfully rendered vision that Melville seems to have attained late in the process of composition and that cannot be said to govern most of the story. 4) Straight readers scant the importance of Melville's enlargement of the surgeon's role, which was not required by any necessity of characterization or plot, while ironists press too heavily on this last-minute revision and impose its insinuations upon doubtfully ironic passages written earlier and left unretouched.

In brief, the burden of the compositional evidence is that *Billy Budd* is not a testament of acceptance *or* a testament of resistance, not metaphysical in theme *or* social in theme, not tragic *or* ironic, but that it was as it evolved, and is as it stands, all of these things, whether one reads it genetically in light of Melville's development from 1886 to 1891 or formalistically as an unfolding action presented in the successive but overlapping perspectives of myth, religion, history, politics, and psychology.

How obligated is the critic to make use of this evidence (which is open to interpretations other than those I have offered here)? Setting aside all questions of a privileged method, the strongest argument for a scholarly criticism of *Billy Budd* — compositional or contextual; ideally both — is the pragmatic one that the present debate has run its course and consists largely of a restatement of old positions in new or not-so-new vocabularies. Disagreements about the story will persist, rooted as they are in extraliterary values that cannot be arbitrated and that find more than enough support in the ambiguous text of a constitutionally ambivalent author. The promise of a scholarly criticism is not that it will resolve the debate but that it will enrich and refine it and render it more adequate to its object: an inexhaustible tale that rays out in all directions and hints at "problems almost as profound as those which puzzle us in the pages of the gospels."[70]

Robert Milder

Washington University, St. Louis

Notes

1. Harrison Hayford and Merton M. Sealts, Jr., editors' introduction, *Billy Budd, Sailor (An Inside Narrative)* by Herman Melville, ed. Hayford and Sealts (Chicago: University of Chicago Press, 1962), 2.

2. Hayford and Sealts, editors' introduction, 2.

3. See Raymond Weaver, ed., *"Billy Budd" and Other Prose Pieces. Vol. 13 of The Works of Herman Melville. Standard Edition* (London: Constable, 1924); Weaver, ed., *The Shorter Novels of Herman Melville* (New York: Horace Liveright, 1928); and F. Barron Freeman, *Melville's Billy Budd* (Cambridge: Harvard University Press, 1948).

4. See Hayford and Sealts, editors' introduction, 12–24.

5. See Milton R. Stern, appendix 1: "Editorial Principles," *Billy Budd Sailor (an Inside Narrative)* by Herman Melville, ed. Stern (Indianapolis: Bobbs–Merrill, 1975), 149–160.

6. E. L. Grant Watson, "Melville's Testament of Acceptance," *New England Quarterly*, 6 (1933):319–327. Watson's essay is the first important and reasonably full discussion of *Billy Budd*, which went virtually unreviewed upon its publication save for a notice by John Middleton Murry in the *Times Literary Supplement*. Part of the neglect may have been due to Raymond Weaver's one-paragraph dismissal of the tale in his biography, *Herman Melville: Mystic and Mariner* (New York: George H. Doran, 1921). In 1926 an English biographer, John Freeman, developed Murry's suggestion of a "last will and spiritual testament" into an assessment of *Billy Budd* as Melville's "everlasting yea," and in 1928 Weaver fell into line in his introduction to *The Shorter Novels of Herman Melville*, which echoes the substance and occasionally the language of Freeman's pages fairly closely. Lewis Mumford's 1929 biography repeats the common estimate with little of the penetration that distinguishes other sections of his book. Building upon these early commentaries, Watson's "testament of acceptance" essay transforms their vague impressionism into an argument of depth, magnitude, and enduring worth.

7. Weaver, *Shorter Novels*, li.

8. John Freeman, *Herman Melville* (New York: Macmillan, 1926), 136.

9. Lewis Mumford, *Herman Melville* (New York: Harcourt, Brace, 1929), 356.

10. Watson, "Melville's Testament," 322.

11. Watson, "Melville's Testament," 327.

12. Warner Berthoff, " 'Certain Phenomenal Men': The Example of *Billy Budd*," *ELH* 27 (1960):349. Berthoff's essay is reprinted with minor changes in *The Example of Melville* (Princeton: Princeton University Press, 1962).

13. Joseph Schiffman, "Melville's Final Stage, Irony: A Re-examination of *Billy Budd* Criticism," *American Literature* 22 (1950):129.

14. See Brook Thomas, "*Billy Budd* and the Judgment of Silence," *Bucknell Review* 27 (1983):51–78.

15. Phil Withim, "*Billy Budd*: Testament of Resistance," *Modern Language Quarterly* 20 (1959):121. Other ironist readings include Leonard Casper, "The Case Against Captain Vere," *Perspective* 5 (1952):146–152, and Karl E. Zink, "Herman Melville and the Forms— Irony and Social Criticism in " 'Billy Budd,' " *Accent* 12 (1952):131–139.

16. Lawrance Thompson, *Melville's Quarrel with God* (Princeton: Princeton University Press, 1952), 387, 360.

17. See Stanton Garner, "Fraud as Fact in Herman Melville's *Billy Budd*," *San Jose Studies* 4 (1978):82–105; Lyon Evans, Jr., " 'Too Good to be True': Subverting Christian Hope in *Billy Budd*," *New England Quarterly* 55 (1982):323–353; and James Duban, *Melville's Major Fiction: Politics, Theology, and Imagination* (DeKalb, Ill.: Northern Illinois University Press, 1983), 221–48.

18. Cleanth Brooks, "Irony as a Principle of Structure," 1949; rpt. in Hazard Adams, ed., *Critical Theory Since Plato* (New York: Harcourt, Brace, 1971), 1043; Brooks, *The Well-Wrought Urn* (New York: Harcourt, Brace, 1947), 214.

19. Richard Harter Fogle, "*Billy Budd*: The Order of the Fall," *Nineteenth-Century Fiction* 15 (1960):168; Fogle, "*Billy Budd*— Acceptance or Irony," *Tulane Studies in English* 8 (1959):109.

20. Fogle, "*Billy Budd*: The Order of the Fall," 190.

21. Fogle, "*Billy Budd*: The Order of the Fall," 191.

22. Fogle, "*Billy Budd*— Acceptance or Irony," 110.

23. Fogle, "*Billy Budd*: The Order of the Fall," 189.

24. Edward H. Rosenberry, "The Problem of *Billy Budd*," *PMLA* 80 (1965):489.

25. Rosenberry, "The Problem of *Billy Budd*," 490.

26. Rosenberry, "The Problem of *Billy Budd*," 490.

27. Schiffman, "Melville's Final Stage," 133.

28. Wendell Glick, "Expediency and Absolute Morality in *Billy Budd*," *PMLA* 68 (1953):103.

29. Stern, "The Politics of Melville's Poetry," from the introduction, *Billy Budd, Sailor*, ed. Stern, xx.

30. C. B. Ives, "*Billy Budd* and the Articles of War," *American Literature* 34 (1962):33.

31. Ives, "Articles of War," 38.

32. Richard I. Weisberg, "How Judges Speak: Some Lessons on Adjudication in *Billy Budd, Sailor*, with an Application to Justice Rehnquist," *New York University Law Review* 57 (1982):59. Weisberg's article appears in revised form in *The Failure of the Word* (New Haven: Yale University Press, 1984).

33. Charles A. Reich, "The Tragedy of Justice in *Billy Budd*," *Yale Review* 56 (1967):389.

34. Christopher W. Sten, "Vere's Use of the Forms," *American Literature* 47 (1975):38.

35. John B. Noone, Jr., "*Billy Budd:* Two Concepts of Nature," *American Literature* 29 (1957):257.

36. Thomas J. Scorza, *In the Time Before Steamships* (DeKalb, Ill.: Northern Illinois University Press, 1979), xxii–xxiii.

37. Scorza, *In the Time Before Steamships,* xxxiii.

38. James R. Hurtgen, "Melville: *Billy Budd* and the Context of Political Rule," in *The Artist and Political Vision,* ed. Benjamin R. Barber and Michael J. Gargas McGrath, 261 (New Brunswick, N.J.: Transaction Press, 1982).

39. Hurtgen, "*Billy Budd* and the Context of Political Rule," 261.

40. John W. Rathbun, "*Billy Budd* and the Limits of Perception," *Nineteenth-Century Fiction* 20 (1965):34.

41. See, for example, James F. Farnham, "Captain Vere's Existential Failure," *Arizona Quarterly* 37 (1981):362–70.

42. Merlin Bowen, *The Long Encounter* (Chicago: University of Chicago Press, 1960), 218.

43. Merton M. Sealts, Jr., "Innocence and Infamy: *Billy Budd, Sailor,*" in *A Companion to Melville Studies,* ed. John Bryant, 425 (Westport, Conn.: Greenwood Press, 1986).

44. For example, Christopher S. Durer calls Vere "a petty mind, held captive by the mores of aristocratic civilization," and likens his execution of Billy to a feudal lord's "punish[ing] by death a serf found guilty of poaching." See Durer, "Captain Vere and Upper-Class Mores in *Billy Budd,*" *Studies in Short Fiction* 19 (1982):9, 16.

45. Ralph W. Willett, "Nelson and Vere: Hero and Victim in *Billy Budd,* Sailor," *PMLA* 82 (1967):370.

46. So Hershel Parker implies in "Evidence for 'Late Insertions' in Melville's Works," *Studies in the Novel* 7 (1975):409.

47. Paul Brodtkorb, Jr., "The Definitive *Billy Budd*: " 'But Aren't It All Sham?,' " *PMLA* 82 (1967):604.

48. Brodtkorb, "Definitive *Billy Budd,*" 611.

49. Barbara Johnson, "Melville's Fist: The Execution of *Billy Budd,*" *Studies in Romanticism* 18 (1979):597. Johnson's article is reprinted in *The Critical Difference* (Baltimore: Johns Hopkins University Press, 1980).

50. Thomas, "*Billy Budd* and the Judgment of Silence," 76.

51. Frank Lentricchia, *Criticism and Social Change* (Chicago: University of Chicago Press, 1983), 11.

52. H. Bruce Franklin, "From Empire to Empire: *Billy Budd, Sailor,*" in *Melville: Reassessments,* ed. A. Robert Lee, 201 (Totowa, N.J.: Barnes & Noble, 1984).

53. Duban, *Melville's Major Fiction,* 237.

54. Martin Bickman, review of Duban, *Melville's Major Fiction, American Literature* 56 (1984):596.

55. E. D. Hirsch, *Validity in Interpretation* (New Haven: Yale University Press, 1967).

56. Sealts, "Innocence and Infamy," 424.

57. Stern, "The Politics of Melville's Poetry," xxiv.

58. Scorza, *In the Time Before Steamships,* xxviii.

59. *The Letters of Herman Melville,* ed. Merrell R. Davis and William H. Gilman (New Haven: Yale University Press, 1960), 127.

60. Robert Milder, "Melville's Late Poetry and *Billy Budd:* From Nostalgia to Transcendence," *Philological Quarterly* 66 (1987):493–507.

61. Newton Arvin, *Herman Melville* (New York: William Sloane, 1950), 281.

62. Edwin Haviland Miller, *Melville* (New York: George Braziller, 1975), 366.

63. Peter L. Hays and Richard Dilworth Rust, " 'Something Healing': Fathers and Sons in *Billy Budd*," *Nineteenth-Century Fiction* 34 (1979):327.

64. Michael Paul Rogin, *Subversive Genealogy: The Politics and Art of Herman Melville* (New York: Knopf, 1983), 295.

65. For Melville's use of myth, see H. Bruce Franklin, *The Wake of the Gods* (Stanford: Stanford University Press, 1963), 188–202, and George B. Hutchinson, "The Conflict of Patriarchy and Balanced Sexual Principles in *Billy Budd*," *Studies in the Novel* 13 (1981):388–98.

66. Stanton Garner, "Melville's Scout toward Aldie," *Melville Society Extracts* no. 51 (1982):5–16.

67. See, for example, Willett, "Nelson and Vere," 372–73, and Edward M. Cifelli, "*Billy Budd:* Boggy Ground to Build On," *Studies in Short Fiction* 13 (1976):463–69.

68. Parker, "Evidence for 'Late Insertions,' " 409.

69. Hayford and Sealts, editors' introduction, 8.

70. Watson, "Melville's Testament," 327.

Commentary on the Text

Growth of the Manuscript
Harrison Hayford and Merton M. Sealts, Jr.*

The manuscript of *Billy Budd* as Melville left it at his death in 1891 may be most accurately described as a semi-final draft, not a final fair copy ready for publication. After his death Mrs. Melville, indeed, called the story "unfinished." She had used exactly the same word in December 1885 when reporting Melville's retirement from his nineteen years of employment as a customs inspector: "He has a great deal [of] unfinished work at his desk which will give him occupation." The "unfinished work" of 1885 may have included the short poem of three or four leaves on which he was working early in 1886, the poem that ultimately became the ballad "Billy in the Darbies" with which the novel concludes. The novel itself developed out of a brief prose headnote setting the scene and introducing the speaker of this poem. An understanding of just how the story took form during the last five years of its author's life has been a major objective of our genetic study of the *Billy Budd* manuscript.

As *Billy Budd* grew under Melville's hand, along with other works both in prose and in verse with which he was engaged, it passed through several distinct stages and substages of development that comprised three major phases, in each of which its original focus was radically altered. Our genetic analysis has followed the course of its growth from the surviving leaves of the ballad and its headnote to Melville's late pencil revisions of his semi-final draft. It has established the fact that more than once, believing his work to be essentially complete, he undertook to put his manuscript into fair-copy form, but each time he was led into further revision and elaboration; what still further changes he might have made had he lived to continue work on the manuscript are of course conjectural. The following section outlines the main phases of the story's development, as established by our analysis of the manuscript. The degree to which *Billy Budd* remained an "unfinished" work is a matter for critical evaluation in

---

*From the editors' introduction to *Billy Budd, Sailor (An Inside Narrative)* by Herman Melville, ed. Harrison Hayford and Merton M. Sealts, Jr. (Chicago: University of Chicago Press, 1962), 1–12., © 1962 The University of Chicago Press. Reprinted by permission of the publisher and authors.

the light of detailed evidence assembled in the table and discussion accompanying our Genetic Text.

Early in 1886, when Melville took up, or perhaps began, the work that became *Billy Budd*, he had in mind neither the plot of a novel nor any one of the characters as they later emerged in the course of his writing. What he did have, in the initial phase of development now represented by four extant draft leaves, was a short composition in both prose and verse that in its complete form ran to perhaps five or six leaves. The focal character was Billy (Billy Budd in the prose headnote), a sailor on the eve of his execution — but a different Billy from the young sailor of the novel who is hanged for striking and killing his superior officer. This Billy was an older man, condemned for fomenting mutiny and apparently guilty as charged, though in his brief initial presentation Melville emphasized the sailor's reverie as he faces death, rather than the events leading up to his condemnation. The prose sketch and ballad thus placed a character in a situation but stopped short of telling a story.

During the first two years of Melville's retirement, 1886–1887, a narrative about Billy Budd emerged out of this material. By November of 1888 Melville had incorporated the ballad and expanded the headnote sketch through several stages into a story that ran to something over 150 manuscript leaves. In constructing its plot he had entered a second phase of development with his introduction of John Claggart, whose presence resulted in a major shift of focus. Billy, no mutineer in this phase, reacts to a false charge of mutiny by striking and killing his accuser, Claggart; this is the act that leads to his condemnation here and in all subsequent stages of the story's growth.

A third and final phase of development, during which the manuscript grew to its ultimate length of 351 leaves, began after November, 1888, when Melville set out (not for the first time) to put his story into fair-copy form. During the ensuing winter months or perhaps in the following spring he made another shift of focus, which involved the full-scale delineation of a third principal character, Captain the Honorable Edward Fairfax Vere, who had previously figured only as the commander in whose presence Billy struck Claggart and by whom the summary sentence of hanging was imposed upon the young sailor. So minor was this commander's part in the second phase of the story's growth that only a few leaves stood between the killing of Claggart and the beginning of the ballad; in the third phase, by contrast, Billy's trial, Vere's long speech to the court, and the dramatized execution and related episodes intervene, and an analysis of Vere's character is now provided in new antecedent chapters. The several stages and substages within this final phase of development occupied Melville until the end of his life, revision being still in progress when he died.

Thus, in the period of over five years between his retirement from the Custom House and his death, Melville had carried the work through a series of developments intricate in detail but clear in their general lines of growth. In three main phases he had introduced in turn the three main characters: first Billy, then Claggart, and finally Vere. As the focus of his attention shifted from one to another of these three principals, the plot and thematic emphasis of the expanding novel underwent consequent modifications within each main phase. Just where the emphasis finally lay in the not altogether finished story as he left it is, in essence, the issue that has engaged and divided the critics of *Billy Budd*.

Within these three broad phases of development, certain of the various stages and substages deserve further attention because of particularly important elements with which they deal and problems which they raise. To the initial phase, in which Billy was the only major character, belong the surviving draft leaves of the ballad and headnote; they are from the first substage of what we designate Stage *A*. Although the situation then presented in the ballad was basically the same as that in its final version, with a sailor speaker already named Billy confronting his execution, there are conspicuous differences. The earlier Billy, as we have said, was an older Billy, for his musings included a dreamy reminiscence of days and ships "no more" and of a larger "general muster" of former shipmates "from every shore" ("Christian Pagan Cannibal breed") than the later and younger Billy could have assembled. This Billy was more like the reminiscing sailors of Melville's *John Marr* volume — John Marr himself, Bridegroom Dick, Tom Deadlight — where the ballad might well have appeared in 1888 had not the story that sprouted from its headnote already overshadowed it. That this early Billy was indeed guilty of mutiny seems clear from his expression "the game is up" and its subsequent revisions: first "The little game," then "My little game," and finally "Our little game"; all these phrases point to his actual implication in some sort of plot. (Even in the final version of the ballad the innocent phrase "Ay, ay, all is up" derives from the incriminating expression of the earlier versions.)

The single draft leaf surviving from the headnote, though a part of this same substage, is of later composition than the material in the ballad leaves which it was designed to introduce in the manner of similar headnotes: those to "John Marr" and "Tom Deadlight" in *John Marr* and also those to other poems Melville never completed or published. It was originally a single long sentence — like some of the headnotes, in the present tense. Much of its language has been carried over into the novel itself and is embedded in the physical description of Billy in Ch. 2, which similarly tells of his beauty, his genial temper, and his evidently noble lineage. In the headnote as in the ballad leaves themselves Melville presented a sailor older than the Billy of the novel. Initially he was not a foretopman — the foretop being a station for the younger men, as the novel was to explain — but "Captain of a gun's crew," a post for a more mature man. In this substage the historical and national setting remained unspecified, but according to the headnote it is wartime, the warship is already a seventy-four, and Billy has been "summarily condemned at sea to be hung as the ringleader of an incipient mutiny the spread of which was apprehended." Whether he was in fact guilty, as seems clear in the ballad draft, the surviving leaf of the headnote does not actually state; in any case, his capital offense is different from what it later became following Melville's introduction of Claggart.

From these four draft fragments antedating the novel itself it is impossible to be sure what main theme and dominant effect Melville had in mind for his ballad as it first stood. Presumably its general form was that of a rambling reverie, as in the other sailor poems on which he was at work. The general situation in all of them is the same: a sailor, usually an old sailor, is musing over bygone days and his own approaching end. Ships and shipmates of the past, the barbaric good nature and genial fellowship of sailors, and some sort of contrast between their simplicity and the way of "the world" are common thematic elements. The opening lines of the original ballad of Billy Budd are a characteristic variation of this last theme. As in the final version, the verse begins abruptly with Billy's comment on the visit and prayer of the chaplain, who, since he is referred to only by pronouns, must have been introduced as a secondary character in the missing portion of the prose headnote.

> Very good of him, Ay, so long to stay
> And down on his marrow bone here to pray
> For the likes of me. Nor bad his story,
> The Good Being hung and gone to glory. —

The major effect here is one of irony, arising from Billy's naïvely thinking it "good" of the chaplain to visit such a lowly prisoner and humbly "to pray / For the likes of me." In his final version of the ballad Melville dropped his direct reference to the gospel story, perhaps after his prose elaboration (in what is now Ch. 24 of *Billy Budd*) of the encounter between Billy and the chaplain, though in the novel he retained and exploited in other ways his suggestive juxtaposition of the condemned sailor with the figure of Christ "hung and gone to glory." Billy's "sailor-way of taking clerical discourse" is compared in the novel to the reception of the Christian gospel "long ago on tropic isles by any superior *savage*, so-called"; as for the chaplain, drawn as a "worthy" man "possessing the good sense of a good heart," he is termed "incongruous" as "the minister of the Prince of Peace serving in the host of the God of War," where he "lends the sanction of the religion of the meek to that which practically is the abrogation of everything but brute Force." This same incongruity between religion and war, repeatedly stressed in Melville's writings from *White-Jacket* through *Clarel* to "Bridegroom Dick" and *Billy Budd*, was evidently a major element in his original conception of Billy's situation.

Nothing in the surviving leaves of the ballad or headnote suggests the presence of Claggart in Melville's first delineation of Billy and his circumstances. When Claggart was either introduced or brought to the fore as the cause of Billy's predicament, the second phase in Melville's development of the work was inaugurated. This phase must have begun as a substage of what we designate Stage A; Claggart's emergence at some point within Stage A can be inferred from the earliest surviving leaves of the final manuscript, those of Stage B, substage Ba, which were copied forward from Stage A. In the new phase, which established the story's setting as the Revolutionary era, just after the mutinies of 1797 in the British navy at Spithead and the Nore occasioned by naval abuses, Melville presented Claggart — mostly from the outside — as a master-at-arms of the period. His original Billy, a mature "Captain of a gun's crew" aboard an unnamed seventy-four, he modified into a young merchant sailor impressed into a British warship, called the *Indomitable*. Opposite Billy, Melville now set an antagonist, Claggart, who, conceiving a mortal dislike for him, begins to scheme actively against him. Billy, described as a model sailor, is brought face to face with the master-at-arms in their commander's presence, where he responds to a false accusation of mutiny by striking and killing Claggart. Melville's juxtaposition of the two characters as protagonist and antagonist evidently led him to heighten Billy's youth, naïveté, heart, goodness, and brightness and to deepen Claggart's antipathetic experience, sophistication, intellect, evil, and darkness. The characterization of Billy was probably carried nearly as far at this phase as Melville was ever to take it, but Claggart's inner nature remained to be studied further in the final phase of the novel's development.

Just how fully Stage A explored the relations between Billy and Claggart is uncertain, since no leaves later than the draft headnote and ballad actually survive from that stage. Probably in the early months of 1888, when Melville was selecting and engrossing the poems he would include in *John Marr and Other Sailors*, he inscribed a fair copy of the story that ran to something over 70 leaves. The surviving leaves of this fair copy, which we designate Stage B, are the earliest still standing in the final manuscript, having been retained and carried forward through the various subsequent copy stages. From the very earliest leaves among them, those of substage Ba, it is clear that by the end of Stage A the story and characters as just outlined were in fact present, and that Melville was then beginning his dramatization of actual scenes. In Ba, Billy's impressment and farewell to the *Rights-of-Man* were described, Claggart's understrappers were said to be stirring up trouble for Billy aboard the *Indomitable*, the interview on deck between the master-at-arms and the captain was related though not dramatized, and Claggart's accusation of Billy and the latter's fatal blow were given their location within the captain's cabin. As the active antagonist, Claggart in the second phase had come to occupy the foreground of the work, as Iago occupies the foreground of *Othello*. Billy, less active, was now somewhat overshadowed; Vere appeared only as the commander who witnessed the false accusation and the retaliatory blow and who thereupon, without ado, imposed the summary sentence of death by hanging. No issue was made of the execution. After relating Billy's death, the story ended not with the ballad, as in Stage *A*, but with the garbled news account now standing in Ch. 29 (the penultimate chapter of the final version).

At this time, early in 1888, it would seem that Melville thought he had completed his story, for he began to make a fair copy, at *Ba;* but even as he inscribed it he was drawn into further elaborations and major expansions which he incorporated on the inserted leaves we designate as substages *Bb* and *Bc* and the closely related Stage *C*. His elaborations at *Bb*, for the most part, sketched the historical background of the story and emphasized the immediate consequences for the British navy of the Nore and Spithead mutinies. Searching for material about these events, he discovered, as he remarks in what is now Ch. 3, that details were not "readily to be found in the libraries." It was evidently at this substage that he came upon the *Naval History of Great Britain* by the historian James, who is named and quoted in that same chapter. At this point too, stimulated by Southey's *Life of Nelson*, he was led into the digression on Nelson and Trafalgar that now constitutes Ch. 4.

The leaves that stood in the manuscript at Stage *Bb* carry many slight secretarial corrections in the hand of Mrs. Melville, which suggest that at this time (perhaps only a little later in 1888 than *Ba*) she was preparing to copy the manuscript, as she later copied that of the *Timoleon* volume of 1891 after making similar corrections. If so, she was forestalled by her husband's launching into still a further series of expansions at *Bc* and *C*. One class of these new additions amounted to a program of dramatizing Claggart's campaign against Billy and included such other dramatized material as the dialogue between Billy and the mustering officer about Billy's paternity, development of the Dansker as observer and confidant, the soup-spilling episode witnessed by Claggart, and—slightly later—the encounters between Billy and the Dansker. Following closely upon these dramatized additions came a series of elaborations of another class, also at substage *Bc* and Stage *C*, in which Melville for the first time ventured into the "murky labyrinth" of Claggart's inner nature and greatly expanded his analysis in what became—after tortuous revisions at later stages—Ch. 11, 12, 13, and 17. Extensive and significant as were these amplifications at *Bb*, *Bc*, and *C*, they are to be seen in perspective as only a continuation of the second, or Claggart, phase of development, in which one class of additions dramatized the outward manifestations of his hostility to Billy Budd and another class began to analyze its inward motivation.

After drafting the elaborations just mentioned, Melville once again sought to put his manuscript into fair-copy form, by the tidying-up copy stage which we designate Stage *D*. At the top of a new first leaf—which still stands as the opening leaf of the story—he penciled "Friday Nov. 16,

1888. / Began"; and on later leaves he noted the dates "Nov 17" and "Nov 18" at intervals that probably marked a day's copy work. The fair-copy sequence of this stage extended only from the opening leaf to the point where the fair-copy sequence of Stage C began—covering, that is, the present Ch. 1–10. Within it, Melville made only a few slight additions: in Ch. 1 he added the Negro sailor and characterizations of Captain Graveling and Lieutenant Ratcliffe; in Ch. 9 he made some revisions in his sketch of the Dansker. At this same time, deciding to exclude from the story his digression on Nelson added at Bb, he removed from the manuscript to a separate folder the leaves of what is now Ch. 4. These various changes, it will be noted, affected only the first ten chapters; the remainder of the story when Melville finished Stage D stood essentially as it did at Stage C, and still ended not with the ballad but with the garbled news account. On the last leaf of that final chapter Melville had by Stage D appended, in pencil, a one-sentence coda to the entire narrative: "Here ends a story not unwarranted by what sometimes happens in this [one undeciphered word] world of ours—Innocence and infamy, spiritual depravity and fair repute." The coda, it seems apparent, was meant to bring out the main point of the story as it then stood: that the judgment and memory of "the world" may attribute to human beings the direct opposite of their true natures; innocence may be consigned to infamy, spiritual depravity may be awarded fair repute.

In the third and final phase of development, another radical shift of focus occurred when Captain Vere was for the first time brought into the foreground. This phase embraced the stages subsequent to D which we designate X, E, F, G, and the late pencil revisions. Though in it Melville made very little change in his treatment of Billy he continued to restate and rework the details of his already extensive analysis of Claggart, especially in Stage E. He also made other revisions, including a tentative restoration of the chapter on Nelson (Ch. 4), the change of the name of Vere's ship from Indomitable to Bellipotent, and a reversal of the order of his two final chapters so as to end the story not with the news account but with the ballad, as in the initial Stage A. (With regard to this last change, incidentally, he neglected to revise the news account to reflect his recent elaboration of the captain's role: specifically to mention the fact of Vere's death in addition to the deaths of Claggart and Budd.) Throughout this phase, the chief effect of his revisions was to transform Vere into a character whose importance equals—and according to some critics even surpasses—that of Billy and Claggart.

In the early part of this third phase, Melville developed Captain Vere in a major role from the point at which Claggart first accuses Billy (Ch. 18 in the final version) through the confrontation scene and the newly created trial and execution scenes (Ch. 19–25), to the now added chapter on Vere's death (Ch. 28). This transformation of the captain's role was made during the extensive pencil-draft substages that constituted Stage X. In the middle of the phase, during Stage *E*, Melville also elaborated his original brief and external introduction of the captain (Ch. 6) and filled out the "sketch of him outlined in a previous chapter" with an altogether new inward analysis of Vere as "an exceptional character," in a chapter "To be inserted after first account of him" (Ch. 7). Finally, in the last part of the third phase, after putting the pencil drafts of Stage *X* into fair copy at Stages *F* and *G*, he made late pencil revisions of his treatment of the surgeon's role which affect the whole interpretation of Captain Vere and his course of action. These late revisions bear so directly on central critical problems, both of interpretation and of evaluation, that they must be described in some detail here.

The crucial revision of the surgeon's role occurred at that point in the story where Billy has struck and killed Claggart and the surgeon has pronounced Claggart dead. At Stage *Ga* the surgeon's part in the scene was purely routine; Vere briefly explained the circumstances to him and instructed him to withdraw, commenting that "before taking action I must have a few moments to mature the line of conduct I shall adopt." When Claggart fell under Billy's blow Vere had said "Fated boy," but he had not decided at once how to act. The case, he remarks to the surgeon, is without precedent and "could not have happened at a worse time either for me or the striker of the blow" (Leaves [229b]356, [229c]357). The surgeon's thoughts—the only ones assigned him at this stage—were reported in narrative summary that shaded into authorial commentary:

> Too well the thoughtful officer knew what his superior meant. As the former withdrew he could not help thinking how worse than futile the utmost discretion sometimes proves in a world subject to unfor[e]seeable fatalities; the prudent method adopted by Captain Vere to obviate publicity and trouble having resulted in an event that necessitated the former, and, under existing circumstances in the navy indefinit[e]ly magnified the latter.
> (Leaf [229c]357, at *Ga*)

Then followed a chapter that began with the three manuscript leaves erroneously printed in all previous editions of *Billy Budd* as the "Preface" (Leaves [229d–f]358–60). Taking up the point about "existing circumstances in the navy," the expository chapter pointed out that in 1797 "it was something caught from the Revolutionary Spirit that at Spithead emboldened the man-of-war's men to rise against real abuses, and afterwards at the Nore to make inordinate aggressive demands, successful resistance to which was confirmed only when the ringleaders were hung for an admonitory spectacle to the anchored fleet," (Stage *Ga*). It was on the basis of these reflections that the narrator then in effect underwrote Vere's view of the case, doing so in the course of an extended passage still standing in the final manuscript (Leaves 238–45), which concluded as follows:

Feeling that unless quick action was taken on it[,] the deed of the foretopman so soon as it should be known on the gun-decks would tend to awaken any slumbering embers of disaffection among the crew, a sense of the urgency of the case overruled every other consideration. But tho' a conscientious dis[c]iplinarian he was no lover of authority for mere authority's sake. Very far was he from embracing opportunities for monopolising to himself the perils of moral responsibility[,] none at least that could properly be referred to an official superior or shared with him by his official equals or even subordinates. So thinking[,] he was glad it would not be at variance with usage to turn the matter over to a summary court of his own officers, reserving to himself as the one on whom the ultimate accountability would rest, the right of maintaining a supervision of it, or informally interposing at need. Accordingly a drum-head court was summarily convened, he electing the individuals composing it . . . (Leaves 244–245 at *Fa*)

As the entire sequence stood at Stage *Ga*, the tenor of Melville's attitude toward Vere was relatively straightforward. Only on the matter of the captain's "circumspectness" in guarding "as much as possible against publicity" did he bring in doubts. Even on this point his narrative voice is noncommittal: Vere "may or may not have erred"; some other officers later criticized him (from jealousy, his friends said); and there was "some imaginative ground for invidious comment" on the temporary secrecy that resembled policy in the palace of Peter the Barbarian. But Melville's subsequent changes have the effect — whatever their intention — of bringing Vere's behavior very much into question.

First, beginning where the surgeon infers that Claggart is already dead, Melville removed six leaves from the manuscript (Leaves [229a–f]355–60, including those later mislabeled "Preface"). In their place he substituted eight other leaves drafted in pencil (leaves 230–37) which emphasize Vere's "excited manner" and "passionate interjections," and the fact that the surgeon ("as yet wholly ignorant of the affair" and "unapprised of the antecedents") if "profoundly discomposed" by them. The surgeon is also now said to be "disturbed" by the captain's apparent "desire for secrecy." Before the surgeon's withdrawal from the cabin, Vere now directs him to apprise the other officers of his intended drumhead court and to enjoin them to secrecy meanwhile. Instead of following this scene with a consideration of "the Revolutionary Spirit," as at *Ga*, Melville reports the surgeon's "disquietude," his reflections on what he has seen and heard, and his ensuing question whether "Captain Vere was suddenly affected in his mind." The surgeon is said to think that instead of convening a drumhead court Vere should "place Billy Budd in confinement and in a way dictated by usage, and postpone further action in so extraordinary a case, to such time as they should rejoin the squadron, and then refer it to the Admiral"; and the officers are said to agree (Leaves 234–36). Finally in two paragraphs that serve as a new introduction to the next chapter (Ch. 21), Melville pushed even further the question of Vere's state of mind, asking as narrator: "Who in the rainbow can draw the line" between sanity and insanity? And he concludes, noncommittally: "Whether Captain Vere, as the Surgeon professionally & privately surmised, was really the sudden victim of any degree of aberration, every one must determine for himself by such light as this narrative may afford."

Which way — if either — Melville expected the reader to determine the question he had thus raised concerning Vere's possible "aberration" is by no means clear. Equally unclear is the larger question of what attitude the story as a whole conveys toward the captain. The lighting afforded by the narrative is not, so to speak, from a single source; it is of the sort characterized in *Moby Dick* (Ch. 3) as from "unequal cross-lights." As Claggart, during the second phase of the story's development, had tended to overshadow its original protagonist, so now in the third and final phase the emerging and ambiguous figure of Vere had moved toward the central position he has since been awarded by many interpreters of the novel. To these complex questions of tone and focus we suggest one avenue of approach in our section below on critical perspectives.

The foregoing alteration in the surgeon's role was the most significant of the numerous local changes Melville made in the course of the final revisions which we term the "late pencil stage." In this stage he appears to have gone through his whole manuscript, now of some 350 leaves, making a series of pencil revisions. He replaced some words and phrases on almost every leaf; he canceled, transposed, and elaborated passages; he added patches and inserted or substituted a few leaves, notably the eight concerning the surgeon. Perhaps Melville made these revisions inconsecutively and sporadically, perhaps in order from beginning to end of the narrative. At some point in the course of them he wrote on the last leaf, below the ballad, "End of Book / April 19th 1891." The notation may have been his last addition to the manuscript. More likely he went back again after the "End," as he had repeatedly done during its five-year growth, to make further pencil revisions during the last summer of his life. The changes affecting the surgeon were likely made then; relevant leaves were not left in good order. Both the second Vere chapter (Ch. 7) and the Nelson digression were still in folders, not yet inserted into the narrative. In short, the manuscript was in a heavily revised, still "unfinished" state when he died, on September 28, 1891.

Early Estimates

Herman Melville's Silence John Middleton Murry*

In 1851 Herman Melville published *Moby Dick;* in the next five years *Pierre*, which was received with cold hostility, *Israel Potter*, and the *Piazza Tales*. Then, to all intents and purposes, there was silence till the end, which did not come till thirty-five years later. The silence of a great writer needs to be listened to. If he has proved his genius, then his silence is an utterance, and one of no less moment than his speech. The silence of a writer who has the vision that Melville proved his own in *Moby Dick* is not an accident without adequate cause; and that we feel that silence was the appropriate epilogue to Melville's masterpiece is only the form of our instinctive recognition that the adequate cause was there. After *Moby Dick* there was, in a sense, nothing to be said, just as after *King Lear* there seemed nothing for Shakespeare to say. Shakespeare did find another utterance in *Antony and Cleopatra:* then he too was silent. For, whatever names we may give to the "romantic" plays of his final period, and however high the praises we sincerely heap upon them, they belong to another order and have a significance of another kind than the great tragedies. They are, essentially, the work of a man who has nothing more to *say*, but who is artist and genius enough at last to contrive a method of saying even that.

Herman Melville could not do that, but then nobody save Shakespeare has been able to work that miracle. Probably Melville knew exactly what Shakespeare had achieved in the faint, far reflection of *The Tempest;* for in the *Battle-pieces, and other Poems*, with which he made scarce so much as a ripple in his own silence in 1866, is this strangely irrelevant verse on Shakespeare: —

> No utter surprise can come to him
> Who reaches Shakespeare's core;
> That which we seek and shun is there —
> Man's final lore.

*From *Times Literary Supplement*, no. 1173 (10 July 1924):433. Copyright 1924 *Times Literary Supplement*, London. Reprinted by permission.

Melville knew where Shakespeare had been: no doubt he also knew where Shakespeare at last arrived; but he could not communicate those mysterious faint echoes of a certitude—that certitude "which we seek and shun"—which are gathered together into *The Tempest*.

Yet Melville was trying to say more during his long silence. How much he struggled with his dumbness we cannot say; perhaps during most of those thirty-five years he acquiesced in it. But something was at the back of his mind, haunting him, and this something he could not utter. If we handle the clues carefully we may reach a point from which we too may catch a glimpse of it; but then, by the nature of things, we shall be unable to utter what we see. We can only indicate the clues. They are to be found, one at the beginning and one at the end of the silence. *Pierre* is at the beginning. It is, judged by the standards, which are traditional in estimating a "work of art," a complete failure. The story is naive, amateurish, melodramatic, wildly improbable, altogether unreal. Let those who are persuaded that a novel is a good story and nothing more avoid *Pierre*. But those who feel that the greatest novels are something quite different from a good story should seek it out: to them it will be strange and fascinating, and they will understand why its outward semblance is clumsy and puerile. Melville is trying to reveal a mystery; he is trying to show that the completely good man is doomed to complete disaster on earth, and he is trying to show at the same time that this must be so, and that it ought to be so. The necessity of that "ought to be so" can be interpreted in two ways: as Melville calls them, horologically or chronometrically. Horologically—that is, estimated by our local and earthly timepieces—the disaster of the good ought to be so, because there is no room for unearthly perfection on earth; chronometrically—that is, estimated by the unvarying recorder of the absolute—it ought to be so, because it is a working out, a manifestation, of the absolute, though hidden, harmony of the ideal and the real. In other words, Melville was trying to reveal anew the central mystery of the Christian religion.

He did not succeed. How could he succeed? Nobody understood *Pierre*; apparently nobody had even a glimmering understanding of it. And the thirty-five years of silence began. At the extreme end of them, moved perhaps by a premonition of coming death, Melville wrote another "story." . . . With the mere fact of the long silence in our minds we could not help regarding *Billy Budd* as the last will and spiritual testament of a man of genius. We could not help expecting this, if we have any imaginative understanding. Of course, if we are content to dismiss in our minds, if not in our words, the man of genius as mad, there is no need to trouble. Some one is sure to have told us that *Billy Budd*, like *Pierre*, is a tissue of naivety and extravagance: that will be enough. And, truly, *Billy Budd is* like *Pierre*—startlingly like. Once more Melville is telling the story of the inevitable and utter disaster of the good and trying to convey to us that this must be so and ought to be so—chronometrically and horologically. He is trying, as it were with his final breath, to reveal the knowledge that has been haunting him — that these things must be so and not otherwise.

Billy Budd is a foretopman, pressed out of the merchant service into the King's Navy in the year of the Nore mutiny. He is completely good, not with the sickly goodness of self-conscious morality, but as one born into earthly paradise — strong, young, manly, loyal, brave, unsuspecting, admired by his officers and adored by his shipmates. And he is hated by the master-at-arms, the policeman of the lower deck. Claggart hates him, simply because he is Billy Budd, with the instinctive hatred of the evil for the good. Melville is careful to explain that there is no reason whatever for his hatred; he puts it deliberately before us as naked and elemental — the clash of absolutes. Claggart is subtle and cool, he works quietly, and he is also a man of courage. He involves Billy Budd in the thin semblance of revolutionary mutiny. The master-at-arms deliberately risks his own life in order to destroy his enemy's. He risks it, and loses it, for in the privacy of his own cabin the captain confronts the accuser with his victim, and in a flash of anger Budd strikes the master-at-arms dead. This moment in the story is unearthly. But Billy Budd is doomed: he has killed his officer in time of war. The captain who understands and loves him presides over the court-martial, and Budd is condemned to be hanged at dawn. Before dawn the crew is piped to quarters.

> Billy stood facing aft. At the penultimate moment, his words, his only ones, words wholly unobstructed in the utterance, were these — "God bless Captain Vere!" Syllables so unanticipated coming from one with the ignominious hemp about his neck — a conventional felon's benediction directed aft toward the quarters of honour; syllables too, delivered in the clear melody of a singing bird on the point of launching from the twig, had a phenomenal effect, not unenhanced by the rare personal beauty of the young sailor, spiritualized now through late experiences so poignantly profound.
>
> Without volition, as it were, as if indeed the ship's populace were the vehicles of some vocal current electric, with one voice, from alow and aloft, came a resonant echo — "God bless Captain Vere!" And yet at that instant Billy alone must have been in their hearts, even as he was in their eyes. At the pronounced words and the spontaneous echo that voluminously rebounded them, Captain Vere, either through stoic self-control or a sort of momentary paralysis induced by emotional shock, stood erectly rigid as a musket in the ship-armourer's rack.
>
> The hull, deliberately recovering from the periodic roll to leeward, was just regaining an even keel, when the last signal, the preconcerted dumb one, was given. At the same moment it chanced that the vapoury fleece hanging low in the east was shot through with a soft glory as of the fleece of the Lamb of God seen in mystical vision, and simultaneously therewith, watched by the wedged mass of upturned faces, Billy ascended; and ascending, took the full rose of the dawn.

> In the pinioned figure, arrived at the yard-end, to the wonder of all, no motion was apparent save that created by the slow roll of the hull, in moderate weather so majestic in a great ship heavy-cannoned.

That is the story, told with a strange combination of naïve and majestic serenity — the revelation of a mystery. It was Melville's final word, worthy of him, indisputably a passing beyond the nihilism of *Moby Dick* to what may seem to some simple and childish, but will be to others wonderful and divine.

[Melville's Everlasting Yea]   John Freeman*

If it seems fantastic to compare *Moby-Dick* with Milton's *Paradise Lost* and assert a parallel conception in each, it will seem fantastic to say that in a shorter story, *Billy Budd*, may be found another *Paradise Regained*.

. . . Exaltation of spirit redeems [the execution scene] from burdens which otherwise might appear too painful to be borne. And beyond this, it is innocence that is vindicated, more conspicuously in death than it could be in life. Melville's MS. contains a note in his own hand — "A story not unwarranted by what happens in this incongruous world of ours — innocence and infirmary [*sic*], spiritual depravity and fair respite [*sic*]";† the ultimate opposition is shown clearly here in this public vindication of the law, and the superior assertion at the very moment of death of the nobility of a pure human spirit. *Moby-Dick* ends in darkness and desolation, for the challenge of Ahab's pride is rebuked by the physical power and the inhumanness of Nature; but *Billy Budd* ends in a brightness of escape, such as the apostle saw when he exclaimed, "O death, where is thy sting?"

Finished but a few months before the author's death and only lately published, *Billy Budd* shows the imaginative faculty still secure and powerful, after nearly forty years' supineness, and the not less striking security of Melville's inward peace. After what storms and secret spiritual turbulence we do not know, except by hints which it is easy to exaggerate, in his last days he re-enters an Eden-like sweetness and serenity, "with calm of mind, all passion spent," and sets his brief, appealing tragedy for witness that evil is defeat and natural goodness invincible in the affections of man. In this, the simplest of stories, told with but little of the old

*From *Herman Melville* (London and New York: Macmillan, 1926), 131–36. Reprinted by permission.

†The phrase should read: "innocence and infamy, spiritual depravity and fair repute."

digressive vexatiousness, and based upon recorded incidents, Herman Melville uttered his everlasting yea, and died before a soul had been allowed to hear him.

[The Highest Kind of Happiness]   Raymond Weaver*

[Melville's] last word upon the strange mystery of himself and of human destiny is *Billy Budd:* "A story," so Melville said in a pencilled note at the end, "not unwarranted by what happens in this incongruous world of ours—innocence and infirmity [*sic*], spiritual depravity and fair respite [*sic*]."[†] It is a brief and appealing narrative, unmatched among Melville's works in lucidity and inward peace. "With calm of mind, all passion spent," Melville turned again to the narrative of one who, like Pierre, reaps death as the wages of virtue. The scene is aboard ship, and the conflict is between the innocence of the handsome young sailor Billy Budd, and the "natural depravity" of Claggart, a subtle, dark, demon-haunted petty officer. Claggart's is the "natural depravity" of Plato's definition: "depravity according to nature." Primarily he had been moved against Billy by his significant personal beauty, but not by that alone; it was, more deeply, the simplicity of a nature which had never willed malice which pricked the malice of the master-at-arms. "One person excepted, the master-at-arms was perhaps the only man in the ship intellectually capable of adequately appreciating the moral phenomenon presented in Billy Budd, and the insight but intensified his passion, which, assuming various secret forms within him, at times assumed that of cynic disdain—disdain of innocence. To be nothing more than innocent!" Melville himself had known this "cynic disdain." For when he wrote *Pierre*, one part of him hated the youthful guilelessness of his earlier self as represented in the hero of that novel, even as Claggart hated Billy Budd. . . .

Just as some theologians have presented the fall of man as evidence of the great glory of God, in similar manner Melville studies the evil in Claggart in vindication of the innocence in Billy Budd. For, primarily, Melville wrote *Billy Budd* in witness to his ultimate faith that evil is defeat and natural goodness invincible in the affections of man. *Billy Budd*, as *Pierre*, ends in disaster and death; in each case inexperience and innocence and seraphic impulse are wrecked against the malign forces of darkness that seem to preside over external human destiny. In *Pierre*, Melville had

*From the Introduction to *The Shorter Novels of Herman Melville* (New York: Liveright Publishing Corp. 1928), xlix-li. Copyright 1928 by Horace Liveright, Inc. Copyright renewed 1956 by Liveright Publishing Corporation. Reprinted by permission of the publisher.

†The phrase should read: "innocence and infamy, spiritual depravity and fair repute."

hurled himself into a fury of vituperation against the world; with *Billy Budd* he would justify the ways of God to man. Among the many parallels of contrast between these two books, each is a tragedy (as was Melville's life), but in opposed sense of the term. For tragedy may be viewed not as being essentially the representation of human misery, but rather as the representation of human goodness or nobility. All of the supremest art is tragic: but the tragedy is, in Aristotle's phrase, "the representation of Eudaimonia," or the highest kind of happiness. There is, of course, in this type of tragedy, with its essential quality of encouragement and triumph, no flinching of any horror of tragic life, no shirking of the truth by a feeble idealism, none of the compromises of the so-called "happy ending." The powers of evil and horror must be granted their fullest scope; it is only thus we can triumph over them. Even though in the end the tragic hero finds no friends among the living or dead, no help in God, only a deluge of calamity everywhere, yet in the very intensity of his affliction he may reveal the splendour undiscoverable in any gentler fate. Here he has reached, not the bottom, but the crowning peak of fortune — something which neither suffering nor misfortune can touch. Only when worldly disaster has worked its utmost can we realize that there remains something in man's soul which is for ever beyond the grasp of the accidents of existence, with power in its own right to make life beautiful. Only through tragedy of this type could Melville affirm his everlasting yea. The final great revelation — or great illusion — of his life, he uttered in *Billy Budd*.

[The Flowering Aloe]   Lewis Mumford*

Billy Budd, [Melville's] final novel, is not a full-bodied story: there is statement, commentary, illustration, just statement, wise commentary, apt illustration: what is lacking is an independent and living creation. The epithets themselves lack body and colour: *Billy Budd* has nothing to compare with the description of boiling whale-oil in *Moby-Dick* — "a wild Hindoo odour, like the left wing of the Day of Judgement."

Billy Budd, which was dedicated to Jack Chase, wherever he might be, alow or aloft, lacks the fecundity and energy of *White-Jacket*: the story itself takes place on the sea, but the sea itself is missing, and even the principal characters are not primarily men: they are actors and symbols. The story gains something by this concentration, perhaps: it is stripped for

*From *Herman Melville* (New York: The Literary Guild, 1929), 353–57. Copyright 1929; renewed 1957 by Lewis Mumford. Reprinted by permission of Gina Maccoby Literary Agency.

action, and even Melville's deliberate digressions do not halt it. Each of the characters has a Platonic clarity of form. . . .

Billy Budd is the story of three men in the British Navy: it is also the story of the world, the spirit, and the devil. Melville left a note, crossed out in the original manuscript, "Here ends a story not unwarranted by what happens in this incongruous world of ours—innocence and infirmity [*sic*], spiritual depravity and fair respite [*sic*]."† The meaning is so obvious that one shrinks from underlining it. Good and evil exist in the nature of things, each forever itself, each doomed to war with the other. In the working out of human institutions, evil has a place as well as the good: Vere is contemptuous of Claggart, but cannot do without him: he loves Budd as a son and must condemn him to the noose: justice dictates an act abhorrent to his nature, and only his inner magnanimity keeps it from being revolting. These are the fundamental ambiguities of life: so long as evil exists, the agents that intercept it will also be evil, whilst we accept the world's conditions: the universal articles of war on which our civilizations rest. Rascality may be punished; but beauty and innocence will suffer in that process far more. There is no comfort, in the perpetual Calvary of the spirit, to find a thief nailed on either side. Melville had been harried by these paradoxes in *Pierre*. At last he was reconciled. He accepted the situation as a tragic necessity; and to meet that tragedy bravely was to find peace, the ultimate peace of resignation, even in an incongruous world. As Melville's own end approached, he cried out with Billy Budd: God bless Captain Vere! In this final affirmation Herman Melville died. September 28, 1891, was the date of the outward event.

---

†The phrase should read: "innocence and infamy, spiritual depravity and fair repute."

Essays

Melville's Testament of Acceptance

E. L. Grant Watson*

Melville finished the short novel, *Billy Budd*, five months before his death in 1891. It was not published until 1924, when it was included in the Constable edition of 750 copies. No other printing has yet appeared.

The style of this product of Melville's last years is strikingly different from the exuberant and highly-colored prose of that great period of more ardent creation (1850 to 1852) which produced *Mardi, Moby-Dick*, and *Pierre*. Though it lacks that fine extravagance of the earlier books, which laid on the color with prodigality, *Billy Budd* is as rich, or even richer, in Melville's peculiar and elaborate symbolism; and this symbolism becomes all the more effective for being presented in a dry and objective manner. The fine flourishes, the purple patches, which scintillate brilliantly in *Moby-Dick*, and the deep sombre melancholy of *Pierre* are not here. The grandiloquence of youth which tempted Stevenson's very partial appreciation is here transformed into the dignity of an achieved detachment. The story develops simply, always unhurried, yet never lagging. Each character is described with the patience which the complex intention of the theme demands — the color of the eyes, the clothes, the complexion, the color of the skin, of the blood under the skin, the past, the present — these are hints at a deep and solemn purpose, one no less ambitious than to portray those ambiguities of good and evil as the mutually dependant opposites, between which the world of realization finds its being.

The title *Billy Budd* is not without significance, and would strike some readers in its crude simplicity as proof that Melville was lacking in a sense of humor. How could any man, they would argue, write a tragedy and call it *Billy Budd?* But a sense of humor, like almost everything else, is relative. Melville certainly lacked it in the crude form; but he was always conscious of those occasions when he might seem, to a superficial view, to be wanting it. He is particularly conscious of the obvious, but not in the obvious manner; and when he uses such a name as *Billy Budd* to set as the hub round which his own philosophy of life must revolve, he does so

*From *New England Quarterly* 6 (1933):319–27. Reprinted by permission of *New England Quarterly*.

41

consciously, choosing the obvious to carry the transcendental. "I have ever found the plain things, the knottiest of all," he has written; and so he has made the simple man, the every-day Billy, the handsome sailor, the hero of a tragedy. Humor is appreciated most easily when larger things contract suddenly to smaller things — as when a man slips on a piece of orange-peel, thus converting his intention of going about his business to the abrupt act of falling on his back-side. Yet a more imaginative intelligence might, with a sense of humor just as true, see in this fall, the destiny of man, with full chorus of pities and ironic spirits. The easy contraction will seem to the sophisticated too facile to provoke a smile, a larger humor is found in the reverse process, namely in a filling in, in an exaggeration from the particular to the general. With such an added pinch of imagination, the obvious thing becomes the centre of mystery. And so, with a sense of humor which perceived both the obvious and the peculiar quality of the name, Melville deliberately chose "Billy Budd." Moreover, he made the hero of this, his gospel story (as it might well be called), a foundling of uncertain parentage, whose "entire family was practically invested in himself."

It is a mistake for critics to try to tell stories which authors must have told better in their texts. The critic's function is rather to hint at what lies beneath — hidden, sometimes, under the surface. Melville called his story "an inside narrative," and though it deals with events stirring and exciting enough in themselves, it is yet more exciting because it deals with the relation of those principles which constitute life itself. A simple-minded-ness unaffected by the shadow of doubt, a divine innocence and courage, which might suggest a Christ not yet conscious of His divinity, and a malice which has lost itself in the unconscious depths of mania — the very mystery of iniquity — these opposites here meet, and find their destiny. But Melville's theme is even larger. All the grim setting of the world is in the battleship *Indomitable*; war and threatened mutiny are the conditions of her existence. Injustice and inhumanity are implicit, yet Captain Vere, her commander, is the man who obeys the law, and yet understands the truth of the spirit. It is significant of Melville's development since the writing of *Moby-Dick* and *Pierre*, that he should create this naval captain — wholly pledged to the unnaturalness of the law, but sufficiently touched, at the same time, by the divine difference from ordinary sanity (he goes by the nick-name of "Starry Vere"), as to live the truth *within* the law, and yet, in the cruel process of that very obedience, to redeem an innocent man from the bitterness of death imposed by the same law. A very different ending this from the despairing acts of dissolution which mark the conclusions of the three earlier books: *Mardi, Moby-Dick,* and *Pierre.*

Melville is no longer a rebel. It should be noted that Billy Budd has not, even under the severest provocation, any element of rebellion in him; he is too free a soul to need a quality which is a virtue only in slaves. His nature spontaneously accepts whatever may befall. When impressed from the merchant-ship, the *Rights of Man,* he makes no demur to the visiting lieutenant's order to get ready his things for trans-shipment. The crew of the merchant-ship are surprised and reproachful at his uncomplaining acquiescence. Once aboard the battleship, the young sailor begins to look around for the advantages of chance and adventure. Such simple power to accept gives him the buoyancy to override troubles and irritations which would check inferior natures.

Yet his complete unconsciousness of the attraction, and consequent repulsion, that his youthful beauty and unsophisticated good-fellowship exercise on Claggart, make it only easier for these qualities to turn envy into hatred. His very virtue makes him the target for the shaft of evil, and his quality of acceptance provokes to action its complementary opposite, the sense of frustration that can not bear the consciousness of itself, and so has to find escape in mania. Thus there develops the conflict between unconscious virtue (not even aware of its loss of Eden and unsuspecting of the presence of evil) and the bitter perversion of love which finds its only solace in destruction.

And not only Billy Budd is marked by this supreme quality of acceptance. Captain Vere, also, possesses it, but with full consciousness, and weighted with the responsibility of understanding the natural natural-ness of man's volition and the unnatural naturalness of the law. In the summing up at the drum-head court-martial of the case for the law against the innocent man, he said:

> Now can we adjudge to summary and shameful death a fellow-creature innocent before God, and whom we feel to be so? — Does that state it right? You sign sad assent. Well, I too feel the full force of that. It is Nature. But do these buttons that we wear attest that our allegiance is to Nature? No, to the King. Though the ocean, which is inviolate Nature primeval, though this be the element where we move and have our being as sailors, yet as the King's officers lies our duty in a sphere correspond-ingly natural? . . . We fight at command. If our judgements approve the war, that is but coincidence. So in other particulars. So now, would it be not so much ourselves that would condemn as it would be martial law operating through us? For that law and the rigour of it, we are not responsible. Our vowed responsibility is in this: That however pitilessly that law may operate, we nevertheless adhere to it and administer it.

In Captain Vere we find a figure which may interestingly be compared to Pontius Pilate. Like Pilate, he condemns the just man to a shameful death, knowing him to be innocent, but, unlike Pilate, he does not wash his hands, but manfully assumes the full responsibility, and in such a way as to take the half, if not more than the half, of the bitterness of the execution upon himself. We are given to suppose that there is an affinity, a spiritual understanding between Captain Vere and Billy Budd, and it is even suggested that in their partial and separate existences they contribute two essential portions of that larger spirit which is man. Such passages as that quoted lie on the surface of this story, but they indicate the depths beneath. There are darker hints: those deep, far-away things in Vere, those occasional flashings-forth of intuition—short, quick probings to the very axis of reality. Though the book be read many times, the student may still remain baffled by Melville's significant arrangement of images. The story is so solidly filled out as to suggest dimensions in all directions. As soon as the mind fastens upon one subject, others flash into being.

Melville reported in *Pierre* how he fished his line into the deep sea of childhood, and there, as surely as any modern psychoanalyst, discovered all the major complexes that have since received baptism at the hands of Freudians. He peered as deep as any into the origins of sensuality, and in conscious understanding he was the equal of any modern psychologist; in poetic divination he has the advantage of most. No doubt the stresses of his own inner life demanded this exceptional awareness. In this book of his old age, the images which he chose for the presentation of his final wisdom, move between the antinomies of love and hate, of innocence and malice. From behind—from far behind the main pageant of the story—there seem to fall suggestive shadows of primal, sexual simplicities. In so conscious a symbolist as Melville, it would be surprising if there should be no meaning or half-meaning in the spilling of Billy's soup towards the homosexually-disposed Claggart, in the impotence of Billy's speech in the presence of his accuser, in his swift and deadly answer, or the likening of Claggart's limp, dead body to that of a snake.

It is possible that such incidents might be taken as indications of some unresolved problem in the writer himself. This may be, but when we remember how far Melville had got in the process of self-analysis in *Pierre*, and when we have glanced at the further analysis that is obvious in the long narrative poem *Clarel*, it seems likely that this final book, written nearly forty years after *Pierre*, should contain a further, deeper wisdom. And as the philosophy in it has grown from that of rebellion to that of acceptance, as the symbolic figures of unconscious forces have become always more concrete and objective, so we may assume that these hints are intentional, and that Melville was particularly conscious of what he was doing.

But let no one suppose that he would ever pin an image to his scale of value, as an entomologist would pin an insect to his board; there is always in his interpretation a wide spaciousness. He lifts some familiar object, holding it to his light, that it may glow and illumine some portion of what must always remain vast and unknown. For his suggestive use of words, and the special values he gives them, and the large implication he can in this way compress into a sentence, the passage which tells how Billy Budd was hanged from the main yard-arm of the battle-ship *Indomitable* is a good example:

Billy stood facing aft. At the penultimate moment, his words, his only ones, words wholly unobstructed in the utterance, were these—"God bless Captain Vere!" Syllables so unanticipated coming from one with the ignominious hemp about his neck—a conventional felon's benediction directed aft towards the quarters of honour; syllables, too, delivered in the clear melody of a singing bird on the point of launching from the twig, had a phenomenal effect, not unenhanced by the rare personal beauty of the young sailor, spiritualised now through late experiences so poignantly profound.

Without volition, as it were, as if indeed the ship's populace were the vehicles of some vocal current-electric, with one voice, from alow and aloft, came a resonate echo—"God bless Captain Vere!" And yet at that instant Billy alone must have been in their hearts, even as he was in their eyes.

At the pronounced words and the spontaneous echo that voluminously rebounded them, Captain Vere, either through stoic self-control or a sort of momentary paralysis induced by emotional shock, stood erectly rigid as a musket in the ship-armourer's rack.

The hull, deliberately recovering from the periodic roll to leeward, was just regaining an even keel, when the last signal, the preconcerted dumb one, was given. At the same moment it chanced that the vapoury fleece hanging low in the east, was shot through with a soft glory as of the fleece of the Lamb of God seen in mystical vision, and simultaneously therewith, watched by the wedged mass of upturned faces, Billy ascended; and ascending, took the full rose of the dawn.

In the pinioned figure, arrived at the yard-end, to the wonder of all, no motion was apparent save that created by the slow roll of the hull, in moderate weather so majestic in a great ship heavy-cannoned.

Here is Melville at his very best, at his deepest, most poetic, and therefore at his most concentrated, most conscious. Every image has its significant implication: the very roll of the heavily-cannoned ship so majestic in moderate weather—the musket in the ship-armourer's rack; and Billy's last words are the triumphant seal of his acceptance, and they are more than that, for in this supreme passage a communion between personality at its purest, most-God-given form, and character, hard-hammered from the imperfect material of life on the battleship *Indomitable*, is here suggested, and one feels that the souls of Captain Vere and Billy are at that moment strangely one.

In this short history of the impressment and hanging of a handsome sailor-boy, are to be discovered problems almost as profound as those which puzzle us in the pages of the Gospels. *Billy Budd* is a book to be read many times, for at each reading it will light up, as do the greater experiences of life, a beyond leading always into the unknown.

Melville's Final Stage, Irony: A Re-examination of *Billy Budd* Criticism

Joseph Schiffman*

The aged Melville, like the Dansker of *Billy Budd*, "never interferes in aught and never gives advice." Melville wrote *Billy Budd*, his last work, without interjecting moral pronouncements; for this reason the story is usually taken as Melville's "Testament of acceptance," or, in the latest and most extended criticism, as Melville's "Recognition of necessity." Most critics, by mistaking form for content, have missed the main importance of *Billy Budd*. Actually, Melville's latest tale shows no radical change in his thought. Change lies in his style. *Billy Budd* is a tale of irony, penned by a writer who preferred allegory and satire to straight narrative, and who late in life, turned to irony for his final attack upon evil. . . . [1]

In almost all respects, *Billy Budd* is typically Melvillian.[2] It is a sea story, Melville's favorite genre. It deal with rebellion. It has reference to reforms, in this case impressment. It is rich in historical background, and concerns ordinary seamen. All those features of *Billy Budd* bear the stamp of the youthful Melville.

In one important respect, however, *Billy Budd* is different from almost all of Melville's other stories. It is written with a cool, detached pen, a seemingly impartial pen.[3] This odd development for Melville has had much to do with launching the "acceptance" theory.

In his preface to *Billy Budd*, Melville speaks of the impact of the French Revolution upon the British Navy, and passes both favorable and unfavorable judgment as to its effects. But, in speaking of the sailors and their conditions of life — Melville's strongest interest — he says: " . . . it was something caught from the Revolutionary spirit that at Spithead emboldened the man-of-war's men to rise against real abuses . . . the Great Mutiny [later at Nore], though by Englishmen naturally deemed monstrous at the time, doubtless gave the first latent prompting to most important reforms in the British Navy."

Thus the scene is set, and though Melville uses a cool pen, he is the Melville of old; his heart still beats quickly for the men in the heat and sweat of the hold.[4]

The main character of the piece, Billy Budd, is regarded judiciously by Melville. He is "at least in aspect" the "Handsome Sailor . . . a superior figure of [his] own class [accepting] the spontaneous homage of his shipmates . . . a nautical Murat" perhaps. He could be "Ashore . . . the champion; afloat the spokesman; on every suitable occasion always foremost." Billy Budd *could* be all these things, but he fails actually to become them. Physically he is well suited for the role, but he is found

*From *American Literature* 22 (1950):128–136. Copyright © 1950, 1977 Duke University Press. Reprinted by permission.

wanting mentally. Unperceptive, in fear of authority, extremely naïve, suffering the tragic fault of a stammer in moments of stress, Billy Budd cannot qualify as a *spokesman*. Melville lets us know this early in the story, and keeps reminding us that "welkin-eyed" Billy is nicknamed "Baby Budd," and is "young and tender" with a "lingering adolescent expression." He is "a novice in the complexities of factious life," so simple-minded that when asked by an officer about his place of birth, he replies, "Please, Sir, I don't know . . . But I have heard that I was found in a pretty silk-lined basket hanging one morning from the knocker of a good man's door in Bristol." Melville warns us that Billy Budd "is not presented as a conventional hero."

Melville regards Billy fondly, admiringly in many respects, but critically. He reminds us of Billy's limitations throughout the tale, so when Billy utters those famous words, "God bless Captain Vere," the reader should be qualified to evaluate those words in the mouth of the speaker.

Billy is an ironic figure, as is Captain Vere. Scholarly, retiring, ill at ease with people, "Starry" Vere is in command of a ship at war. Painfully aware of the evil in Claggart, and pronouncing Billy's killing of him the blow of an "angel," Vere nevertheless forces through the death sentence against Billy. A student of philosophy, he ironically rules out all inquiry into the motives for Billy's act and insists that he be tried for striking and killing a petty officer, an approach that can only result in Billy's hanging under the naval code. At heart a kind man, Vere, strange to say, makes possible the depraved Claggart's wish — the destruction of Billy. "God bless Captain Vere!" Is this not piercing irony? As innocent Billy utters these words, does not the reader gag? The injustice of Billy's hanging is heightened by his ironic blessing of the ironic Vere.

Herein lies the literary importance of the tale. The aged Melville had developed a new weapon in his lifelong fight against injustice. Charles R. Anderson put it very well:

> The earlier Melville would have railed against the "evil" of such a system [the hanging of Billy], and the "inhumanity" of Vere being willing to serve as a vehicle of it . . . This is the wonder, the thing that makes *Billy Budd* significant, since Melville discovered so little along this line — that irony is a subtler and finer device for the fiction writer than headlong attack on social abuses.[5]

Billy Budd gives us added proof of Melville's great capacity for growth as a writer. However, his development of a new tool had its ironic counterpart in Melville criticism; many critics mistook Melville's irony for a change in his thinking, rather than a richer development in his craft.

F. Barron Freeman, rejecting the "Testament of acceptance" theory, has substituted the "Recognition of necessity" theory. In an intensive study of the aged Melville's thought, Freeman finds "a calm acceptance of the necessity of earthly imperfection and original sin." In Billy, Freeman sees a

"Christian hero" practicing resignation and achieving final, heavenly reward. To Freeman the "importance . . . in the tale of *Billy Budd* lies in the optimistic way in which it suggests an acceptance of Fate."[6]

Thus it becomes clear that Freeman's "Recognition of necessity" theory is not greatly different from the older "Testament of acceptance" theory. In both cases the rebellious Melville ends his days "chastened and subdued." Gone are the mad tossings of the *Pequod,* moored are the homesick soliloquies of Starbuck, in ashes are the beautiful wild fires of the "hot old man," Ahab. The aged Melville became reconciled. To Watson, Weir, Mumford, Sedgwick, and Thorp, it was achieved in bitterness. To Freeman it came happily in a rediscovery of traditional religious faith. In finally approving "the religious concept of earthly imperfection and heavenly goodness" the old sea dog had found his comfortable niche at the ancestral hearth. But Melville's complex tale offers a quite different theme for analysis as well.[7]

Freeman sees in "the calm description of Billy's ascension" Melville's considered judgment of "hope and triumph in death . . . "[8] Again, style, tone, and form are mistaken for content. For Billy's triumph is not personal, it is social, and so of this world.

As Billy stands on deck with the rope around his neck, "A meek shy light appeared in the East, where stretched a diaphanous fleece of white furrowed vapor. That light slowly waxed . . . " About to die, Billy, who could not conceive of malice or ill will, offers his humble benediction to Vere. And here the main point of Melville's ironic tale is revealed. The sailors, brought on deck to witness the hanging, echo Billy's words. "Without volition as it were, as if indeed the ship's populace were the vehicles of some vocal current electric, with one voice from alow to aloft, came a resonant sympathetic echo — " 'God bless Captain Vere.' " But this is not intended for Vere, for: "yet at that instant Billy alone must have been in their hearts, even as he was in their eyes." The men blessed Billy, not Vere, with the words "God bless Captain Vere." Though hanged as a criminal, Billy is lovingly remembered for his martyrdom. The bluejackets keep track of the spar from which Billy was suspended. "Knowledge followed it from ship to dock-yard and again from dock-yard to ship, still pursuing it even when at last reduced to a mere dock-yard boom. To them a chip of it was a piece of the Cross." Billy dies in helpless defeat only to become ironically reincarnated as a living symbol for all sailors.

And finally Billy is immortalized in a ballad composed by his shipmates. It is a tender ballad, mournful and affectionate, and sings of identification of all sailors with Billy.

> . . . Through the port comes the moon-shine astray!
> . . . But 'twill die in the dawning of Billy's last day.
> A jewel-block they'll make of me to-morrow,
> . . . Like the ear-drop I gave to Bristol Molly —
> . . . Sure, a messmate will reach me the last parting cup;

. . . Heaven knows who will have the running of me up!
. . . But Donald he has promised to stand by the plank;
So I'll shake a friendly hand ere I sink.
. . . Sentry, are you there?
Just ease these darbies at the wrist,
And roll me over fair.
I am sleepy, and the oozy weeds about me twist.

Thus Billy becomes — under Melville's ironic pen — something he never intended becoming: a symbol to all bluejackets of their hardship and camaraderie. He stammered in life, but spoke clearly in death.

So ends Melville's last book, with the sailors singing "Billie in the Darbies," honoring him as one of their own. In this song Melville sings to bewildered Wellingsborough [sic] of Redburn; to Jack Chase, the Great Heart of White-Jacket; to Steelkilt of Moby-Dick, to all the breathing, bleeding characters he ever put on paper.

In Billy Budd, Melville presents a picture of depravity subduing virtue, but not silencing it. Billy is sacrificed, but his ballad-singing mates seize upon this as a symbol of their lives. They never accepted natural depravity as victor, and they lived to see the end of impressment.

Melville knew that. He wrote the story of mutinies in the British Navy almost a full century after they took place. He had the tremendous advantage of historical perspective, a fact almost all critics have overlooked. By 1888 one could correctly evaluate the events of 1797. Melville could appreciate the legacy of the impressed Billy Budds and their mates: "the Great Mutiny, though by Englishmen naturally deemed monstrous at the time, doubtless gave the first latent prompting to most important reforms in the British Navy."

Billy Budd, forcibly removed from the ship Rights-of Man, helped bring the rights of man to the seamen of His Majesty's Navy. His shipmates aboard H.M.S. Indomitable made this possible, along with the generations of seafaring men who followed.

Notes

1. The present writer owes his thanks to Professor Gay Wilson Allen for first suggesting that Billy Budd might best be understood as a work of irony.

2. Lewis Mumford, Herman Melville (New York: Harcourt, Brace, 1929), p. 333, says; "Billy Budd contain[s] the earlier themes . . . of [Melville's] life, now transformed and resolved."

3. Melville had once before used a seemingly impartial pen. "Benito Cereno" is a tale of irony.

4. It is instructive to observe how Melville reworked his background source, The Naval History of Great Britain, by the British historian, William James, into a defense of the mutinying sailors at Spithead and Nore [F. Barron Freeman, ed., Melville's "Billy Budd" (Cambridge, Mass.: Harvard University Press, 1948), pp. 39–40].

5. From his critical comments upon reading this paper. Professor Anderson had begun approaching the irony in *Billy Budd* in his article, "The Genesis of *Billy Budd*," *American Literature*, XII, 329–346 (Nov., 1940).

6. Freeman, *op. cit.*, pp. 115–124.

7. Since this paper was begun, one critic has attacked the "Testament of acceptance" theory, while another has attacked Freeman's "Recognition of necessity" theory. Richard Chase says: " . . . it is my impression that Melville made his definitive moral statement in *Moby Dick, The Confidence Man*, and *Clarel*, and that the moral situation in *Billy Budd* is deeply equivocal." See his article, "Dissent on *Billy Budd*," *Partisan Review*, XV, 1212–1218 (Nov., 1948). Alfred Kazin, discussing Freeman's interpretation, says: "F. Barron Freeman . . . tries to blunt Melville's sharp edge . . . did Melville make through Billy's rapturous death an affirmation of Christian belief? . . . In *Billy Budd* he [Melville] had obviously agreed to accept the whole mysterious creation at last, with the weariness of an old man for whom all questions of justice end in death . . . But it does not follow from this that he forgave God for just possibly not existing." See his review, "Ishmael in His Academic Heaven," *New Yorker*, Feb. 12, 1949, 84–89.

8. Freeman, *op. cit.*, pp. 125–126.

Billy Budd: The Order of the Fall

Richard Harter Fogle*

Interpretation of *Billy Budd* has been copious and elaborate, with the natural result that in some instances at least it has reached the stage of overrefinement. Two views of Melville's novelette are interesting heresies, disastrous in their implications but persuasive enough so that they cannot be ignored. One is the notion that the irony which *Billy Budd* unquestionably contains is of a type which directly reverses the overt meaning of the story; the other, closely related, asserts the presence of a hidden interior narrator behind the apparent third-person narrator whom we would generally identify with Melville. According to this reading, the ostensible narrator is shallow, conventional, and platitudinous, while the concealed narrator is keen and malignant, a bitter mocker behind a bland façade. Both of these views are provocative, and both are destructive and false. At the risk of unfairness, however, they will be dismissed without formal refutation in this essay. Tracking down heresies is dangerous and disagreeable. One is likely to get lost in the process, and in notably unpleasant surroundings. I will therefore offer a few observations only.

The irony imputed by some critics to *Billy Budd* would if it existed be cheap, puerile, and perverse. This masterpiece of Melville's old age contains ironies and ambiguities aplenty, but they are such as arise naturally from profound meditation upon a tragic theme of great magni-

*From *Nineteenth-Century Fiction* 15, 3 (December 1960):189–205. © 1960 Regents of the University of California Press. Reprinted by permission of the Regents and of the author.

tude. They do not reverse the direct statements upon which our sense of the meaning rests, but modify, enrich, and complete them. Likewise the division of the narrator into two is unwarranted by any evidence, and lessens rather than enhances the interest and aesthetic value of the story. The teller of *Billy Budd* is not Melville in any abstraction of Melville "the man," but Melville in relation to the imaginative stuff he is working, and this Melville-the-man-and-the-artist is quite complex enough to encompass both assertion and negation, the hope and the fear, the generality and its completion by the particular. The "hidden narrator," in fact, is merely a fabrication of the critic to convey his own sense of "Melville the man" as a secret malcontent too cowardly to speak out. Acceptance of him would make an intellectual and artistic chaos of the story.

Rejection of these heresies, however, need not deny the complexity of *Billy Budd*. Melville has no fixed beliefs to guide him through the fundamental and tremendous issues of good and evil, of innocence and experience, indeed of basic reality that his story engages. One is concerned, not to minimize its difficulties, but to reassert the good faith along with the value of Melville's final pursuit of truth. Much is positive in *Billy Budd*: the sense of tragedy, the celebration of heroism, the commemoration of the past, the archetypal pattern of the Fall of Man, the meaning of political events, and the ultimate acceptance of the principle of divine justice. It is a story not of diminution but of magnification: not of Aristotelian comedy but of Aristotelian tragedy. . . .

This essay proposes to emphasize the large affirmative elements of *Billy Budd*, which make of it a celebration rather than a condemnation of reality and its mysterious Master. Melville, however, in keeping with his time and his own nature, is dealing with an ultimately unknowable universe which it is nevertheless his paradoxical purpose to know. Given the scope and complexity of the problem and the subtlety and range of the author's mind (to separate them arbitrarily), no easy certainties can be expected. All the issues, in fact, are as difficult as possible. Here a critic might protest that *Billy Budd* is an image, an aesthetic object, and not a metaphysical treatise. One critic at least has persuasively so protested. Yet there are many avenues toward truth, and without rearguing the dispute of literature and belief one can accept the coexistence of a final with a formal cause. Thus assuming the validity of the inquiry, I proceed to the difficulties that complicate the affirmative interpretation of *Billy Budd* that is to be advanced here.

Perhaps the chief of these concerns Captain Vere of the British ship of the line *Indomitable*, aboard which Billy is impressed from the merchantman *The Rights of Man*. Vere is figuratively the God of *Billy Budd*, although we must be cautious in applying the metaphor, so as to avoid a full and literal identification. Much depends, then, upon the reader's interpretation of him. Is he well-intentioned, beneficent? Is his judgment to be respected? He is certainly used as a symbol for order: nicknamed

"Starry" Vere, he represents the steadfast, well-regulated system of the heavens, the ideal of conservatism. Yet it may be asked, "Is this good?" To William Blake it would not have been good; his Urizen, the God of repression and negation, was lord of the stars in their courses, and Melville knew Blake:

> Prison'd on wat'ry shore,
> Starry Jealousy does keep my den:
> Cold and hoar,
> Weeping o'er,
> I hear the father of the ancient men.

Vere might conceivably be the inexorable agent of the principle of tyranny. Also, if he is well-intentioned, he may be misguided. In carrying out the provisions of the naval code by which he is bound, he apparently violates it in a number of instances. He takes judgment into his own hands; at the fatal court-martial he is arbitrary, so that his officers are seriously disturbed; the procedure at Billy's execution, which is carried out with masterly forethought, is subtly irregular. He could have waited—it would have been more customary to wait—upon the judgment of his admiral, but he hurries Billy to his death.

These are possibilities, for which Melville makes full allowance. Nevertheless the weight of both the internal and the external evidence is strongly against them. As to the evidence in *Billy Budd* itself the question, very frequent in modern criticism, may be asked, is it possible to draw a conclusion at all? Is not Vere a dramatic character in an imagined fictional work, whom the author treats with dramatic objectivity? One answers that no such objectivity is possible to any creator but God himself—the writer aspires to objectivity, he tries to free himself from the limits of his individual mind, but if he succeeded he would be more or less than human, and his work would be more or less than literature. He cannot and should not transcend the limitations of his own vision and emphasis, which are also his identity and his power. Absolute objectivity would be simply confusion and meaningless, dead neutrality. The writer tells us, "Here is the way I see things, here is the evidence. You may if you like interpret my evidence differently." So Melville offers us ample material for divergent interpretations of Captain Vere, but his own is accessible to us in the text of *Billy Budd*. To deny that it can be determined is in my opinion a disastrous conclusion based upon a half-truth.

Captain the Honorable Edward Fairfax Vere is a bachelor of forty at the time of the action of *Billy Budd*. Melville uses a dialectic method of balanced oppositions to describe him: he is of noble birth, but his advancement has not been altogether owing to his family connections; a stern disciplinarian, he is also mindful of the welfare of his men; he is "intrepid to the verge of temerity, though never injudiciously so"; a thorough seaman and naval officer, he never uses nautical terms in ordinary conversation, and is notably unobtrusive as commander of his ship. In politics he is an enlightened conservative. He represents a golden mean.

He has salient traits and qualities, however, which characterize him more sharply as an unusual man. Though practical enough when occasion demands it, he "would at times betray a certain dreaminess of mood." He is exceptionally bookish, and he reads deeply, in "confirmation of his own more reserved thoughts," and to establish settled principles by study of the past. His fellow officers find him a little pedantic; he cannot quite accommodate his thought and conversation to the "bluff company" of men "whose reading was mainly confined to the journals." Thus he has not quite the tact of a man of the world; he is too honest and direct to pay careful heed to immediate circumstances. His nickname, "Starry" Vere, has come upon him accidentally from a kinsman who had been reading Marvell's "Appleton House," with the lines

> This 'tis to have been from the first
> In a domestic heaven nursed
> Under the discipline severe
> Of Fairfax and the starry Vere.

The connection is casually made, but the association of "discipline severe" with the captain is nevertheless worth pointing out. A lover of order, he is devoted to duty and discipline, and certainly to self-discipline.

Vere is a bachelor, and Melville frequently attaches symbolic importance to the distinction between the bachelor and the married man—to which categories of humanity the monk might also be added. Carefree detachment from the deeper problems of life, however, is generally the hallmark of Melville's bachelors; in particular, they disbelieve in evil and are untouched by it. Captain Delano of "Benito Cereno" and Stubb in *Moby Dick* are bachelors, symbolically though not literally; the Templars of the sketch "The Paradise of Bachelors" are bachelors who have in The Inner Temple found the perfect freedom from trouble. Captain Vere is not quite like these; his is the disengagement of one set apart for a high and strange destiny. Uninvolved, *Billy Budd* involves him in complex tragedy. This sense of destiny is presumably the reason for his otherwise unexplained "dreaminess of mood." The trait both isolates and exalts him, as one who is to be the priest of dreadful rites and mysteries. Though unconsciously, he looks forward to his great central act.

One notices that Vere resembles Melville himself, in his reading, in his respect for the lessons of the past, especially the history of classical antiquity; perhaps in what ordinary men think of as his pedantry. Melville's well known disinclination for society in his later years was partly attributable to his hopelessness of being understood. Like Vere no man of the world, he sought some genuine meeting of minds, and was impatient of the usual pleasantries of social intercourse. Most important for our reading of Captain Vere's character, his conservative love of order is shared by the later Melville. This statement is no doubt debatable, but the evidence in support of it is very strong: within *Billy Budd* itself in the introductory sections on the mutinies at Spithead and the Nore, and in the general attitude toward the French Revolution. The Nore Mutineers "ran up with hurras the British colors with the union and cross wiped out; by that cancellation transmuting the flag of founded law and freedom defined, into the enemy's red meteor of unbridled and unbounded revolt. Reasonable discontent growing out of practical grievances in the fleet had been ignited into irrational combustion as by live cinders blown across the Channel from France in flames." This and comparable passages, I maintain, are to be taken at their face value.

Melville's writing from *Battle-Pieces* onward supports this argument for Captain Vere. The heavily boding introductory poems of the *Battle-Pieces* volume are darkened by the prospect of civil disorder—

> When ocean-clouds over inland hills
> Sweep storming in late autumn brown,
> And horror the sodden valley fills,
> And the spire falls crashing in the town,
> I must upon my countries ills. . . .
> "Misgivings"

The impressive "The House-Top" is unequivocal in its condemnation of the New York draft rioters:

> The Town is taken by its rats—ship-rats
> And rats of the wharves. All civil charms
> And priestly spells which late held hearts in awe—
> Fear-bound, subjected to a better sway
> Than sway of self; these like a dream dissolve,
> And man rebounds whole aeons back in nature.

True, the suppression of the riots by martial law is partly regrettable, a "grimy slur on the Republic's faith implied," but Man's dignity, "never to be scourged," is as "Nature's Roman," living in freedom under law. "Bridegroom Dick" of "John Marr and other Sailors" acquiesces to naval authority as the earlier White-jacket had not, as an inescapable necessity, and one may mention in passing the many signs in the massive *Clarel* of Melville's revulsion from materialist and naturalistic doctrines of unfettered democratic rule and inevitable progress. In the late *Timoleon* volume "Fragments of a Lost Gnostic Poem" reads like a direct attack upon Blake's exaltation of energy unrestrained—

> Indolence is heaven's ally here,
> And energy the child of hell:
> The Good Man pouring from his pitcher clear,
> But brims the poisoned well . . .

and "The Age of the Antonines," when "Orders and ranks they kept degree," is set up as an example for Americans to ponder. Melville praises "Greek Architecture" for

> Not magnitude, not lavishness,
> But Form — the Site;
> Not innovating wilfulness,
> But reverence for the Archetype.

Far more could be cited from the poems and prose of the later Melville to demonstrate their kinship with the convictions of Captain Vere, but these instances may suffice.

So much for Vere's character. To proceed to his actions, their wisdom and their honesty are open to question, but this must always be true of any man's conduct when faced with a tragic dilemma. We sense that the Captain must play his predestined part in the tragic drama. If he is guilty of a tragic error, it is in his insistence upon secrecy throughout, or perhaps more largely in his acceptance of all responsibility for decisions. Yet here again, the tragic circumstance is unusual, the natures of the men he deals with exceptional, and chance by accumulation takes on the purpose and the power of fate. . . .

[When Billy strikes and kills Claggart] Vere immediately foresees the full consequences, as his first word indicates. " 'Fated boy,' breathed Captain Vere in tone so low as to be almost a whisper, 'what have you done!' " Henceforth he is to be the agent of the Fates, or perhaps the banishing angel of the latter Fall.

The Captain's behavior in the following moments is suspicious, almost mad, to the eye of an observer. The ship's surgeon is immediately summoned. A prudent, poised, and experienced man, he is an excellent witness. His shock, however, comes from his limited understanding of what he witnesses. Vere's conduct is perfectly intelligible by the light of his own superior insight.

> Suddenly, catching the Surgeon's arm convulsively, he exclaimed pointing down to the body — "it is the divine judgment of Ananias! Look!
> . . ." Captain Vere was now again motionless standing absorbed in thought. But again starting, he vehemently exclaimed — "Struck dead by an angel of God. Yet the angel must hang!"

The surgeon is further disturbed by Vere's disposition of the body in a compartment of his cabin, as implying an unaccountable desire for secrecy; and, as we have seen, in this respect Vere is consistently laid open to suspicion. The possibility that he is wrong, or even that he is evil, is steadily before us. Yet a reasonable reading demonstrates that Vere's estimate of the situation, affected as it is by mutiny and war, is correct. A fallen and corrupted world can only be governed by the stern provisions of the Mutiny Act, carried out with the utmost speed and decision. No time can be permitted for doubt or speculation by those who might mutiny; in his secrecy Vere is defending an indispensable order. The surgeon is a calm and experienced man of the world, but Vere is more than a man of the world. He is as it were a seer and priest, endowed with intuitive knowledge of the human heart and spirit, well-fitted, and alone well-fitted on the battleship *Indomitable*, to comprehend two such extraordinary human beings as Claggart and Billy Budd. Along with them he belongs to a different order of nature from common humanity, and he is of tragedy the ideal spectator as well as the agent.

Melville specifically distinguishes, in his discussion of Claggart's character, between the man of the world and the wise man: "I am not certain whether to know the world and to know human nature be not two distinct branches of knowledge, which while they may coexist in the same heart, yet either may exist with little or nothing of the other. Nay, in an average man of the world, his constant rubbing with it blunts that fine spiritual insight indispensable to the understanding of the essential in certain exceptional characters, whether evil ones or good." Such an exceptional character is Captain Vere, as is made utterly clear in the account of his final interview with the condemned Billy. This interview is private—the narrator himself does not venture to intrude upon it, so that its precise nature is left in obscurity. Its general purport, however, is unmistakable: "But there is no telling the sacrament, seldom if in any case revealed to the gadding world wherever under circumstances at all akin to those here attempted to be set forth two of great Nature's nobler order embrace. There is privacy at the time, inviolable to the survivor, and holy oblivion the sequel to each diviner magnanimity, providentially covers all at last." The solemnly hieratic quality of *Billy Budd* is epitomized in the vocabulary of this passage, with "sacrament," "great Nature," "privacy . . . inviolable," "holy oblivion," "diviner magnanimity," and "providentially." The story is concerned both literally and more largely with a mystery. The reference to "great Nature" might lead us to one further reflection: despite the grounds for suspicion of him which Melville himself carefully implants, we can confidently exculpate Captain Vere from the guilt that inheres in the code he carries out because he so thoroughly understands its limitations, and so clearly distinguishes between its empirical measures and the absolute values of divine justice. Vere is genuinely disinterested because he comprehends the entire truth. He himself dies in battle not long after the execution of Billy, and his last words are the murmured " 'Billy Budd, Billy Budd,' " but "That these were not the accents of remorse, would seem clear . . ." His death, fighting the French battleship *Atheiste*, is a fitting consummation of a solemn observance, and is ironic only in the largest sense of tragic irony, a mode quite devoid of mockery.

Melville properly declines to make a definitive statement, although one would suppose that the import of the passages cited above was definite enough. "Whether Captain Vere, as the Surgeon professionally and primarily surmised, was really the sudden victim of any degree of aberration, one must determine for himself by such light as this narrative may afford." The light afforded is surely sufficient, both as regards Vere's wisdom and his good faith. Yet the situation is enormously complex, even in a sense perverse: "In the jugglery of circumstances preceding and attending the event on board the *Indomitable* and in the light of the martial code whereby it was formally to be judged, innocence and guilt personified in Claggart and Budd — in effect changed places." This jugglery, of course, affects not merely Claggart and Billy but Captain Vere as well, so that the better may frequently seem to be the worser part. Thus at the court-martial all his officers take a more lenient view than Vere's; they seek some compromise to avoid invoking the penalty of death. They are, however, "well-meaning men not intellectually mature," too weak to confront the logic of tragedy. " 'But surely,' " says the good-natured officer of marines, " 'Budd purposed neither mutiny nor homicide.' " " 'Surely not, my good man,' " Vere replies. " 'And before a court less arbitrary and more merciful than a martial one that plea would largely extenuate. At the last Assizes it shall acquit. But how here? We proceed under the law of the Mutiny Act.' " It is to be remarked, incidentally, as part of the jugglery of circumstances by which Vere is made to act outside the code he would enforce in order to achieve the purposes for which it exists, that the presence of a marine "in a case having to do with a sailor" is an infraction of the general custom of the Navy. It is worth noticing, too, that Melville does not spare Vere at the court-martial the tinge of pedantry he has earlier mentioned as one of his attributes. As has been asserted, however, this slight disharmony of Vere's with ordinary minds should be interpreted, although it could be otherwise interpreted, as a mark of his strength and distinction and not of his weakness. One feels that in this matter Melville comes very close to identifying himself sympathetically with his character.

At the court-martial Vere is at first slow to speak, but his hesitation comes of considering how best to fit his words to the capacities of his hearers. "Similar impatience as to talking is perhaps one reason that deters some minds from addressing any popular assemblies."

> When speak he did, something both in the substance of what he said and his manner of saying it, showed the influence of unshared studies modifying and tempering the practical training of an active career. This, along with his phraseology now and then was suggestive of the grounds whereon rested that imputation of a certain pedantry socially alleged against him by certain naval men of wholly practical cast . . .

Vere thus represents something of Melville's own isolation in his age and society, and symbolized in the circumstances of the writing itself of *Billy Budd*, a work for long unpublished. This isolation does not at all preclude an anxious solicitude for the times, and a desire to set men right. Vere may be said to be preaching the necessity of tragedy to his good-natured and reluctant officers, and so, on the whole, is Melville. In a complacent and optimistic age he asserts the doctrine "now popularly ignored," of the Fall of Man, and directs attention to the neglected words of Holy Writ, to which he recurs.

> And, indeed, if that lexicon which is based on Holy Writ were any longer popular, one might with less difficulty define and denominate certain phenomenal men. As it is, one must turn to some authority not liable to the charge of being tinctured with Biblical element. . . . Dark sayings are these, some will say. But why? Is it because they somewhat savor of Holy Writ in its phrase mysteries of iniquity? If they do, such savor was foreign from my intention for little will it commend these pages to many a reader of today.

The irony is minatory. Vere also uses the phrase, "a mystery of iniquity," in lecturing to his officers.

Neither Melville nor Vere is denying the possibility of progress and the existence of Providence. The rejection of materialist optimism does not preclude the hope that all may yet be well. More than once in *Billy Budd* it is said that the French Revolution, once deemed an unmixed evil, has functioned in a design to bring about an ultimate good, in which the sacrifice of Billy has its mysterious place as well. But Melville and Vere maintain that this good can come about only through suffering and tragic action; there are no short cuts, no easy solutions. The Original Sin has alienated man from nature, and therefore no natural code can fitly govern human society. War is a sin; the mutiny at the Nore is a sin against order; and their consequences are the Articles of War and the Mutiny Act. Yet the alienation is not total, we are not wholly estranged from the natural and the divine; and sacrifice can redeem. At the court-martial Captain Vere's movements symbolize his resistance against an inappropriate yielding to nature, his acceptance of the hard and bitter way: "Turning, he to-and-fro paced the cabin athwart; in the returning ascent to windward, climbing the slant deck in the ship's lee roll; without knowing it symbolizing thus in his action a mind resolute to surmount difficulties even if against primitive instincts strong as the wind and the sea." His argument re-emphasizes this separation: " 'Though the ocean, which is inviolate Nature primeval, though this be the element where we move and have our being as sailors, yet as the King's officers lies our duty in a sphere correspondingly natural?' "

In connection with the verdict of the court-martial, a verdict of death directed largely by Vere, the famous American case of the brig-of-war *Somers* is referred to as a parallel, although on the *Somers* the sentence of death was carried out "in a time of peace and within not many days sail of home." This case, in which Melville's cousin Gert Gansevoort, an officer on the *Somers*, figured prominently, is "here cited without comment." Yet the following paragraph constitutes a powerful justification of the decision, or at least the decider, in each instance:

> Says a writer whom few know, "Forty years after a battle it is easy for a non-combatant to reason about how it ought to have been fought. It is another thing personally and under fire to direct the fighting while involved in the obscuring smoke of it. Much so with respect to other emergencies involving considerations both practical and moral, and when it is imperative promptly to act. The greater the fog the more it imperils the steamer, and speed is put on though at the hazard of running somebody down. Little ween the snug card-players in the cabin of the responsibilities of the sleepless man on the bridge."

The writer "whom few know" is of course Melville himself.

The quotation suggests, in addition to its obvious sympathy with the man in authority, the terrible directness and nakedness of his responsibility. In executing his constituted law he himself stands outside it. Vere as well as Billy Budd must be the sacrifice, as is indicated by the private interview after the verdict, which associates the two as father and son, Abraham and Isaac (or God the Father and God the Son). Immediately after the interview the senior lieutenant of the *Indomitable* encounters his Captain: "The face he beheld, for the moment one expressive of the agony of the strong, was to that officer, though a man of fifty, a startling revelation. That the condemned one suffered less than he who mainly had effected the condemnation was apparently indicated. . . ." And Vere's duty is to remain agonizing and to a degree equivocal, in the tragic jugglery of circumstances. "In this proceeding [the burial of Claggart] as in every public one growing out of the tragedy strict adherence to usage was observed," it is said. Yet, as has been hinted earlier, this is in a sense not true. Original Sin has set all askew, as man is apart from nature; the order of the Mutiny Act is an order subtly distorted, a little perverse. To maintain it Vere must in some degree violate it. Or, to put the action on another level, Vere is the priest-celebrant of a mysterious ceremonial sacrifice, which he must perform with decorum in despite of imperfect assistants and a confused and turbulent congregation, the crew of the *Indomitable*.

Until the sacrifice is consummated the Original Sin is in power. Its consequences cannot be evaded. "Their Captain's announcement was listened to by the throng of standing sailors in a dumbness like that of a seated congregation of believers in hell listening to the clergyman's announcement of his Calvinistic text." Extraordinary measures are taken, therefore, to ensure that the ceremony is fitly carried out. Special precautions are taken that none shall communicate with Billy (save the Chaplain, whose services as Christian priest are irrelevant at this grim observance and unneeded by the victim himself). Certain parts of the ceremony are imperceptibly altered or hastened as the immediate circumstances dictate; regularity is consistently preserved by slight irregularities. Thus at a threatening murmur of the crew its entity as a congregation is suddenly destroyed by calling the starboard watch. "Shrill as the shriek of the sea-hawk the whistles of the Boatswain and his Mates pierced that ominous low sound, dissipating it; and yielding to the mechanism of discipline the throng was thinned by one half." The comparison suggests the cruel bird of prey, perhaps the exultant emissary of a fierce sky-god, like the hawk that was dragged to destruction with the sinking *Pequod* in *Moby Dick*. This, with its implications, is an aspect of the meaning that cannot be ignored, but at the same time it is only one aspect of a very complex totality. To return to the progress of events, Billy's body is then buried with all expedition, "with a promptitude not perceptibly merging into hurry, though bordering that." But "a second strange human murmur was heard" when sea birds pass close to the ship and hover over the spot where the body has vanished into the sea. Immediately the drum beats to quarters, "at an hour prior to the customary one."

> That such variance from usage was authorized by an officer like Captain Vere, a martinet as some deemed him, was evidence of the necessity for unusual action, implied in what he deemed to be temporarily the mood of his men. "With mankind" he would say "forms, measured forms are everything; and that is the import couched in the story of Orpheus with his lyre spellbinding the wild denizens of the woods." And this he once applied to the disruption of forms going on across the Channel and the consequences thereof.

Here again form as it were violates form to secure the ends of form. The actions of the sea birds present a complex situation to us. They represent a natural and in some degree a divine order, as the superstitious sailors intuitively sense; they are akin to the "primitive instincts strong as the wind and the sea" against which we have seen Captain Vere resolutely combating. The imagery of this passage is strongly reminiscent of Melville's impressive ballad of "The Haglets," the fatal birds that follow the doomed flagship of the Admiral of the White. These seafowl are notable at once for their apparent purposiveness and their absolute alienation from the purposes of man; they are "the seafowl . . . whose hearts none know," the "inscrutable haglets," the "shadowing three" that ". . . follow, follow fast in wake, / Untiring wing and lidless eye. . . ." Thus the birds that come to the burial of Billy Budd have a dual significance. They are supernatural, but do they mourn or exult? Are they the emissaries of a god of nature who is outraged and pitiful, or of an authoritarian sky-god, like Shelley's Jupiter, who forever oppresses the natural man, the "people" of the *Indomitable* and of the world? For Melville's purposes they are both, though these meanings are contradictory; since the possibilities of the situation itself are ambiguous and contradictory.

Immediately upon the second murmur of the crew the drum beats to quarters. "At this unwonted muster at quarters, all proceeded as at the regular hour." The religious ceremony in which Billy Budd has been sacrificed to the observance of the Mutiny Act concludes formally, in terms specifically liturgical: "The band on the quarter-deck played a sacred air. After which the Chaplain went through with the customary morning service. That done, the drum beat the retreat, and toned by music and religious rites subserving the discipline and purpose of war, the men in their wonted orderly manner dispersed to the places allotted them when not at the guns." There is plainly a sharp irony in this mingling of Christianity and war. Vere is the real priest, the Chaplain only a simulacrum. Yet the tragedy must be played out, the redemption must be bought by the blood of the Lamb, and Vere and Billy must take their allotted parts.

Critics have frequently noted the supernatural aura surrounding the death of Billy, so that he becomes momentarily a second Christ. At the last signal, "it chanced that the vapory fleece hanging low in the East, was shot through with a soft glory as of the fleece of the Lamb of God seen in mystical vision simultaneously therewith, watched by the wedged mass of upturned faces, Billy ascended; and ascending, took the full rose of the dawn." Some physical aspects of the execution are so unusual as to seem miraculous. And at full day, "The fleece of low-hanging vapor had vanished, licked up by the sun that late had so glorified it. And the circumambient air in the clearness of its serenity was like smooth white marble in the polished block not yet removed from the marble-dealer's yard." This latter manifestation is not free from ambiguity, with the vanishing of the fleece and the suggestion of a tombstone in "the marble-dealer's yard," but the clearness and serenity remain.

[Captain Vere and the Weakness of Expediency]

Merlin Bowen*

There has been for many years a tendency to see in *Billy Budd* Melville's last "testament of acceptance," his long-delayed recognition of necessity — almost, as it were, the deathbed recantation of his "absolutist" errors: the author becomes his own chastened Babbalanja, kneeling on the Serenian sands to beg forgiveness for his past impiety and madness. (One wonders here to what extent this judgment may rest upon a too unqualified identification of Melville with the more intransigent of his heroes.) In

*From *The Long Encounter* (Chicago: University of Chicago Press, 1960), 216-33. ©
1960 The University of Chicago Press. Reprinted by permission of the publisher and
author.

such a view, at any rate, Captain Vere commonly assumes the stature of a tragic hero. He is seen as a brooding and compassionate Lincoln, courageously facing up to the hard necessities of action and responsibility, as a sort of latter-day Abraham "resolutely offering [young Isaac] up in obedience to the exacting behest."[1] What somehow goes unnoticed is that the action of hanging Billy is undertaken in clear opposition to Vere's own conscience and in obedience to "the exacting behest" not of God but of social expediency.

There are, it is true, several considerations that would seem to invite such an interpretation: the circumstances of the work's composition, so like those of that other supposed farewell to life, Shakespeare's *Tempest;* the quiet, unrhetorical, and "reasonable" character of the style; the frequently equivocal nature of the narrator's comments; and, finally, one may guess, the experience of our own generation with a like crisis of civilization so immense as to dwindle, as it seems, all merely personal values and standards.

Surely, though, it must come as a shock to any reader of Melville to find him here at the end of a long and deeply considered life with nothing more to show for it than this sorry wisdom of resignation to a forced complicity in evil. Nothing in the earlier writings — certainly not in *Clarel* — could have led one to predict so complete a reversal of attitude. And when one remembers the motto — "Keep true to the dreams of thy youth" — glued to the inside of the writing box on which *Billy Budd* was composed, one's doubts of such an interpretation grow.

Fortunately, there is no need to rely upon external probabilities in disputing such a view. The pages of *Billy Budd* themselves contain sufficient evidence upon which to base a quite different estimate of Captain Vere. According to this view, he appears as a uniformed and conscientious servant of "Cain's city," an overcivilized man who has stifled the sound of his own heart and learned to live by the head alone as his calling requires, who has abdicated his full humanity in the interests of a utilitarian social ethic and postponed the realization of truth and justice to some other and more convenient world. Neither the Christian gospel nor the modern doctrine of the rights of man has, in his opinion, any place in the government of this man-of-war world. And when the simple and loyal-hearted sailor, Billy Budd, left speechless by Claggart's accusation of treason, impulsively knocks the liar down and so kills him, the practical Vere knows his duty at once and resolutely proceeds to hang, for the greatest good of the greatest number, a man innocent in all but the most technical sense of the word.

To state the facts thus baldly is to express perhaps too harsh a judgment. One must admit that there is something deeply pathetic in the spectacle of a man fundamentally good, as Vere is, being led by the logic of his assumptions into so false a dilemma and so fatal a resolution. But to go beyond pity, as some critics do, and to discover in his collaboration with admitted evil the elements of heroism or philosophic wisdom is surely to infer beyond the presented evidence and to slide over the book's many indications of Vere's narrowness and rigidity. *Billy Budd* will appear as a much more coherent, though still puzzling, work of art if regarded as a study in the possible consequences of a commitment to a fixed and theoretic pattern rather than to patternless life itself with all its contradictions, crosscurrents, and inescapable risks.

In the book's central opposition of civilization and nature, head and heart, there can be no real question where Captain the Honorable Edward Fairfax Vere stands: quite clearly, and despite his own instinctive feelings in the matter,[2] he stands with Claggart and against Billy. By both temperament and training, he is much closer to the petty officer he despises than to the young foretopman he admires. There does exist, of course, an obvious difference of intention (or wish) between the two officers; but this difference remains, by Vere's insistence that "private conscience" must not oppose the naval code, a purely theoretical one, with no slightest influence upon conduct, and for this reason it can hardly be called a moral difference at all.

Captain Vere's political faith is here very much to the point. As he is described to us, he appears as a Burkean conservative of the strictest sort, whose faith lies neither in man nor in "novel opinions" but in proved and "lasting institutions."[3] Billy, it will be recalled, has been forcibly impressed into the service of these institutions from aboard the merchantman "Rights-of-Man," named for Thomas Paine's famous "rejoinder of Burke's arraignment of the French Revolution."[4] Recent disorders in France and even within the British navy itself have seriously alarmed Vere. Distrustful of his own men,[5] he has even less confidence in the general mass: " 'With mankind' he would say 'forms, are everything; and that is the import couched in the story of Orpheus with his lyre spell-binding the wild denizens of the wood.' And this he once applied to the disruption of forms going on across the Channel and the consequences thereof."[6] Nature has for him the connotation of disorder, and he fears it accordingly. When, anxious for an immediate conviction of Billy and alarmed by what he considers the "scruples" of his court, he reminds his officers that " 'our allegiance is [not] to Nature [but] to the King,' " he is not speaking metaphorically: the king he has in mind is George III, and he is calling upon his officers to reject the natural in favor, not of the supernatural, but of the artificial, in the form of a particular, imperfect social order. They have in fact, he reminds them, already made that choice, for

> "in receiving our commissions we in the most important regards ceased to be natural free agents. When war is declared, are we the commissioned fighters previously consulted? We fight at command. If our judgments approve the war, that is but coincidence. . . . So now. For suppose condemnation to follow these present proceedings. Would it be so much we ourselves that would condemn as it would be martial law

operating through us? For that law and the rigor of it, we are not responsible. Our vowed responsibility is in this: That however pitilessly that law may operate in any instance, we nevertheless adhere to it and administer it."[7]

Billy, on the other hand, has participated in no such compact, has signed away nothing. Born outside the law as a natural child, he remains "little more than a sort of upright barbarian, much . . . as Adam presumably might have been ere the urbane Serpent wriggled himself into his company." He wears, it is true, though not by choice, "the external uniform of civilization," but this is a matter of the surface only: his peculiar virtues, "pristine and unadulterate," derive "from a period prior to Cain's city and citified man."[8] Yet, he is no anarchist. His loyalty is no less true than Vere's, but it is a simpler and far less abstract thing — essentially a sort of heartfelt personal gratitude and love: " 'I have eaten the King's bread and I am true to the King.' "[9] Such a sentiment has much less to recommend it to the "thoroughly civilized" mind than has the "austere patriotism" of Claggart[10] — so serviceable to authority, so zealous for order, so irrespective of persons. And where artificial virtues are thus honored above the natural, evil is certain to prosper: "Civilization, especially if of the austerer sort, is auspicious to it. It folds itself in the mantle of respectability."[11] Each finds that it can make use of the other. A sense, upon a prior occasion, of something "superserviceable and strained" about Claggart's zeal has not led Vere to dispense with the informer's services. And in the end it is through Vere that Claggart's wish for Billy's destruction is accomplished, and by Vere's refusal to publish the truth that the lie of Claggart's fidelity and Billy's depravity gains acceptance as the authorized account.

Vere's excessive intellectuality is a second consideration aligning him with his despised but useful master-at-arms. The simple and unsophisticated Billy is an illiterate, endowed only with "that kind and degree of intelligence going along with the unconventional rectitude of a sound human creature, one to whom not yet has been proffered the questionable apple of knowledge."[12] But Claggart's "general aspect and manner" hint of an education quite above the demands of his office, and "his brow [is] of the sort phrenologically associated with more than average intellect."[13] (It is upon this forehead, "so shapely and intellectual-looking a feature in the master-at-arms," that Billy's fatal blow is later to fall.)[14] Billy's face, on the other hand, is "without the intellectual look of the pallid Claggart's, [but] none the less [is] it lit, like his, from within, though from a different source. The bonfire in his heart [makes] luminous the rose-tan in his cheek."[15]

Lacking as he is in any qualities that might be called brilliant,[16] Captain Vere is one of those who live by the head. His "philosophical austerity"[17] leaves little room for feeling. Exhibiting "a marked leaning toward everything intellectual," he reads much and thoughtfully, if within a rather narrow range, preferring those books which treat of "actual men and events" — the world as it is — to those which address the imagination.[18] These "unshared studies [,] modifying and tempering the practical training of an active career," have the effect of making him seem to certain of his fellow officers somewhat "pedantic" and remote from life — "a dry and bookish gentleman."[19] "A certain dreaminess of mood" comes over him at times which, when unavoidably broken in upon by a subordinate, may be transformed into a flash of unexpected but instantly controlled anger. Control is perhaps his most marked characteristic. Habitually grave in his bearing, he has "little appreciation of mere humor," and is by rigorous training, if not by nature, "the most undemonstrative of men."[20] His is "a mind resolute to surmount difficulties even if against primitive instincts strong as the wind and the sea."[21] The problem which Billy's impulsive act has placed before the court appears to him a practical one to be settled on purely rational grounds. Fearful of the still insufficiently "formalized humanity" of his officers, he warns them not to admit the heart to their councils:

> "But the exceptional in the matter moves the hearts within you. Even so too is mine moved. But let not warm hearts betray heads that should be cool. Ashore in a criminal case will an upright judge allow himself off the bench to be waylaid by some tender kinswoman of the accused seeking to touch him with her tearful plea? Well the heart, sometimes the feminine in man, here is as that piteous woman, and hard though it be, she must here be ruled out."[22]

The officers, less intellectually agile than he, seem not to notice the flaw in his analogy — at any rate do not venture to point out that what the heart asks in this case is not gratuitous mercy but ordinary justice, which is never disregardful of intent. But they remain "less convinced than agitated by the course of [his] argument."[23] When, finally, they do yield, it is not because their "scruples" have been dissipated but because they have been overawed by Vere's superior mind and crowded into action by his representations of urgency.[24] They have been given, too, their captain's personal assurance that he sympathizes with his victim as deeply as they; and in that knowledge there is perhaps some comfort for them, if no help for Billy. " 'Budd's intent or non-intent [Vere has earlier instructed them] is nothing to the purpose' "; their concern must be with his deed alone.[25] Fortunately, it is quite otherwise with the judges' act: here it is the intent and not the deed that matters. " 'I feel as you do for this unfortunate boy [Vere assures them]. But did he know our hearts, I take him to be of that generous nature that he would feel even for us on whom in this military necessity so heavy a compulsion is laid.' "[26]

The nature of that alleged compulsion deserves a more careful examination. Vere, is, to begin with, no simple impressed seaman but an officer and therefore a volunteer. He is also, as Melville is at some pains to emphasize, a mature, thoughtful, and morally sensitive man who presumably knew what he was doing when he accepted his commission and so placed himself in the service of a military code whose brutishness he abhors.[27] If, as he now intimates, his buttons and epaulets were purchased at the cost of his independence as a moral being, it must be admitted that the bargain was his own. His reason for making it seems clear enough from the evidence furnished us: he is deeply, indeed fanatically, committed to the maintenance of the established order as the sole means of preserving "the peace of the world and the true welfare of mankind."[28] And as the happiness of the human species seems to him dependent upon "lasting institutions," so these in turn rest upon the disciplined strength of the British fleet, "the right arm of a Power then all but the sole free conservative one of the Old World."[29] With so clear a view of the steps leading to "the true welfare of mankind," it is not surprising that in what seems to him a grave emergency Vere should dismiss the voice of conscience as an irrelevance,[30] relegate the whole question of moral intent to the leisured speculations of casuists and "psychologic theologians," and resign himself with an almost Plinlimmonish acquiescence to the unattainability of true justice this side of " 'the Last Assizes.' "[31]

Clearly, it is for this world that Captain Vere's most anxious cares are felt. The interests of the next world are represented locally by the chaplain, and the captain is no doubt happy to reciprocate that gentleman's religious care not to over-step the limits of his jurisdiction.[32] Like every sensible commander, he takes the navy as he finds it, accepting philosophically such established evils as impressment, spying, and flogging.[33] He conducts the business of his ship strictly according to China time; and if God chooses to send one of His Greenwich chronometers aboard, He does so at His own risk. " 'Struck dead by an angel of God,' " Vere exclaims as he looks down at the fallen Claggart. " 'Yet the angel must hang!' "[34] One is reminded of the answer of another practical man in an earlier book when begged to intercede for the life of a boy condemned to death for a cause of conscience: " 'Speak not,' said Media. " 'His fate is fixed. Let [the world] stand.' "[35]

But one must be careful — as Meville himself is — not to make a monster of Vere. He is neither a sadist nor a conscious hypocrite. If he is cruel, if he is sometimes not wholly honest with himself and others, these faults are rather the consequences of a principled expediency and an excessive caution.

Caution is, of course, constitutional with him. As the rule of the heart declares itself in an impulsiveness bordering at times on rashness, so the rule of the head is commonly evidenced by a habit of guarded circumspection. Claggart, for instance, is gifted with "an uncommon prudence" and brings to the accomplishment of his irrational aim "a cool judgment[,] sagacious and sound."[36] And Captain Vere, on his part, would seem to be the very soul of caution. Of his personal courage, of course, there can be no serious question: that has already been proved in a number of naval engagements.[37] But where the safety of his ship — and, by extension, of the fleet and civilization — seems to him concerned, he becomes suspicious and fearful in the extreme.

The master-at-arms, it appears, knows this trait of his captain well enough and plays upon it adroitly — almost too adroitly, since he arouses his anger — when giving "evidence" against Billy at the mainmast.[38] Vere impatiently brushes aside the imputation of fear on his part; but the seed has been planted with Iago-like cunning and almost immediately begins to put forth shoots. Fearfulness certainly lies behind Vere's strange decision to test the informer's truthfulness by a private confrontation with the accused rather than by a formal examination of witnesses.[39] What legally admissible evidence he could hope to obtain by such a confrontation is not at all clear, but what does in point of fact happen is that he himself thereby sets up the fatal situation and invites disaster. The point was not lost upon that "self-poised character of . . . grave sense and experience," the ship's surgeon. Leaving Vere's cabin under a strict injunction of secrecy after certifying the death of the master-at-arms, "he could not help thinking how more than futile the utmost discretion sometimes proves in this human sphere, subject as it is to unforeseeable fatalities; the prudent method adopted by Captain Vere to obviate publicity and trouble having resulted in an event that necessitated the former, and, under existing circumstances in the navy, indefinitely magnified the latter."[40] And with Claggart now dead at Billy's hand, the same spirit of fearfulness dictates the secrecy and precipitation of Vere's action in calling a drumhead court-martial: "Feeling that unless quick action were taken on it, the deed of the Foretopman, so soon as it should be known on the gun-decks, would tend to awaken any slumbering embers of the Nore [Mutiny] among the crew, a sense of the urgency of the case overruled in Captain Vere every other consideration."[41] Justice, clearly, is such a consideration. He has known from the first that " 'the angel must hang,' "[42] and in the light of this prejudgment of the case the body he convokes appears less a court of law than a convenient instrument of his will.

A not entirely disinterested prudence, the narrator hints, underlies Vere's decision to proceed against Billy by court-martial rather than by the open exercise of those summary powers legally his as captain:

> . . . though a conscientious disciplinarian he was no lover of authority for mere authority's sake. Very far was he from embracing opportunities for monopolizing to himself the perils of moral responsibility — none at least that could properly be referred to an official superior or shared with him by his official equals or even subordinates. So thinking, he was glad it would not be at variance with usage to turn the matter over to a summary court of his own officers, reserving to himself as the one on whom the ultimate accountability would rest, the right of maintaining a supervision of it, or formally or informally interposing at need.[43]

And interpose he does, repeatedly and in such a manner as to make the trial seem little more than the rehearsal of a written script. So far as actual function is concerned, the members of the court are mere bystanders: Vere is at once Billy's accuser, his jury, and his judge. The officers he has chosen, not without some misgivings of their good nature,[44] are simple, honest and modest men, "without the faculty, [almost without] the inclination to gainsay one whom they [feel] to be an earnest man, one too not less their superior in mind than in naval rank."[45] As a result, Vere is able to manipulate them as he will, reducing the moral problem to a mere question of the mechanical infraction of a law, misrepresenting their desire for justice as overscrupulosity or baseless sentiment, confusing the issue by making the real question of the prisoner's intent seem to depend upon an understanding (by definition impossible) of "the mystery of iniquity" in Claggart, and — which proves decisive with them — impressing them with his own fears of "the practical consequences" of either an acquittal or a mitigation of the full penalty.[46] In brief, Billy Budd was formally convicted and sentenced to be hung at the yard-arm in the early morning-watch. . . ."[47]

It is sometimes argued in Vere's defense that his fears, viewed in context and without the benefit of hindsight, are entirely reasonable and proper: he has not simply imagined either the revolutionary unrest of Europe or the recent mutinies in the British fleet. And if this is so, his defenders continue, the action he takes must be considered both wise and courageous: he has no other meaningful alternative.

Now to argue in this way is of course to beg the question of the rightness of expediency as a principle of action. The conclusion follows from the given premise only for him whose watch is set to China time. Another man, less firmly committed to the ultimate value of particular institutions, might admit Vere's estimate of the situation to be entirely correct and yet regard his choice of a course of action as unquestionably wrong.

But coming down, as White-Jacket offered to do in the manner of flogging,[48] "from the lofty mast-head of an eternal principle" to the practical level of the quarter-deck, one may note in *Billy Budd* several passages that seem plainly intended to cast doubt on the necessity for Vere's action even on grounds of expediency.

For one, Vere has not the least grain of particular evidence that disaffection actually exists aboard his ship. Claggart, for all his "ferreting genius" and his obvious wish to frighten his commander, has been able to bring forward nothing of a specific nature beyond his vague charge against Billy — which charge Vere does not believe.[49] Nor does the reader — and surely this is no oversight on Melville's part — have any evidence withheld from the captain. The general situation, it is true, is such as to justify watchfulness, but not alarm.[50] Mere possibility is a long step from that near-certainty of impending revolt which moves Vere at the trial to insist upon the death penalty.[51] The *might-be*, like the *might-have-been*, "is but boggy ground to build on."[52] Vere's surmise gains little support from the behavior of the men at those three later moments when the greatest strain is placed upon their loyalties. They receive his announcement of the death sentence with the unprotesting "dumbness . . . of a seated congregation of believers in hell listening to the clergyman's announcement of his Calvinistic text."[53] At the moment of Billy's execution, they echo, like good Calvinists, "with one voice from alow and aloft," the prisoner's last cry, " 'God bless Captain Vere!' "[54] And when their shipmate's body is tipped into the sea, their mood appears less one of anger against their officers than of awe before the seeming prodigies of Billy's peaceful death and that strange "croaked requiem" of the seabirds continuing to circle "the burial-spot astern."[55] Taking all in all, it is hard to see in the captain's fears anything more than the fantasies of a mind by nature somewhat pedantically abstract[56] and by the usages of office walled off from any direct contact with the particular realities of life aboard his ship.

But were one to admit the existence of latent discontent aboard the "Indomitable," one could still question the assertion that Vere has no reasonable alternative to the course he takes. He himself, before the convoking of the court, briefly considers one such alternative: to defer "taking any action whatever respecting it, further than to keep the Foretopman a close prisoner till the ship [now on detached duty] rejoined the squadron and then submitting the matter to the judgment of his Admiral."[57] The same has already occurred, and independently, to the ship's officers and to the surgeon, the latter at least a man most guarded in the drawing of inferences.[58] But Captain Vere dismisses the thought almost as soon as it comes, "feeling that unless quick action were [to be] taken on it, the deed of the Foretopman, so soon as it should be known on the gun-decks, would tend to awaken any slumbering embers of the Nore among the crew."[59] The word *any* seems not without significance here: Vere knows of no such embers; but he is fearful, and that fear itself dictates a secrecy which forbids his seeking evidence.[60] He is in this not unlike Claggart whose covert hatred, feeding upon a suspected injury, by its very "secretiveness voluntarily cuts [itself] off from enlightenment or disillusion; and, not unreluctantly, action is taken upon surmise as upon certainty."[61]

A still strong indication of the narrator's belief that an alternative — and a practicable alternative — exists is given us, with an elaborate apology for "divergence" from "the main road," in the implied comparison of Vere and Lord Nelson.[62] Although Vere is nowhere explicitly compared with the admiral, the qualities attributed to this " 'greatest sailor since the world began' " bring the lesser man's own qualities, by the force of contrast, unavoidably to mind.[63] When we read of Nelson's almost vainglorious splendor of appearance, we are reminded of Vere's civilian look, his "unobtrusiveness of demeanor," as of "some highly honorable discreet envoy" visiting the quarter-deck.[64] The description of Nelson as a "reckless declarer of his person in fight" reminds us that Vere is "intrepid to the verge of temerity, but never injudiciously so."[65] Nelson — for all that he is "painfully circumspect" in his preparations for battle — invites by his rashness and bravado the reproof of the "martial utilitarians" and "the Benthamites of war."[66] The lodging of such a charge against Captain Vere would strike us as preposterous; but he does not by this immunity rise in our estimation: "Personal prudence, even when dictated by quite other than selfish considerations, surely is no special virtue in a military man; while an excessive love of glory, impassioning a less burning impulse[,] the honest sense of duty, is the first."[67]

But all this is in preparation for the passage which most unmistakably points up the contrast between the two men:

> Discontent foreran the Two Mutinies, and more or less it lurkingly survived them. Hence it was not unreasonable to apprehend some return of trouble sporadic or general. One instance of such apprehensions: In the same year with this story, Nelson, then Vice-Admiral Sir Horatio, being with the fleet off the Spanish coast, was directed by the Admiral in command to shift his pennant from the *Captain* to the *Theseus*; and for this reason: that the latter ship having newly arrived on the station from home where it had taken part in the Great Mutiny, danger was apprehended from the temper of the men; and it was thought that an officer like Nelson was the one, not indeed to terrorise the crew into base subjection but to win them, by force of his mere presence and heroic personality, back to an allegiance, if not as enthusiastic as his own, yet as true. So it was that for a time on more than one quarter-deck anxiety did exist.[68]

But how different the actions to which these apprehensions led!

To " 'respect the omens of ill' " is of course never unreasonable: " 'evil is the chronic malady of the universe; and checked in one place, breaks forth in another.' "[69] So "discontent" in some sense "lurkingly survived" its suppression at the Nore, and the possibility of its reappearance is something no responsible commander can safely ignore. This much is true. But what is perhaps " 'the grand error' " of Captain Vere, as of other doctrinaire and wholly committed men, is " 'the general supposition, that the very special Diabolus is abroad; whereas, the very special Diabolus has been abroad ever since [the world] began.' "[70] The year A.D. 1797 is not the first time the world has stood in crisis:

> "By Fate's decree
> Have not earth's vitals heaved in change
> Repeated? some wild element
> Or action been evolved? the range
> Of surface split? the deeps unpent?
> Continents in God's cauldrons cast?
> And this without effecting so
> The neutralising of the past,

> Whose rudiments persistent flow,
> From age to age transmitting, own,
> The evil with the good."[71]

And if the world has rallied from these convulsions sufficiently to continue, this is to be credited less to human foresight than to the presence, in that "persistent flow," of a " 'good which lets [the] evil last.' "[72] Since no man reads the future, "let us revere that sacred uncertainty which forever impends over man and nations."[73] The ebb and flow of good and evil is a movement to be traced not only in the general advance and retreat of tides but in the thrust and withdrawal of each separate wave. Melville found this truth of sufficient importance to what he was saying in *Billy Budd* for him to devote his entire preface to it:

> The opening proposition made by the Spirit of that Age, involved the rectification of the Old World's hereditary wrongs. In France to some extent this was bloodily effected. But what then? Straightway the Revolution itself became a wrongdoer, one more oppressive than the Kings. Under Napoleon it enthroned upstart kings, and initiated that prolonged agony of continual war whose final throe was Waterloo. During those years not the wisest could have foreseen that the outcome of all would be what to some thinkers apparently it has since turned out to be, a political advance along nearly the whole line for Europeans.
>
> Now as elsewhere hinted, it was something caught from the Revolutionary Spirit that at Spithead emboldened the man-of-war's men to rise against real abuses, long-standing ones, and afterwards at the Nore to make inordinate and aggressive demands, successful resistance to which was confirmed only when the ringleaders were hung for an admonitory spectacle to the anchored fleet. Yet in a way analogous to the operation of the Revolution at large the Great Mutiny, though by Englishmen naturally deemed monstrous at the time, doubtless gave the first latent prompting to most important reforms in the British Navy.[74]

Could one forbid events, as the censor forbids books, the task of choosing those events would not be easy. For "in all things man sows upon the wind, which bloweth just where it listeth; for ill or good, man cannot know. Often ill comes from the good, as good from the ill."[75]

There is a sense in which *Benito Cereno* and *Billy Budd* may be said to complement each other. Each is essentially a study in blindness: as Captain Delano in the one is blind to the strength and permanence of evil, so in the other Captain Vere cannot see that good has the power to maintain itself, if never wholly to prevail, in a world where it seems always at the point of extinction. Still less does Vere realize that it is by its own intrinsic power that it survives and not through any devices borrowed from its opposite. The good which in this instance eventually comes from the evil of the young sailor's death owes nothing at all to Vere's supposed foresight — with regard to which that death must appear wholly futile and meaningless — and everything to the simple fact of Billy's own goodness silently operating upon the hearts of men. It is the crowning weakness of expediency that it so often turns out not to have been expedient at all. Captain Vere, dying of his wound at Gibralter, is perhaps fortunate in being cut off before attaining to this humiliating knowledge and to the remorse which must have followed it.[76] The rest of us, realizing what little control man has over the consequences of his actions, may find in Vere's story encouragement to risk the luxury of at least following our own conscience.

Notes

1. *Billy Budd*, in *The Portable Melville*, ed. Jay Leyda (New York: Viking Press, 1952), p. 720.

2. *Ibid.*, pp. 693, 696–97.

3. *Ibid.*, pp. 660–66.

4. *Ibid.*, pp. 644–45.

5. *Ibid.*, pp. 698–99, 707, 717–18.

6. *Ibid.*, p. 734.

7. *Ibid.*, pp. 714–15.

8. *Ibid.*, pp. 647–49; see also p. 696.

9. *Ibid.*, p. 709.

10. *Ibid.*, p. 666.

11. *Ibid.*, pp. 674–75.

12. *Ibid.*, pp. 648–49.

13. *Ibid.*, p. 662.

14. *Ibid.*, p. 702.

15. *Ibid.*, p. 677.

16. *Ibid.*, p. 659.

17. *Ibid.*, p. 736.

18. *Ibid.*, p. 660.

19. *Ibid.*, p. 661.

20. *Ibid.*, pp. 658–59.

21. *Ibid.*, p. 713.

22. *Ibid.*, p. 715.

23. *Ibid.*

24. *Ibid.*, pp. 717–18.

25. *Ibid.*, p. 716.

26. *Ibid.*, p. 717.

27. *Ibid.*, p. 716.

28. *Ibid.*, pp. 660–61, 734.

29. *Ibid.*, p. 651.

30. *Ibid.*, pp. 715–16.

31. *Ibid.*, pp. 711–12, 714, 716.

32. *Ibid.*, p. 727.

33. *Ibid.*, pp. 696–97, 666, 695, 666–67.

34. *Ibid.*, p. 703.

35. *The Works of Herman Melville* (16 vols.; Standard Edition; London: Constable & Co., 1922–24), *Mardi*, II, 30 (chap. cxliii). Unless otherwise noted, all references hereafter to the text of Melville's writings will be to this edition.

36. *Billy Budd*, in *The Portable Melville*, pp. 680, 675.

37. *Ibid.*, pp. 657–58.

38. *Ibid.*, pp. 695–96.

39. *Ibid.*, pp. 698–99.

40. *Ibid.*, p. 704.

41. *Ibid.*, p. 707.

42. *Ibid.*, p. 703; see also p. 711.

43. *Ibid.*, pp. 707–8.

44. *Ibid.*, p. 708.

45. *Ibid.*, pp. 717–18.

46. *Ibid.*, pp. 711–12, 714–15, 712–14, 718, 716–17.

47. *Ibid.*, p. 719.

48. *White*-Jacket, p. 184 (chap. xxxvi).

49. *Billy Budd*, in *The Portable Melville*, pp. 695–98.

50. *Ibid.*, pp. 656–57.

51. *Ibid.*, p. 717.

52. *Ibid.*, p. 655.

53. *Ibid.*, p. 722.

54. *Ibid.*, p. 729.

55. *Ibid.*, p. 733.

56. *Ibid.*, p. 661.

57. *Ibid.*, p. 707.

58. *Ibid.*, pp. 704–5, 730–31.

59. *Ibid.*, p. 707.

60. *Ibid.*, pp. 698–99, 706–7.

61. *Ibid.*, p. 680.

62. *Ibid.*, pp. 653–57.

63. The quoted phrase is twice repeated (*ibid.*, pp. 653, 655), as if for emphasis. We may note also that the guarded praise of Vere by his fellow officers (*ibid.*, p. 661) is so phrased as to invite the comparison with Lord Nelson.

64. *Ibid.*, pp. 656, 658.

65. *Ibid.*, pp. 655, 658.

66. *Ibid.*, pp. 654–55.

67. *Ibid.*, p. 655.

68. *Ibid.*, pp. 656–57. One may recall also that in an earlier book of Melville's "the Great Sailor" is called to the stand as an expert witness against flogging, a mode of discipline to which Vere (*ibid.*, pp. 666–67) has shown himself not wholly averse: "It is well known that Lord Nelson himself, in point of policy, was averse to flogging; and that, too, when he had witnessed the mutinous effects of government abuses in the navy . . . which to the terror of all England, developed themselves at the great mutiny of the Nore: an outbreak that for several weeks jeopardized the very existence of the British navy" (*White–Jacket*, p. 186, chap. xxxvi).

69. *Mardi*, II, 244 (chap. clxi).

70. *Ibid.*, p. 238 (chap. clxi).

71. *Clarel*, I, 137 (Part I, canto xxxiv).

72. *Ibid.*, II, 240 (Part IV, canto xix).

73. "Supplement" to *Battle-Pieces*, in *Poems*, p. 186.

74. *Billy Budd*, in *The Portable Melville*, pp. 637–38.

75. "The Encantadas," in *The Piazza Tales*, p. 227.

76. *Billy Budd*, in *The Portable Melville*, p. 736.

"Certain Phenomenal Men": The Example of *Billy Budd*

Warner Berthoff*

"Ah, who can say what passes between people in such a relation?"
— Henry James, *The Golden Bowl*

I

In the case of *Billy Budd* it may be well to ask at the start what kind of performance we are dealing with. First of all, it is a story — whatever else we may say must take account of it in its proper form. More exactly, it is, in Melville's own phrase, an "inside narrative"; we are to take it as decisively identifying the characters and events it describes. It is of course an extraordinarily poignant narrative, and one which most readers have felt to be peculiarly meaningful. The difficulty, to judge from what has been written about it, comes in trying to say what exactly does happen in it and what the meaning is. A great deal of Melville's work, early and late, seems often to have an unsettling effect on the judgment of his readers, not least the more responsive and sympathetic among them. His writing has proved perilously attractive to certain extravagant fashions in present-day criticism, especially that of appealing to mere literature for moral and even religious authority; or of imputing systems of meaning such as could not practicably be secured within the form and scope of the work in question. No claim of immunity in this respect is made for the present essay, which can only take its chances with the rest.

The ground common to most discussion of *Billy Budd* is the assumption that the story is allegorical — a narrative representation of some universal truth or law or balance of contraries, a parable of Good and Evil, a re-enactment of the Fall, a projected myth of a ritual killing which is also a resurrection, and so on. Such interpretations do not have to be scrambled for. The evidence from which they are adduced is undeniably there. The trouble is rather that the statement of them will miss what one

*From *ELH* 26 (1960): 334–51. Reprinted by permission of The Johns Hopkins University Press.

feels, as one reads and re-reads, to be the governing concentration and emphasis of the actual telling. *Billy Budd* is indeed full of quickening intimations as to the larger, the perhaps universal circumstance of human life — intimations which are typical of Melville's imagination, as his explicitness in articulating them is typical of his best performance as a writer. But the decisive narrative logic and cogency of the story are, I think, to be found elsewhere. They are to be found in an effort which Melville characteristically troubled to furnish precise words for, the effort to "define and denominate certain phenomenal men" (ch. 11). To render in force and detail through all the incident and commentary of his narrative the essential feature and bearing of these men, to name and make authoritative the example of character manifested in them — this is what seems to me to lie at the heart of Melville's enterprise. In *Billy Budd* he undertakes to define not universal truth but certain specific and contingent examples of being and behavior.

The question is not only, what does Melville do in *Billy Budd*, but, what kind of writer is he? After all our commentary and analysis we still have no very clear notion. Even his style has eluded definition. We note its overflowing energy and vivacity, its expansiveness, its confidential charm, its abundant originality, its rare attentiveness to the material capacity, so to speak, of the vocabulary and idiom of written English as well as to prose cadence — all of which are impressive and ingratiating qualities surely but are not peculiar to Melville, not even in the "poetic" concentration of his highest flights. They sum up a general fashion of high nineteenth-century prose (we may be reminded of the broad influence, not usually salutary, of Carlyle) and do not help much to identify Melville's special achievement. But if we concern ourselves with what is most durably exciting in his work, if we have in mind those crowded, substance-rough passages in which he shows himself most tenaciously respectful of his material and in which his full though sometimes awkwardly com-pacted effort is to express accurately and completely the restless progress of his understanding, the nervous pressure of his inquisitiveness, then I think we may come closer to the manner of his greatness. So I should argue that the decisive virtue in Melville's best writing is its insistent thrust toward an entire explicitness, an unstinting exactness — a virtue not limited to special operations like description or characterization or mock-enyclopedism or dramatic climax but generic and constitutional. Without it, the energy, expansiveness, charm, originality, would have been largely wasted (though it is also the source of much overwriting). "Thrust toward explication" might be more exact: he will lay it all open and he will get it all said. Like so many of the major Americans he is an explainer, and his stories are very often most satisfying, contrary to Jamesian dogmas of dramatization, when most explanatory. His art (not always under control) is in keeping his explanations in the service of his prime narrative objects. In the manner of his time he lusted after analogies and correspondences, and the meanings they tantalized him with — but not to build the kind of private philosophical system which beguiled so many of his ambitious contemporaries. His concern was rather to express the full march and grasp of his unappeasable imagination.

And what he was moved to express he found words for — with a thoroughness and consistency, I think, that are matched by no other of our prose masters except Emerson. This seems to me the prime truth about Melville as a writer. So in inquiring into what happens in *Billy Budd*, we can fairly assume that Melville tries to say as best he can. His explanations are not simple, but they are not short-circuited or evasive, and they are not obscure; he summons the energy, the patience, to carry them through. What mystification or ambiguity may seem to invest his story are in his subject, the types of "moral phenomenon" (ch. 13) he has set himself to render, and not finally in the rendering. No single notation, for example, more effectively establishes Melville's full idea of the "something defective and abnormal" in Claggart than, at the confessed limit of observation and analysis, a reference to the Scriptural "mysteries of iniquity." What Melville was trying to express seems to me sufficiently identified in that precisely climactic phrase — though he knew and characteristically specified the risk he was taking in falling back on the "lexicon of Holy Writ" in an age which had grown indifferent to it. But the sufficiency, the persuasiveness of the phrase, as we reach it in the narrative, derive in turn from the impulse toward entire explicitness which is felt to stand back of it. This delivered impulse, this unintimidated thrust, seems to me to be at the heart of Melville's greatness as a writer — and also to constitute, in calling up all his rare genius for specification, the commanding *formal* lesson of his art. It stands before us in his work, it is to be felt, as a moral quality, too — a condition of the "adult health" (Emerson's phrase) necessary to great performances. Certainly it is a main part of what we speak of as Melville's natural genius, and that one part in particular without which his genius could not have so splendidly discovered and expressed itself.

II

I do not mean to dismiss out of hand the various allegorical interpretations of *Billy Budd*. If only in their sheer variety and equal conviction, they have much to tell us — about the nature of Melville's writing, about the excitements and hazards of criticism. No one has worked along this line of approach more discerningly than Professor Norman Holmes Pearson, whose findings have the merit of standing near the center of sensible opinion on the story and may serve briefly — I hope not unfairly — as a stalking horse.[1] To Professor Pearson, *Billy Budd* is best understood by analogy to Milton's heroic poems: "What Melville was doing was to try to give in as universalized a way as possible . . . another redaction of the myth which had concerned Milton . . . in the trilogy of his three major works" — the Christian myth, that is, of the fall from innocence and the promise of redemption.

There is of course much evidence to support this judgment, and Professor Pearson and others have mustered it cogently; it need not be reviewed here. What does need to be said is commonplace enough: that the analogies Melville brings forward in support of his story — Billy as Adam, his hanging as a kind of Ascension, the yardarm as the True Cross, and so on — prove nothing in themselves about either his intention or his achievement. We may bear in mind for one thing that we are reading a nineteenth-century, not a seventeenth-century writer; for in Melville's time the literary apprehension of Christian myth was nearly as divorced from sacramental religion, and as merely moral and pathetic when not wholly sentimental, as the apprehension of classical myth. But first of all we need to look to the whole development of Melville's actual narrative and to the particular disposition and intensity of its insistences. The question is: how do these evidences operate in the story? do they determine the action and constitute its first meaning? or are they at most a kind of illustrative commentary, suggesting by familiar analogy the appropriate pitch of feeling?

There is little doubt that Melville meant his story to be in some manner exemplary and that as he worked on it he found it profoundly moving, he "believed" in it. The strength of intimation in an inveterate explainer like Melville is in some proportion to the weight and spur of his own perplexities. The religious metaphors in *Billy Budd* do indeed confirm our sense of a religious depth in Melville's sensibility. But we must be wary of abstracting the stuff of these metaphors from his immediate deployment of them — the obvious temptation, but somehow especially insidious with this work. Our time is not so much skeptical of religious doctrines and symbols — certainly not passionately and burdensomely skeptical as Melville was — as it is ignorant of them, which Melville was not. Perhaps the first truth about us in this respect is that we are the embarrassed receivers of (in Carlo Levi's phrase) a civilization which used to be Christian. We respect, we are in a civil way habituated to, the positions of Christian belief; but the norms of our experience no longer reinforce them. And finding in a document like *Billy Budd* that this half-forgotten vocabulary (the lexicon of Christianity Melville apologized for appealing to) has been restored to use, we may be overimpressed, mistaking mere unembarrassed familiarity with it for a reconstitution of its prime significance. But to make of *Billy Budd* an attempt, and an attempt comparable to Milton's to reanimate the Christian myth of human destiny under divine law is to respond less to the limiting and authenticating particulars of Melville's story than to the pathos of its corroborative analogies and allusions, or perhaps to the transferred pathos of our own progressive disregard of them. Also it is to claim for Melville the kind of positive testament or settled belief which seems inconsistent with what we know of him; which all his tenacity in doubt, his frank and courageous ignorance, his respect for the discomforts of truth and the phenomenal ambiguities of existence, would have gone to keep him from taking refuge in, even for the space of a story, even at the end of his life.

No, the actual telling of *Billy Budd* will not bear so grand a burden of meaning, and was not intended to. What its limiting circumstances are, Melville is concerned to say as precisely as he can. His use of the military setting in constraint of the events of his story is to the point here. The martial law by which Billy goes to his death is usually held to be symbolic of some universal law or authority, such as divine providence: I think mistakenly. Nor can I follow Professor Richard Chase in comparing it with the "abstract legality" confronted by Antigone or the "inhumanly enforced legality" of *The Winter's Tale;* for the official agencies of justice in these plays are to be understood as wrong precisely in that, being "abstract" and "inhuman," they are other than what they ought to be. But Melville is at some pains to present martial law as morally *sui generis*, and in its own terms morally unimpeachable. It is designed, he reminds us, solely to subserve the extraordinary circumstance of war. It is "War's child," as Captain Vere tells the court, and must of its nature look "but to the frontage, the appearance" of things — and not wrongly. As against moral or divine law it can have no regard to questions of motive or judgments of virtue: "The prisoner's deed — with that alone we have to do." It is for this terrible eventuality alone, otherwise it would be indefensible. But in the circumstances Melville sets out, there is no appeal from it.

Why Melville's story is at home in this rigid context, and what it gains from it, are absorbing questions, but beyond the restricted compass of this essay.[2] My point now is simply that in *Billy Budd* martial law and the "military necessity" are accepted in their own right, without ulterior design. Melville does not choose, as he did in *White Jacket*, to judge the martial discipline by a higher moral law; he makes such a standard available neither to Vere and the court in their search for the right action (though they reach out to it) nor to the reader in judging what has happened. Christian conscience, mercy, the judgment of God — these are neither directly opposed to martial law nor put aside as meaningless; Melville has Vere speak of such considerations as having the force of "Nature" in the hearts of men but as being, in the "singular" given case, inapplicable. Doctrines of Christianity are invoked in full support of the pathos of the story, but assent to them is not at stake in the story. It interested Melville, indeed it profoundly moved him, to point out in passing how one part of his narrative confirmed the Calvinist doctrine of depravity or how another suggested the "heresy" of natural innocence, but these propositions are not, as such, his subject or argument. The whole movement of suggestion in Melville's narrative seems to me the reverse of allegorical; the words and names for the action of the story, the thoughts and analogies that help define it, follow from it and are subject to it. The image of the action itself, of a particular occurrence involving particular persons, stands first.

In *Billy Budd* this image is constituted first of all by the three main characters, and the action proceeds from the capacity of spirit painstakingly attributed to each of them. Each is set before us as a kind of natural force; in fact Melville's probing curiosity projects what might seem a thoroughly deterministic explanation of their behavior if it was not so clearly in the service of a stubborn and wondering sense of their free agency. "Character" is in general rather curiously exhibited here, Melville's language repeatedly suggesting that it is best apprehended at any single moment by a kind of *savoring*. A man's character derives from the accumulated conditions (the seasonings, so to speak) of his whole life, and so registers as a "taste" or "flavor" on the "moral palate," as though too subtly compounded for stricter definition. It may be that no sequence of dramatic events will wholly communicate this distinguishing savor of character; the necessities of action, in art as in life, show little enough respect for person. But the mode of exposition Melville turned to has other resources than dramatization, other ways of declaring its meanings. So the climax of this minutely specifying narration is reached in an episode in which the actual event is withheld, and we are referred instead to the *character* of the participants.

This is the episode in which, the trial over, Vere privately tells Billy the court's decision. Given in very nearly the shortest chapter of the narrative (ch. 23), it follows the longest and most detailed; and in contrast to the thorough exposition just concluded (of Vere's distress, the hesitant proceedings of the court, the ambiguities of the evidence, and all Vere'e patient argument) it moves instead by conjecture and reticence. "Beyond the communication of the sentence," its main passage begins, "what took place at this interview was never known." Yet on this elliptical passage the full weight of the narrative, accelerating after its slow-paced beginnings into the drama of the middle chapters, centers and falls, its steady simple movement coming full stop. By working so sensible a change of pace and manner, and by explicitly likening the hidden event to what must happen wherever in the world the circumstances are "at all akin to those here attempted to be set forth," Melville appears for a moment to be concentrating our attention on the very heart of his whole conception. What we are told is what it chiefly concerns him to have us know—the phenomenal quality of character in his two heroes. In their essential being Vere and Billy are as one, "each radically sharing in the rarer qualities of our nature—so rare indeed as to be all but incredible to average minds however much cultivated." On this basis and in these limited terms the narrator will risk "some conjecture." But insofar as his conjecture accords with this rarity of spirit by which he had identified his protagonists, it may lead into the profoundest truth, it may be definitive.

So the chapter's central paragraph begins: "It would have been in consonance with the spirit of Captain Vere. . . ." The capacity of spirit being known, the weight and bearing of the event may be measured and its meaning grasped. And what capacity of spirit Melville meant to set before us begins to be confirmed in the virtues he gravely imagines as "not improbably" brought into play in the interview: in Vere, utter frankness and unselfishness, making him confess his own part in Billy's sentencing, and intensifying into the compassion of a father; in Billy an equal frankness, and bravery of course, but also joy, in the realization of his Captain's extraordinary trust. Yet these important virtues are in a way incidental. What draws the narrator on is the magnitude of the capability they speak for. Translated out of their customary stations, Vere and Billy meet as "two of great Nature's nobler order." Their entire competence of spirit before the event is assumed; only the immediate exercise of it goes past saying. Though the narration here makes a show of drawing back even from conjecture, the quality and the significance of the action continue to be defined; exact terms are used. Melville writes that "there is no telling the sacrament" when two such spirits embrace, but the very word "sacrament" precisely advances his explanation. The same tactic directs the closing sentence of this astonishing paragraph: "There is privacy at the time, inviolable to the survivor, and holy oblivion, the sequel to each diviner magnanimity, providentially covers all at last." Here again the withholding is according to the inmost nature of that which is being disclosed; the "privacy" of the scene is a consequence of the rare virtue, the "magnanimity," at work in it.[3]

May we not take this explanation, and the word that thus concludes it, as literally as we can? As with martial law, Melville's purpose was not to universalize the particular phenomenon, the capacity of spirit generating this encounter, but simply to identify it, to declare it in its own name. In Vere and Billy, the passage affirms, we have to do with magnanimity, with greatness of soul, a quality which, though "all but incredible to average minds however much cultivated," is nevertheless according to nature, and is touched with divinity — or whatever in human conduct is suggestive of divinity. Though it is constrained by Claggart's spiritual depravity (also "according to nature") and has still to undergo the pitiless operation of the "military necessity," this greatness of soul in the two heroes achieves in the sacrament of their coming together an "inviolable," a "diviner" magnanimity. As there is a mystery of iniquity in Claggart, there is a mystery of magnanimity in these two. It is given no power to prevent the now settled outcome of the story. Yet its radiance is beyond catastrophe. It is such as can survive those decisive accidents of individual existence — age, health, station, luck, particular experience — which Melville consistently presented the lives of his characters as being determined by. Now the narrative has come to its defining climax. Here the tone is set for what remains to be told, and not at the pitch of tragedy — the tone of exalted acceptance and muted patient joy which will be heard in the account of Billy in irons like a "slumbering child," in Billy's "God bless Captain Vere!," in Vere's dying with Billy's name on his lips (not in remorse, Melville specifies), and finally, and with what sure art, in the gravely acquiescent music of the closing ballad.

III

This view of the action of *Billy Budd* (a view not discouraged by the dedication to the "great heart" of Jack Chase) does not, I think, deny the story any power of suggestion or degree of achievement. Perhaps it may remove the sense of disproportion between theme and occasion which Professor Pearson's and kindred readings leave us with, yet at the same time increase the interest of Melville's actual accomplishment. For an idea of natural greatness of soul lies, as we know, at the center not only of classical tradition in moral philosophy and literature but of Christian tradition as well. It lies also (as securely as ideas of equality and civil liberty) at the heart of the democratic ethos. The great-souled man — what significant reckoning of our duty and destiny, whether in the mode of tragedy or satire or prophecy or simple witness, does not somehow take account of him? And what more momentous question can be put to the democratic writer than the question of greatness of mind and soul in a mass society?

To follow out this view of the story might well lead into discussion of Melville's "Americanism," an absorbing matter certainly though just at present a little shopworn. Just as usefully it may lead us back to a parallel which I have made some point here of questioning — the example of Milton. The Milton who matters here, however, is not the Christian poet of *Paradise Lost* and regained but the prideful humanist whose dedication to the idea of magnanimity is proverbial in English letters. For Milton's concern with this virtue in his writings, and his explicit pride in the pursuit of it in his life, are foremost among the qualities which have given him his peculiar personal aura and earned him so much gratuitous personal hostility. They are also of the essence of his Protestantism, and it can not be altogether accidental that the two writers of epic imagination and enterprise in the Protestant camp (if we may imagine one) of Anglo-American literature should show a common concern, a considered preoccupation, with magnanimity.[4]

As we might expect, Milton was confident and unembarrassed in deploying the term. He used it consistently and (according to his lights) precisely, to denote a summary condition of virtuousness in which the lesser particular virtues were gathered up and lifted to grandeur; in this he followed the Aristotelian definition of magnanimity as the "crowning ornament" of the virtuous character (Nich. Ethics, IV, iii, 16). What is especially Miltonic is his emphasis on rational self-consciousness in the exercise of magnanimity. For him the concept signifies the highest reach of that "pious and just honoring of ourselves" which is a duty of the virtuous man second only to love of God. Cultivation of magnanimity thus becomes the great end of education—so we find him saying in this famous and characteristic sentence: "I call therefore a compleat and generous Education that which fits a man to perform justly, skillfully and magnanimously all the offices both private and public of Peace and War." But to describe the ideal education is to consider what end man was born for; and it is in the account of the creation of Adam that we come to the furthest reach of Milton's idea:

> There wanted yet the Master work, the end
> Of all yet don; a Creature who not prone
> And Brute as other Creatures, but endu'd
> With Sanctitie of Reason might erect
> His Stature, and upright with Front serene
> Govern the rest, self-knowing, and from thence
> Magnanimous to correspond with Heav'n . . .

In magnanimity, so conceived, natural creation rises to its greatest beauty and supreme fulfillment. Would any nineteenth-century transcendentalist or mystical democrat ever claim more than this for the instructed soul of man?

Of these associations some were still viable for Melville but not all. It was precisely a doctrinal confidence in what the great-souled man might "correspond with" that, two hundred years later, his intelligence despaired of. At the same time certain outwardly passive virtues like humility and disinterestedness had come to seem positive and potentially heroic as they had not to Milton (who in the *Tetracordon* made "humble" and "magnanimous" sharply antithetical). So Melville could specify in Vere a "certain unaffected modesty of manhood" without diminishing his general "ascendancy of character" or his Miltonic readiness for all private and public offices of peace and war. It is still, however, a traditionally heroic image of magnanimity that we are shown at the beginning of *Billy Budd* in the chapters on Nelson. Nelson's greatness in command is assumed; what concerned Melville was his personal behavior at Trafalgar and the charge of "vainglory" and "affectation" it lay open to. And though Melville was on the defensive here, he unequivocally championed the impulse of the great-hearted hero to display his greatness and love the glory of it. Given "a nature like Nelson" and the opportunity of Trafalgar, then the "sort of priestly motive" that directed Nelson's conduct was, Melville insisted in one of his showiest sentences, altogether natural and fitting, coming from that "exaltation of sentiment" which is the mark of the truly heroic action.[5]

The point is not that Milton's conception of magnanimity is a "source" of *Billy Budd*. What we are considering is not a case of "influence" but a comparable turn and reach of mind, formed in a broadly common moral tradition though expressing very different stages in its devolution. To Milton magnanimity was within the achieving of every wise and good man, a condition of completed moral being to be reached through rational procedures of education and piety. To Melville it was a rarer thing—much less a condition to be achieved, much more a mysterious distillation of certain transactions and contingencies in certain men's lives. At the high tide of his creative energy he could imagine it as naturally resulting from that "unshackled, democratic spirit of Christianity" in which America seemed destined to lead the world; we know how quickly this confidence went out of him. He found himself unable to assume even a moral efficacy in magnanimity, since he could not be sure in the first place of the moral order of creation, any more than he could have much faith in the moral justness of American society; both seemed paralysingly indifferent to degrees of virtue. Nor could he take refuge in ideas of the infinitude of the private man or of the priesthood of the individual soul, as the simpler protestant and democratic optimisms of his time would encourage him to. This being so, his undertaking in *Billy Budd*, and his success in it, are all the more impressive.

But did he in fact succeed? The character and role of Captain Vere fit well enough the traditional notion of magnanimity, but what about the character of Billy Budd? What has Miltonic magnanimity to do with the "mindless innocence" (as Professor Chase has put it) of the boy sailor? Given the character Melville presents, how much can be claimed for it? "To be nothing more than innocent!"—Claggart's "cynic disdain" may not be unreasonable; in one form or another it has been shared by most critics of the story. Have we not, in Billy, an expression of sentiment poignant in itself but unassimilated and unresolved in the narrative, and best explained (as Professor Chase would explain it) by the life history and personal necessities of the author?

But magnanimity, we may note again, is not a substantive virtue. No particular actions prove it or follow from it. What the word describes is a certain dimension of spirit which the virtuous man may rise to and which any moral event may conceivably participate in. Whatever has a soul (and to Melville's excruciating animism anything can seem to) may in certain extraordinary circumstances grow into the condition of magnanimity, the soul that is called innocent not less than the soul instructed by experience. If innocence is compatible with virtuousness—and in characterizing Billy, Melville did not doubt that it is: "a virtue went out of him"—then it too is capable of its own kind of magnanimity.

Here again we may appeal to Melville's explicitness; for in working out his conception of the character of Billy Budd—a "child-man" not incapable of moral reflection yet mysteriously uncorrupted, able to conceive of death but like a savage warrior "wholly without irrational fear of it"—Melville does in fact "denominate" it categorically. This is in a passage of explanation added to Chapter 16 of the revised draft, just after

Billy has been approached by an apparent conspiracy of mutiny (though in his innocence he has hardly understood it as that). Melville, first specifying that the thought of reporting these overtures never entered Billy's mind, pushes on to a more positive claim, though at the moment a superfluous one: even if the step of reporting what he had heard *had* been suggested to him, "he would have been deterred from taking it by the thought, one of novice-magnanimity, that it would savor overmuch of the dirty work of a tell-tale." A special sort of magnanimity, awkwardly qualified and, though capable of choosing between evils, not yet decisively tested: nevertheless Melville makes it the defining motive in his conjecture here. Notice, too, that the term is introduced to attribute to Billy a natural revulsion from the role of informer; for in this he is sensibly at one with Captain Vere, who will respond to Claggart's accusations in the same way. To the magnanimous man, conscious of his nature and of the reputation it rightfully deserves, there may be a greater sin than breach of the ninth commandment but there is none more loathsome. It is a sudden intuition that Claggart is bearing false witness which goads Vere into the intemperate threat of the yard-arm-end, and so gives the master-at-arms his right to a full hearing; it is "horror" of his accuser, as against mere "amazement" at the accusation, that paralyzes Billy in Claggart's presence.

Can Melville's intention be doubted — to show Vere and Billy as bound to one another in a complementary greatness of soul?[6] As the story moves on to the music of its close we are shown how each in his own way has instructed the other; how, so to speak, the magnanimity possible to virtuous innocence has fulfilled itself and in turn given its mysterious blessing to the world-sustaining magnanimity of experienced and commissioned virtue. The first represents the part of man which, being born to nature, remains of nature; the second represents the part of man which is uniquely of his own making, his defining burden as a moral and historical creature. Melville is explicit about what has happened. The "tension of agony" in Billy, he wrote, "survived not the something healing in the closeted interview with Captain Vere"; in turn Billy, restored to the role of "peacemaker," has lifted Vere, for all his anguish, beyond remorse. The motions of magnanimity under the most agonizing worldly duress: that is Melville's image and his theme.

By way of elaboration, we have been shown three fulfillments of human nature — on one side depravity (or "monomania," his word for Claggart as for Ahab), on the other these two forms of magnanimity self-realized through recognition of one another. No exact balance is struck. We sense some division of intention or disequilibrium. Midway in the story, for example, it is the conflict between the two sides that engrosses interest. But in the showdown Claggart is not allowed to be any real match for the other two,[7] and we see that Melville's most profound intention lies further along. It is seldom observed how pitiable Claggart is, in a way in which Billy and Vere are not. Once acting in the open he can not really deceive the Captain or leave any lasting scar on Billy—though his own understrappers deceive him at will (ch. 14), as indeed he deceives himself; it is not usually pointed out that Claggart believes his absurd accusation. He is envious and despairing, an embodiment of those life-denying "sins refined" which in *Clarel* were Melville's vision of Sodom and Gomorrah. But he is not a hypocrite (as was Bland, the master-at-arms of *White Jacket*). In such a nature, Melville made a point of explaining, conscience functions not in restraint of its terrible determinations but as their helpless agent. Also it is not usually observed how abruptly and entirely Claggart and what is embodied in him are dismissed from the story. After the trial he is barely mentioned again; no trace of his concerted malignity is allowed to survive the interview between Vere and Billy. It is as though Melville's conception of the radically opposing crystallizations possible to human nature—confidence and envy, love and hate, frankness and dissimulation, assurance and despair, magnanimity and depravity—had swung clear of his tormenting search for belief, so that he was free to rise at the climax of his story to a different and surer theme: the conjunction of the two magnanimities, making sacrifice to the military necessity.

IV

"The only great ones among mankind are the poet, the priest, and the soldier; the man who sings, the man who blesses, and the man who sacrifices, and sacrifices himself." It is not, I think, the grand design of Christian myth nor the example of Greek tragedy or Miltonic epic but this confessional aphorism of Baudelaire's that stands nearest the logic and authority of *Billy Budd*.[8] Strong judgments of life-in-general, of good and evil and law and justice, may throb through Melville's narrative, but its work is not to prove them. It asks not, "what is life?" or "what are the ways of God?" or even "what is justice?" but, "given this imaginable event in these circumstances, what power of response is there in certain phenomenal men?" So we are shown one kind of greatness of spirit in Vere, the soldier-priest of the military necessity, joining with another kind in Billy Budd, whose power to bless transfigures not only his own life. We observe, as in Baudelaire's journal or Vigny's *Servitudes et Grandeurs Militaires*, how an apprehension of the moral chaos and inscrutability of the experienced world has been held in balance by an austere intuition of honor and of personal abnegation. Yet for all their poignancy the specific terms of Melville's narrative do not require our option. Far less than in *Moby-Dick* or *Pierre* or *White Jacket* or *The Confidence Man* are we asked to subscribe to some world-view. This is only a story, a narrative of "what befell" certain men in the year of the Great Mutiny. What does require our option, however, is the manner of the telling, the compassion and patiently exact utterance of the writer who has "sung" the story; for it is through these that we are brought to "believe" in the degree of virtue claimed for its protagonists.

"What one notices in him," E. M. Forster said of the Melville of *Billy Budd*, "is that his apprehensions are free from personal worry."[9] His imagination and compassion work immediately, taking fair and full measure of their impressive objects. This can not be said of all of Melville's work, in much of which (most damagingly in *Pierre*) his thrust toward explicitness rather puts before us the features of his own discomposure. And given the circumstances of the writing of *Billy Budd* — his career as an author of books thirty years behind him, his life closing down, his own two boys dead and his old energies gone — we might reasonably expect incoherence, failure of control. Instead we find a concentration, and integrity, of performance that match the best in his earlier career. The achievement, and the act of mind it speaks for, are indeed extraordinary. The particulars of this story positively invited misconstruction, as they still invite misinterpretation. Straining after dramatic effect or insistence on an allegorical lesson could only have diminished its grave authority. Mere indignation or pity would have left it no more than a parable of injustice, an exercise in resentment. But there is no indignation or outrage in the telling of *Billy Budd* — no quarrel at all, with God or society or law or nature or any agency of human suffering. Rather there is a poise and sureness of judgment (but at no loss of the appetite for explanation); a compassionate objectivity which, claiming no credit for itself, keeps its fine temper before the worst appearances; most of all, a readiness of apprehension possibly only to an actual, measurable greatness of mind. That is to say, there is intellectual magnanimity — which Milton proposed in his treatise on Christian doctrine as the greatest of that "first class of special virtues connected with the duty of man towards himself."

This is the example the Melville of *Billy Budd* offers as a writer. A personal example, of course, but also a formal example, and of the most radical sort — as Henry James would remind us in declaring that "the deepest quality of a work of art will always be the quality of the mind of the producer." If we add that this quality does not come full-blown into the world but must be made and exercised, like any rational creation, then we may at least imagine how Melville's still barely tapped capacity to "influence" might yet be productively exploited, and his legacy as a writer husbanded and renewed.

Notes

1. Norman Holmes Pearson, "*Billy Budd*: 'The King's Yarn,' " *American Quarterly*, III (Summer 1951), 99–114.

2. The search for answers might begin with Vigny's *Servitudes et Grandeurs Militaires* (1835), which provides, I think, a much truer parallel to *Billy Budd* than Milton's great

poems. The resemblances are striking. Both Vigny and Melville (having elsewhere, in *Stello* and *Pierre*, dramatized the Romantic theme of the suffering and heroism of the creative imagination) discovered in obedience to the martial discipline a more compelling occasion for moral drama; both responded to the resignation and self-effacement of military service as a more profoundly moving symbol of imaginable virtue. Indeed Vigny's notation of "a certain puerility" in the military character sheds light on a controversial aspect of the character of Billy Budd, as his portrait of Collingwood (whom Melville also paid his respects to, and for the same reasons, in *White Jacket*), in which we are asked specifically to apprehend "all that the sense of duty can subdue in a great soul," sheds light on the treatment of Captain Vere.

Curiously it is Vigny's book which is the more didactic, being openly concerned to advance a general moral discipline for a post-Christian culture. "Is anything still sacred?" Vigny asked: "in the universal foundering of creeds, to what wreckage can brave hands still cleave?" His answer was that "creeds are weak, but man is strong." and he went on in his closing chapter to describe a "religion of Honor," characterized by "manly decency" and the "passive grandeur" of personal abnegation: "Whereas all other virtues seem to be sent down from heaven to take us by the hand and raise us up, this alone appears to be innate and to be straining heavenwards. It is a wholly human virtue, born of the earth and earning no heavenly reward after death. It is indeed the virtue of the life of this world." The implicit logic of Melville's rendering of his two heroes could not be stated more sympathetically.

3. This view of what Melville was driving at in *Billy Budd*, and of his deliberateness in getting to it, is reinforced by examination of the extant drafts of this passage (in the Houghton Library). In its first form the paragraph is differently phrased: Vere and Billy are called simply "two of the nobler order," and the passage ends: "and holy oblivion the desirable thing for each diviner magnanimity, naturally ensues." Rewriting—his corrections are pencilled in—Melville brought into sharper focus the suggestion of "naturally" by crossing out the adverb itself but then enlarging the preceding phrase to "two of great Nature's nobler order." This allowed him to introduce a further perspective with "providentially," as if to call to mind an ultimate scope of being within which not only the life of man but the encompassing life of all creation is circumscribed. The change in the last clause corresponds. In speaking of what would be the "desirable thing," Melville had rounded off his idea too restrictively; with the apparently neutral word "sequel" he reached out past subjective wish to an indifferent order of nature and providence which to his imagination all human actions belong to and gain dignity from, and which an event so charged as this with emotion and with necessity would most vividly exemplify.

What he did not change is also significant. In both versions, it will be noticed, the center of gravity in the closing sentence is the same "each diviner magnanimity."

4. See Merritt Y. Hughes, "The Christ of 'Paradise Regained' and the Renaissance Heroic Tradition," *Studies in Philology*, XXXV (1938), 254–277.

5. This defence of Nelson, it may be noted, fits perfectly the Aristotelian concept of greatness of soul, according to which, "honor is the object with which the great-souled are concerned, since it is honor above all else which great men claim and deserve." Also, "he that claims less than he deserves is small-souled . . ." *Nichomachean Ethics*, IV, iii, 8 and 11, Loeb Classical Library edition.

6. The question of Billy's moral nature, and its progress through the story, may need a few words more. At several points in the narrative Melville takes time to describe the exact blend of character in Billy as it affects the action then going forward; each time he shows Billy occupied in positive moral considerations (chs. 17, 22, 25). In chs. 25 and 26 it is suggested that Billy has undergone a degree of visible (or only just not invisible) change as a result of his "tension of agony." His "rare personal beauty" is "spiritualized," the skull begins "delicately to be defined" beneath the skin. But these suggestions are muted and unforced. An allegorical demonstration of the progress of the soul does not seem intended. By way of contrast, think how Hawthorne might have handled this action; did handle it, in fact, in *The Marble Faun*.

7. One of Melville's revisions is worth nothing in this respect. Describing Claggart's response to "the moral phenomenon presented in Billy Budd" (ch. 13), he struck out this too schematic sentence: "In him he recognized his own direct opposite . . ."

8. *Mon Coeur Mis à Nu*, #48.

9. E. M. Forster, *Aspects of the Novel* (New York, 1927), 206.

Billy Budd and the
Articles of War

C. B. Ives*

Allegory is often so patent in *Billy Budd* that many critics have found in the novel not a story but Melville's philosophical generalizations about man's fate and others have read the book as a statement regarding the nature of the struggle between good and evil. It seems to me, however, that the novel contains realistic elements worth examining and that one of these is Captain Vere's appeal to the Articles of War to justify his hanging Billy.

Did Melville make his captain's case . . . so strong that every reasonable captain would have acted as he did? If so, the story has lost some of its realistic appeal. Vere's position was exactly that; he said that he had no choice and that, in fact, he was faced with no problem at all.[1] I believe that the reader is mistaken if he accepts Vere's position at face value. Let us analyze it somewhat.

Vere's argument was founded mainly on the Articles of War, a combination of enactments by Parliament and regulations by the Admiralty. He appealed also to the Mutiny Act, but the body of laws falling under that title applied only to the army[2] and were without significance to his situation.

Examine, then, that section of the Articles of War that applied to Billy's act: "If any Officer, Mariner, Soldier or other Person in the Fleet, shall strike any of his Superior Officers . . . on any Pretense whatsoever, every such Person being convicted of any such Offense, by the Sentence of a Court Martial, shall suffer Death. . . ."[3] This provision makes it clear that Billy Budd's offense was punishable by death under the Articles, but it is equally clear that Vere was wrong in asserting that the Articles required him to hang Billy forthwith. They required no such thing. On the contrary, they provided the punishment of death only upon conviction by a "Court Martial," by which term was meant a general court-martial, called by the commander of a detachment, a squadron, or a fleet.[4] The Articles of War provided nowhere for such summary court-martial as was held by Captain Vere.[5]

In an emergency, however, and in the event of a mutiny, a captain

*From *American Literature* 34 (1962):31-39. © 1962 Duke University Press. Reprinted by permission.

might hang the mutineers as a matter of necessity, in disregard of the Articles of War.[6] In such cases it was normal to secure the advice and judgment of his officers in a summary court. That was the situation supposed to obtain on the *Somers;* and, although the acquittal of Captain Mackenzie in that case might serve as precedent only for American ships, it was based on the traditions that the American navy had inherited from England.

But Billy Budd was not a mutineer and was not hanged for mutiny. Mutiny required a "combination of two or more persons,"[7] and, besides, Vere declared emphatically, "I believe you, my man," when Billy protested his loyalty. Nor was he hanged for murder, since Vere agreed that intent was lacking. Vere's stated reasons for the hanging were that Billy had struck his superior and that there was *danger* of mutiny by some other members of the crew.

For his decision, Vere could undoubtedly find support in the British naval customs that allowed latitude to a captain's authority even in defiance of statute, the attitude of naval officers being, as one might expect, that politicians knew nothing about discipline at sea and that even the Admiralty was too much of an ivory tower for its members to make consistently sensible regulations. Thus, for example, although printed instructions of the Admiralty limited captains of ships to imposing punishments of not more than a dozen lashes,[8] in practice these autocrats seldom gave less than the allowance and frequently gave several dozen more.[9]

Discretion was customarily allowed in the direction of leniency also. The faults of sailors sometimes passed without punishment at all,[10] and sometimes received lighter punishments than the Articles called for.[11] Thus, a captain might impose a minor punishment for desertion although the Articles demanded that a court-martial try the offender for his life;[12] and not only was sleeping on watch regularly overlooked (though punishable under the Article by "Death or such other Punishment as a Court-Martial shall think fit to impose, and as the circumstances of the case shall require," 22 George II, c. 33, II, 27), but, according to at least one experienced officer of those days, it was actually encouraged.[13] Billy's offense, striking a superior officer, for which the Articles allowed no alternative to death, did not always receive that punishment.[14]

In short, a captain of a man-of-war was godlike and might exercise his disciplinary discretion or even his disciplinary whims freely with little expectation of reproof.[15]

Was Captain Vere aware of his broad powers? The considerable argument that he made to the officers of his drumhead court-martial implies that he was; and when he said, "one of two things we must do — condemn or let go," he explicitly recognized the power to let go that he — advised, though not bound, by his court — possessed by naval custom. His appeals at one moment to the Articles of War and at the next to the "practical consequences" demonstrate his own confidence that the Articles did not control him.

In addition to the alternatives of hanging and acquittal, his officers also recognized the availability of two other lines of action: conviction with a penalty less than hanging or reference of the case to the Admiral as provided by the Articles. The first of these was called to Vere's attention by the junior lieutenant; and Vere was aware of the second,[16] though he did not discuss it at the trial.

We must, then conclude that Captain Vere, contrary to some of his statements to his officers, had, as a matter of fact, the broadest powers in dealing with Billy. He could let him off, he could impose a minor punishment, he could refer the case to a general court-martial, or he could hang him. He chose to hang him.

Consider now some of the irregularities in the so-called trial ordered by Captain Vere. When Vere told the surgeon of his determination to call a drumhead court-martial immediately, the surgeon thought Vere was "suddenly affected in his mind." He recalled Vere's "excited exclamations so at variance with his normal manner." The lieutenants and the captain of marines "fully shared" the surgeon's "surprise and concern." The misgivings of these men were undoubtedly roused in part by the precipitancy of the "trial," the best procedure even in cases of minor crimes being to delay the decision as to punishment for at least twenty-four hours;[17] but mainly their anxiety seems to have come from Vere's decision to try Billy at all, since they saw no reason not to comply with the provisions of the Articles of War. The "sense of the urgency of the case" that "overruled in Captain Vere every other consideration" did not possess his officers.

They also saw, no doubt, a violation of at least the spirit of the law in the secrecy with which Vere hurried on to his conviction of Billy. General courts-martial were required by the Articles of War to be held in the greatest possible publicity.[18] Since drumhead courts were not provided for by statute, only by custom, nothing explicitly required Vere to give publicity to his trial; yet the general policy was made clear by the Articles, and, after news of the hanging got abroad in the fleet, Vere was criticized for this secrecy "in the confidential talk of more than one or two gun-rooms and cabins."

Finally, Vere's officers must have recognized that a basic element of judicial inquiry and trial was defied by Vere's predetermination to hang Billy. It is true that they did not hear him address Billy as "Fated boy" the moment after Claggart gave his last gasp; but the surgeon had hardly confirmed Claggart's death when he heard the Captain exclaim that Billy must hang. The members of the court could not help seeing that the proceedings were sham, dominated and directed by Vere, who required them only for the sake of form—" 'With mankind' he would say 'forms, measured forms are everything. . . .' "

There is no reason for the reader to suppose that these officers of

Vere's were foolish men. The surgeon not only was by profession something of a student of abnormal behavior but was also, as Melville takes pains to make clear, a man of the most matter-of-fact judgment, not given to flights of fancy or imagination. Although Melville says that Vere regarded the members of his court as "well-meaning men not intellectually mature" and had special doubts about the captain of marines (the commander of the police force on the ship, who one might expect to know something of the demands and limitations of discipline) for being "an extremely good-natured man, an enjoyer of his dinner, a sound sleeper, and inclined to obesity," are not these strictures more revealing of Vere's own character than of the characters of his officers?

What was there in the character of Vere that brought him to adopt his extraordinary course? Why, though appealing to the Articles of War, did he disregard them? And why did he disregard the advice of his officers, the suggestions of common sense, and the strong inclination of his own heart?

Melville gives the Captain many virtues, which need not be denied in putting emphasis on that side of his nature that seems to have been the chief cause of Billy's summary hanging.

Vere was a bachelor of "forty or thereabouts," who had "ruled out" the feminine in his personal life just as he demanded of the members of his court that they rule it out in deciding Billy's fate. He was not given to colorful talk or gestures, for when ashore "he never garnished unprofessional talk with nautical terms," and when afloat he might have been mistaken by any landsman for a civilian rather than the captain of the ship. He was undemonstrative and humorless. His bookishness was marked — "dry and bookish" some called him — and it was biased towards "actual men and events" rather than fiction or poetry. In his reading he "found confirmation" of certain "positive convictions" that he was determined never to change. So pedantic was his interest in historical fact and so stubborn his lack of interest in human nature that even with those of his fellow officers whose intellectual inclinations were thoroughly alien to his he freely alluded to his bookish research. In short, although the life he led was vigorous and dramatic, Vere turned from the enjoyment of it to books; and, although his reading might have been even more impressed with color and vitality than his adventurous life, he turned away from literary art or imagination or feeling to the dryness of recorded fact.

At Billy's trial, Vere's arguments were aimed primarily at making the decision that would be most difficult for human sympathy, most difficult for man as a living being having a natural love of life. He cited the Articles of War (which did not, in fact, support him), the Mutiny Act (which did not apply), the practicalities of the situation (which to every other judgment called for delay at least), and the necessity, as he said, of doing what no one wanted to do, of suppressing Nature, of injuring the heart — "the feminine in man" — even of violating the conscience. When he announced the court's decision to his sailors, they received his statement "like believers in hell listening to the clergyman's announcement of his Calvinistic text."

In all this, Vere was guided not by the mind, as he professed, but by the heart turning against itself. Note well that in spite of his devotion to the facts of books, to a colorless simplicity of personal speech and appearance, to the coldest duties of his profession and rank, emotion was not always entirely concealed; for a "certain dreaminess of mood" revealed itself at times, signifying that, even before his surprising emotional outbursts in the case of Billy Budd, Vere had never been entirely as dry as dust.

Give full weight also to Melville's chapter on Nelson, inserted with no casual intent. At Trafalgar, says Melville, Nelson dressed himself out in all his decorations, advertising his identity to the enemy and suffering death in consequence. His was "a sort of priestly motive," says Melville, and the admiral "adorned himself for the altar and the sacrifice." A similar priestly motive and a similar sacrifice is declared in Melville's comparison of Vere to Abraham preparing to offer up Isaac. Although Abraham's sacrifice was not literally of himself, like Nelson's, it was of his son, whom he loved and who was, in no remote sense, a part of himself. Similarly, Vere loved Billy Budd and spoke to him in "fatherly" tone.

A review of these aspects of Vere's nature justifies the conclusion that the Captain's sudden decision to hang Billy was a sacrificial gesture, born of a kind of self-punishment that had become habitual in Vere's life, the sacrifice and denial that are involved in man's search for the comprehension of fact that destroys fancy, in man's search for the experience that gives him truth but robs him of innocence. All of his life Vere had devoted himself abnormally to this emphasis, killing repeatedly the affections that manifested themselves only in moments of dreaminess, moments that embarrassed and irritated him when they were discovered. Billy represented all of this nearly-destroyed side of him—the affectionate side, the heart, the feminine—and stirred him to such a pitch that when the innocent sailor delivered the death blow to Claggart, Vere's suppressed love for Billy and for all that Billy stood for rose suddenly to the surface. However, Vere's self-disciplinary passion for the harshness of fact-searching and heart-denial rose equally fast and dominated his will as it always had done.

A more normal captain would never have been so eager to hang Billy Budd, and a more practical one might not have hanged him at all, in view of his great value to the morale and efficiency of the crew. Billy's destruction was doomed not only by the abnormal malevolence of Claggart but also by the abnormal "inside narrative" of Vere's personality.[19] The customs of the sea did not require it; and the Articles of War provided only a deceptive excuse for the exercise of Vere's extraordinary "priestly motive," which, as Melville suggests at the beginning of Chapter XXII, may well have contained the elements of true insanity.

Notes

1. Most critics agree with Vere.

2. The Mutiny Act arose out of the loyalty of Scotch regiments to James II after the accession of William and Mary. Charles M. Clode, *The Administration of Justice under Military and Martial Law* (London, 1874), p. 20. Its application was not extended beyond the army and other land forces. *Ibid.*, pp. 31–32.

3. 22 George II, c. 33, II, 22 (1749).

4. Admiralty may grant Commissions for Courts Martial to any Officer commanding in Chief any Fleet or Squadron of Ships of War. 22 George II, c. 33, VI. Commanders in Chief may impower commanders of a Squadron or Detachment ordered on separate service to hold Courts Martial. *Ibid.*, VIII.

5. J. E. R. Stephens, C. E. Gifford, F. Harrison Smith, *Manual of Naval Law and Court Martial Procedure* (London, 1901), pp. 21, 69; formal prohibition of the power in ships' captains to give sentences of loss of life or limb were contained in official instructions as early as 1653. *Ibid.*, pp. 18–19.

6. John Masefield, *Sea Life in Nelson's Time* (2nd ed.; London, 1920), p. 213; even J. F. Cooper, strongly critical of Mackenzie, conceded the right to hang if that was the only way a captain could save the ship, himself, or his officers. *Proceedings of the Naval Court Martial in the Case of Alexander Slidell Mackenzie . . . to which is Annexed an Elaborate Review by James Fennimore Cooper* (New York, 1844), p. 272.

7. Stephens and others, p. 143.

8. *Regulations and Instructions Relating to His Majesty's Service at Sea* (11th ed.; London, 1772), Article IV, p. 46; A Surgeon's-Mate of 1803, *Sketch of the Punishments to Which Common Seamen and Marines are Liable in the Royal Navy* (London, n.d.), pp. 9–10; Admiral Philip Patton, perhaps naïvely, said that custom imposed the limitation, *Strictures on Naval Discipline* (Edinburgh, n.d.), p. 86.

9. A Surgeon's-Mate of 1803, p. 10; Lieut. Thomas Hodgskin, R.N., *An Essay on Naval Discipline Shewing Part of Its Evil Effects* (London, 1813), p. 60; Graham Hewlett, "Discipline and Punishments in the Royal Navy," *United Service Magazine*, N.S., XLIV, 613 (March, 1912); T. H. Wintringham, *Mutiny* (London, 1936), pp. 68–69. However, such excessive flogging as two hundred or eight hundred lashes might, when they resulted in death, bring conviction for murder against the captain; Louis B. Davidson and Eddie Doherty, *Strange Crimes at Sea* (New York, 1954), pp. 69–90.

10. Patton, pp. 82–83; leniency in cases involving the death penalty seems to have been the normal practice in the early days of the Articles; one authority says that although the Articles of War of 1652 provided the death penalty for a great number of offenses, "up to the time of the Restoration there is no known instance of a death sentence pronounced under it having been carried out. Even the fomenters of mutiny escaped." Sir William Laird Clowes, *The Royal Navy* (London, 1898), II, 103. In the army, even the sentences of courts-martial were sometimes disregarded; Clode, p. 32.

11. Patton, pp. 82–83.

12. A Surgeon's-Mate of 1803, pp. 5–6.

13. Hodgskin, p. 40.

14. Masefield says (p. 213) that a man who struck an officer in Nelson's time was only "*fairly* certain to be hanged or flogged through the fleet." Italics added.

15. ". . . they [ships' captains] are legislators, they are judges, they are juries, and they are very often parties and executioners," Hodgskin, pp. 29–30. ". . . the discipline of each ship depends upon what is called the captain's natural disposition," *ibid.*, p. 35.

16. *Billy Budd*, Chapter XXII: "The case indeed was such that fain would the

Indomitable's captain have deferred taking any action whatever respecting it further than to keep the foretopman a close prisoner till the ship rejoined the squadron and then submitting the matter to the judgment of his Admiral."

17. Patton, pp. 31–32, 84–85; William N. Glascock, *Naval Sketch Book* (London, 1826), I, 243.

18. *Regulations and Instructions Relating to His Majesty's Service at Sea* (11th ed.; London, 1772), Article III: "Courts Martial shall always be held in the Forenoon, and in the most public Place of the Ship, where all, who will, may be present . . ."

19. The struggle between Claggart and Billy is re-enacted on a wholly different plane within the nature of Vere himself," says F. O. Matthiessen (*American Renaissance*, [New York: Oxford University Press, 1941], p. 509); and he seems to put the Captain on Claggart's side of the conflict when he adds, "He [the Captain] had the strength of mind and the earnestness of will to dominate his instincts."

Billy Budd and the
Limits of Perception

John W. Rathbun*

With the publication by Harrison Hayford and Merton Sealts of a new reading text of *Billy Budd*, accompanied by a complete transcription of the genetic text, an excellent introduction, and awesomely complete notes, we are now possessed of the most reliable text that can reasonably be expected.[1] Several changes, such as the substitution of *Bellipotent* for the British man-of-war, *Indomitable*, and the excision of the Preface, are changes to which we will become habituated only after long acquaintance, although one can recognize the force of the editors' arguments. But the primary materials included offer the first real opportunity to come to grips with the central significance of Melville's compact masterpiece. Here the genetic text compiled by Hayford and Sealts is invaluable, for it gives solid clues to Melville's increasingly sharpened purposes in writing the novel. In addition, by providing us with the chronologies of the various drafts, the editors make it possible to be conscious of inherent difficulties in the text, which, if they cannot be resolved, can at least serve as a restraint on ingenious attempts to impose an absolute order on materials that finally must remain recalcitrant.

The last point is important. Despite the vast amount of commentary on *Billy Budd*, I think there has persisted in most scholars' minds an uneasy feeling that our imaginations have failed to comprehend Melville's novel. The ambiguous, ranging, and habitually ironic mind of Melville, coupled with textual difficulties, defeats us. We have rendered tribute to this defeat, especially in recent commentary, through close and intense readings of the text. These have contributed much to our understanding.

*From *Nineteenth-Century Fiction* 20, 1 (June 1965):19–34. © 1965 Regents of the University of California Press. Reprinted by permission of the Regents.

But they have also encouraged fashions of analysis (such as the current preoccupation with Captain Vere) that have become increasingly narrower in focus. This article proposes to explore the novel as a whole. To achieve this, I have worked within the novel's structure as it establishes a logic of action and have analyzed the thematic imagery as it supports this action.

I would like to declare at the outset that I have avoided two sets of assumptions or expectations which I do not think especially helpful in reading *Billy Budd:* one, that the story is a tragedy; two, that the focus of the story is on any one character. I offer two alternative views. These are, first, that the story captures something of the quality and intention of a saint's play, with some modification of the term that will become apparent in the article; and second, that Melville's tale revolves about the point that social forms and conventions radically narrow the range of individual perception and response. What Melville is telling us, I think, is that society elaborates social forms and conventions to render the individual subordinate to social norms. When on occasion there emerges a man of individual nobility of heart, one who is as incapable of social "reconstruction" as Billy, it is testimony to our pathetic social condition that we intuitively recognize his superior excellence but suffer a terrible incapacity to comprehend him completely or to emulate him at all.

Social Convention, War, and the State

In the opening pages of the novel, Melville skillfully contrasts those citizens who wear the "external uniform of civilization" and the upright innocence of sailors dissociated from the land whose vices are only "frank manifestations of natural law" (pp. 52–53). The "pristine and unadulterate" virtues found in the figure of the "Handsome Sailor" are "out of keeping" with the "thoroughly civilized" man reared according to "custom and convention" (p. 53). Virtue is antecedent to culture and is a matter of individual rectitude. Therefore, no virtue can inhere in society. In the absence of virtue, society must rely on culture to induce uniform conduct. And culture is no more than the sum total of customs and conventions that encourage a kind of Pavlovian response in men. The natural tendencies of the individual, says Melville, are transformed into a cultured crookedness of heart that leads to moral obliquity (p. 52). The free, self-determining individual simply disappears. In his place, we find man in the aggregate, unquestioning, responding mechanically to external stimuli, living in "Cain's cities" (p. 53).

This effort on the part of society to compromise innocence constitutes much of the tension of Melville's novel. Billy throughout consistently tries to correspond to the standards established by the state. On leaving the *Rights of Man* of Captain Graveling, Billy says farewell to his individual rights, as many commentators on the text have pointed out. He becomes, Captain Vere later asserts, a "King's bargain." When asked about the accusation Claggart had lodged against him, Billy replies that he has loyally eaten the King's bread, an unwitting parody of the Christian ritual. But for all his effort, Billy fails to become "civilized." He suffers no deterioration of individual character despite his various temptations. And this partially accounts for his downfall, since it prevents him from understanding the antipathy of the "urbane" Claggart.

Billy's inability to lose his own spontaneity of character stands in opposition to his shipmates. More than landsmen, they possess a residue of natural innocence. But long service aboard a man-of-war, dedicated to the service of the state, has brought them into conformity to the disciplined obedience that state must demand. Aboard the *Bellipotent*, "usage" serves as a synonym for regulative custom or convention. Usage standardizes action and at the same time reduces men to the point where they are amenable to social control. It is necessarily the official representatives of the state who must see to it that usage is observed. Captain Vere, when acting in his official role, habitually observes usage. He goes by the book. Following Claggart's death, it is apparent from the thoughts of the surgeon and the assembled officers that "usage" would allow mere confinement of Billy until land is reached and the matter referred to the Admiral.[2] But Vere, mindful that usage, inflexible in its particulars, must be seen in strict relation to circumstance, and mindful too that the atmosphere of the time is mysterious, foreboding, and prodigious, decrees the summary court martial as permitted in the Mutiny Acts.[3] And it is perfectly in keeping with usage that his officers hear the case while he reserves to himself the right to supervise the proceedings and to intervene at need.

In all the measures taken by the ship's officers, the ultimate motive is to exercise usage as a control over the seamen. Chapters xxiii and xxvii are studies in depth of the social role of usage. In the former, the crew listen to the announcement of Billy's death-sentence as Calvinist laymen might listen to a Calvinist clergyman, without protest or surprise, with full knowledge and understanding of the code. But when their "native-sense" of right becomes operative a low murmur of protest rises.[4] The officers are equal to the danger. Instantly, there is the shrill piping of whistles, piercing and imperative, and the men, who themselves are the "greatest sticklers for usage," promptly respond because of their habituation to duty.[5] Similarly, in chapter xxviii, which is concerned with events immediately following Billy's execution, the whistles and drums serve to suppress the crew's innate sense of justice and to bring them into line. And lest this point is not clear, Melville makes the point specific. "True martial discipline long continued," he says, "superinduces in average man a sort of impulse of docility whose operation at the official sound of command much resembles in its promptitude the effect of an instinct" (p. 127).[6]

Aboard the *Bellipotent*, these habituations to duty exist in the cause of war. As the story progresses, it moves from Billy's world of the yardarms and upper decks, with their sense of freedom and space, to the ghostly clutter of the upper decks at night and to the depths within. There are increasing references to shot, subterranean rooms and passages, darkness, and the heavy cumbersome guns. We move downward through various spirals of horror as we do in Dante, until we reach the heart of the matter below the luminous surface. The *Bellipotent* is a special kind of hell in which custom and usage exist in the cause of evil. With the interview between the Chaplain and Billy, we find that even peace, ironically, is conscripted to war. Melville raises the question as to why the Chaplain did not act to save Billy and drives his point home. Sea protocol would have rendered the attempt futile. The Chaplain knew that Billy was to become a "martyr to martial discipline" (p. 121), but he occupied the "incongruous" position of being a minister of the Prince of Peace expected to obey the code of the Host of God of War. Hence the Chaplain subserves the same cause as the cannon. We see the terrible irony of a minister who professes love and attachment serving a god who through "brute Force" would destroy those ideals. He lends the "sanction of the religion of the meek" to an abomination (p. 122).[7]

The cause of war is an enormously complicated and darksome thing, reinforced by Melville's imagery of blackness and the fact that Billy's temptations, trial, and condemnation occur at night. Billy's first temptation, the incitement to mutiny, takes place on the moonless "tarry balcony" of the lee forechains. Everything is shadowily outlined, and at Billy's repulse the unknown man flees into the dark shade of the booms. The sense of mystery, intrigue, and betrayal is overwhelming. Then in close order occur Claggart's night-time accusation of Billy, the confrontation of the two below decks, the garish trial with its jail-house and dead-house so near, and the moonlight announcement of the sentence to the crew. Billy's death-vigil, muted and quiet in tone, is reinforced by a dark oppressiveness. Billy lies between two guns as if nipped in the "vice of fate." Surrounding him on the upper gun-decks are all the impedimenta of war. Everything is heavy, huge, painted black as was "customary" or tarred the same color. It all appears as an "upland cave's black mouth." Even the lantern gives off a "dirty yellow light" that stains the moonlight, and around Billy are the "obscurer bays." The white ducks worn by Billy contrast dramatically with this pervasive "funereal hue." The darkness imagery is continued in the following morning scene. The black night covers the ship. The "cavernous" decks below are like the "tiered galleries in a coal-mine." (Again the evocation is in terms of Dante.) Racks of heavy shot are everywhere. The black booms tiered on the deck cast an eerie shadow. Then a "metallic" stroke follows the sounding of eight bells. Immediately, the preemptory whistles blow, and the men flood obediently out of the ship's bowels onto deck. The whole scene stands impressively against the exalted moment that follows, when Billy pronounces his benediction on Captain Vere and is raised to take the full rays of the sun.

Coincident with this bleak view of the state in terms of convention and war, Melville criticizes the state as a source of legal despotism over the individual.[8] As Melville develops this aspect of the novel, the principles of universal justice are seen to principally affirm man's transcendental individualism (as this is apotheosized in the upright seamen and Billy's Adamic character). The state, therefore, viewing man solely as a social creature, is impelled to set up a secular code of justice in opposition to the divine order.[9] This has the effect of cancelling out man's individualism and molding him into a social pattern that assures first rank to the state. The state becomes an end in itself, its citizens pawns in the intricate moves of statecraft. Pervasive throughout the novel, the theme of state supremacy is clearly delineated by Melville in the trial scene. Captain Vere is the spokesman for the new attitude. As an English sea-commander, he has committed himself to the primacy of state policy. His "vows of allegiance" are to "martial duty," which means in effect that he is "not authorized" to consider abstract principles of guilt and innocence. Consequently, prudence and rigor must be his primary attributes. Captain Vere can look only to the external act. Scruple and compassion, which might be operative under the terms of universal justice, are matters for "psychologic theologians" and are outside state concerns (p. 108). In "practical" matters (and in the world of the state all matters are practical), one cannot afford the stance of moralist or casuist (p. 110). As Vere tells his own officers, their allegiance is not to the natural law but to the King. In serving under the King, no man is a free-agent. The state pre-determines everything (pp. 110-111). A man's only duty is to obey.

Here, of course, there is no correspondence between God's law and state law. The very idea of correspondence, that an intimate relationship exists between man's rage for order and the objective world, is denied. A King's representative, Captain Vere points out, must distinguish between the King's concerns and God's concerns. Private conscience must yield to imperial law (p. 111). This last statement reverses the authorities of God and King that had obtained in past times, and it testifies to the superiority of the King in all issues affecting the state. A new divinity has come into existence, not to shape the best ends of man, but to secure its own interests and self-perpetuation.[10]

The Religious Symbolism

The religious symbolism of the characters has been explored by a number of scholars. I simply propose to examine it here in terms of what I have already said about the state's ability to counteract man's nature, the state's authority, and its code of justice. Much of Melville's story is couched in Biblical and religious terms. As the novel progresses, Billy takes on in turn the characters of the pre-Fall Adam, Isaac, and Christ, but with results radically different from the original Biblical versions. Billy becomes the Adam who does not fall, the Isaac who is not saved, the Christ who does not redeem. One comes away from the book with a sense of the immense futility of Billy's death. One comes away too with a sense of the immense sadness and aloneness that Melville must have experienced in civilized man's incapacity to imaginatively realize an experience of transcendental significance to all men.

As a pre-Fall Adamite figure, Billy is primarily intended to represent unperjured innocence and guilelessness, qualities in which the crew partially share as "upright barbarian" Adams (p. 52). Opposed to Billy is the depraved and deceitful Claggart. The two men are polar exemplars of good and evil, each phenomenal in his own way. Neither man possesses a known parentage, so that their "true antecedents" remain obscured in mystery (pp. 51, 65). Billy, a "peacemaker" who might have "posed for a young Adam before the Fall," is a "child-man" possessed of an "essential good nature" (pp. 86, 81). Claggart is the "direct reverse of a saint," a man who does not have a "normal" nature (p. 74). These differing natures lead to differing attributes. Billy is a rosy-hued, vivacious man of "significant personal beauty" (p. 77), while Claggart's complexion testifies to something "defective or abnormal" in the blood (p. 64). Claggart's superior intellectual capacity, his constitutional sobriety and ingratiating deference to superiors, his "austere" patriotism, are all the antithesis to Billy's animal-like fatalism and "unconventional" rectitude.

In both men, the heart dictates their attitudes, but those attitudes are put into action in different ways. The "bonfire" in Billy's heart is heroic and innocent. He does not try to force events nor has he learned from experience. He has not tasted of the "questionable apple of knowledge" (p. 52). The result is that Billy's innocence does not sharpen his faculties or enlighten his will (p. 70). Claggart's heart, on the other hand, is filled with envy. His "innate" depravity folds itself in the "mantle of respectability" (a "manufacturable" thing closely associated with the "moral obliquity" of the city), and he uses his reason to effect "the irrational" (p. 76). His conscience is "lawyer to his will," so that a fancied provocation can provide the motive for various acts against Billy (p. 80).

Billy does not exclusively possess the qualities endowed by the figures of Adam and the "handsome sailor," which are complementary images. The figure of the "handsome sailor" is to be found aboard a number of ships (p. 43). A sort of natural regality obtains in such men. The handsome sailors, whom seamen recognize and to whom they respond, possess a strength and beauty in excess of that of ordinary men, and their moral natures correspond closely to their physical beauty (p. 44). Their natural habitat is the upper deck and the shrouds, swinging airily over the decks and living in the natural sunshine of the day.

Claggart's nature is common enough to have been defined by Plato, and he enlists subordinates in his cause who share in his qualities. Claggart too belongs to a class. Where Billy's world is the world of the upper decks, Claggart's world is the lower gun-decks, where he serves as a sort of chief of police (p. 64). In this lower world, he controls "various converging wires of underground influence" that allow him to function as the inquisitorial arm of the state. Obviously endowed with intelligence and a good education, he displays a "ferreting genius" which is the hallmark, according to Melville, of civilized man at his worst. The "austere" civilized man is corrupt and untrustworthy. All the more reason, then, for Claggart's "austere" patriotism to employ itself in fashioning a maze of deceit for the entrapment of individuals. For this purpose, he employs subordinates like Squeak, who have the ferreting aptitude of a "rat in a cellar" (pp. 67, 79). In the dark gloom of the lower decks, such men mine their network of deceit and betrayal and work assiduously against those of the topside.

Caught between these two levels of moral experience is the world of convention. The conventional world, committed as it is to set patterns of response and pedestrian wisdom, lacks the requisite tools to comprehend either Billy's innocence or Claggart's satanism. Both men are "exceptional" creatures, moral phenomena who transcend man's ordinary way of knowing (pp. 74, 78). The world of convention "blunts that fine spiritual insight" which is needed to understand "certain exceptional characters" (p. 75). Claggart cannot be understood in terms of a knowledge of the world (p. 75), and only Vere and Claggart have any inkling of the richness of spirit possessed by Billy. This indictment of a world committed to custom and convention is harsh, and it relegates the world to the position of onlooker as the two exemplar figures clash and destroy one another.[11]

Billy's very lack of knowledge contributes to an innocence which is his blinder (p. 88). His virtues are all the more extraordinary because he is so absolutely unaware that he possesses them. Before Claggart's satanism, saintly Billy can only express blank puzzlement. Melville makes clear that Claggart's antipathy and evil are mysterious even while spontaneous and profound. Like Satan looking at Adam in *Paradise Lost*, Claggart knows a "soft yearning" for Billy and experiences despair, melancholy, and sadness over that unattainable station (p. 88). And so recoiling upon himself, he uses all the deceits, stratagems, and temptations he can to destroy Billy. Since culture is "auspicious" to depravity, Claggart utilizes the attributes of the landsman—his finesse, his liking for intricate moves, indirection, and obliqueness—to bring about Billy's fall.

One must be aware, however, of the complex ironies that control the fall motif. It is fairly certain that Billy does not re-experience Adam's original fall from grace. Billy does not taste of the tree of knowledge, nor does he lose his primeval innocence. This can be seen in Captain Vere's statement that at the Last Assizes Billy will be acquitted before the bar of divine justice, and seen too in the imagery attending Billy's execution, where Billy is transfigured by "the full rose of the dawn." Yet Melville is specific in attributing a human flaw to Billy in his stutter. I think the stutter serves two functions. It first establishes Billy as a finite human being and therefore no idealized "conventional" hero of romance (p. 53).

His innocence is therefore "natural," just as Claggart's depravity is natural; philosophers like Rousseau and Calvin are alike wrong in plumping for one to the exclusion of the other. His stutter, secondly, is a flaw only in the eyes of man. Speech, after all, is man's method of civilized communication. To that extent, language itself is arbitrary, restricted, exclusive, deliberately regulated. Billy represents all that is uncoerced, free, and spontaneous. He transcends the reductions language must make in order to communicate. Billy must be known intuitively, not logically. His agonized attempt to talk, and his inability to do so, when Claggart makes his accusation, leads then to a fall only in the eyes of the state and its code of temporal justice. Before heaven, Billy is innocent. But in terms of the secular code Billy has fallen, and he must be punished.

With the conclusion of the trial scene, Billy's betrayal by the forces of evil is concluded and the Adam symbolism completed. Following the trial, Melville suggests a second Biblical parallel. At this point Billy acquires a father in Captain Vere, who becomes Abraham to Billy's Isaac. Again, Melville's departure from the Biblical story is as significant as his suggestion of its relevance. Captain Vere possesses many of the attributes of the established order. He is a sailor of distinction, intrepid but not injudicious, modest and aristocratic, dreamy at times, sturdy but not brilliant in his actions (p. 60). He is inherently conservative and believes in institutionalism as a control of the social order. Of a markedly intellectual temperament, he reads history, biography, and "unconventional" (therefore honest and self-reliant) writers like Montaigne. In the process, he has come to some considered opinions on how "lasting institutions" might be established that an ordered society can live in peace (p. 63).

In his contacts with other men, Captain Vere again displays a wide range of abilities. The state recognizes his tact and initiative and gives him extra duties to perform. In the interview with Claggart, he is impatient and conscious of a "vaguely repellent distaste" for the man (p. 91). Ordinarily, he can intuitively understand other men's motives and their "essential nature" (p. 96). These are all fine qualities and certainly in Vere's favor. He is not the villain of the novel, as some recent commentators have tried to suggest. But Vere is not the hero either. He takes Claggart's measure accurately and sensibly. But he cannot fathom the guile of the man. Claggart finally perplexes Vere. In an unfamiliar situation, he resorts to the familiar position of policy and tact. He resolves to "practically" test Claggart's veracity. His learned trust in overt proof brings about the confrontation and from that the crisis ensues. Then during the trial scene Vere becomes the authoritarian representative of the state, winning out over his officers' more humane instincts (pp. 109-110).

Vere's inclinations, when he allows himself to slide away from his "formalized humanity" and to abandon his "austere" devotion to military duty, are all toward love (p. 115). In his imagined description of the private interview between Captain Vere and Billy, Melville is explicit in pointing out that both Vere and Billy are two of "Nature's nobler order" (p. 115). They share radically in the "rarer qualities of our nature," so radically, indeed, that we can hardly conjecture the extent. Vere's capacity to realize the virtue of love, although finally limited, makes the last moments between him and Billy "sacramental."

Yet there is for Vere the "exacting behest," as there was for Abraham. Vere's tragedy, finally, is that he is in the service of a dread sovereign. Abraham, in the service of a greater sovereign, was stayed in the execution of God's command: Abraham's intent was sufficient. No such stay is granted Vere. It constitutes a failure of the only authority he knows, the state. In a society where laws are promulgated to govern the whole rather than to protect the individual, their infraction must necessarily be unquestioningly punished. No melioration is possible. Indeed, such melioration is impossible, for the state is distant and indifferent. Only the Mutiny Acts figure, and they allow (if they do not decree) the sacrifice of Billy.[12]

The suggestion of sacrifice evokes the memory of the greatest sacrificial victim of all, and with Billy's death Melville turns to the symbol of Christ. The symbol works in two ways. Just as Christ was condemned by the laws of temporal justice so Billy is condemned. The injustice of what happens to Billy is accentuated through the various references to Christ's agony and execution. Second, through his death Billy achieves a spiritual father and transcendental significance. As one of "Nature's nobler order," Billy stands for all that is good, natural, and noble in mankind. He has been spiritualized by his experience. His agony is over. Resignation and peace possess him. In the final climactic moment, the darkness is dissipated, and Billy ascends to his death. But the full significance of Billy's nature and death, as the last chapters indicate, is ultimately lost on society, on Captain Vere, and on the seamen.

The Final Chapters

As Melville quite correctly points out, in terms of dramatic action the story should end with Billy's death. But if a reader has been sensitive to Melville's organization of his narrative, it soon becomes apparent that Melville has interwoven various strands which can more or less be reduced to a counterpoint of authority (the stage, usage, and war) and freedom (primeval innocence, human community, and Billy's triple role as sacrificial victim).[13] These strands are not resolved with Billy's death. The final chapters constitute an ironic epilogue, in which in a series of tonally contrasting events we see the impact of Billy's death on the state, Captain Vere, and the seamen.

The reaction of the state occurs in the conversation of the Purser and the surgeon and in the official version of Billy's death. In both chapters there is a deliberate downgrading of tone from the drama of Billy's death to a flat and literal level. The Purser and Surgeon are utilitarian and unimaginative. They see Billy's death as a natural event, a phenomenon but not phenomenal. Their whole concern is with a "scientific" knowledge of the externals of the event, especially the absence of spasmodic movement as Billy hung at the end of the rope. Their conversation is ridiculous, pompous, and arrogant. For every natural event, a natural cause must be predicated. Here is the tell-tale clue. On the mundane level, Billy's death should *be* a natural event. But even the physical death somehow escapes definition. There is a mystery to it that resists rational explanation. Their failure to get beyond the literal is a failure of the imagination, and here no power on earth can help.

In conjunction with this scene, we have the juggling of history for the convenience of the state. At various points in the narrative, Melville prepares us for this eventuality. In discussing the Nore mutiny, he points out that England was chary about all reference to mutinies. The official need was to write history selectively, to avoid facts, to gloss over facts, or to ignore facts completely. Melville's sober realism acknowledges that this is sometimes necessary. He is less lenient in discussing the *Somers* incident in chapter xxi, where he is clearly out of sympathy with the Captain's procedure in an incident nearly like the one that occurred aboard the *Bellipotent*. And then there are the ambiguities of circumstance themselves, in which appearance does not always correspond to reality. The official need is to recognize only the externalities of events. This leads necessarily to changing the consideration from Billy's essential innocence to Billy's circumstantial guilt. When, therefore, the official version of Billy's execution is published, all relation to the truth is lost, even though the account is "for the most part written in good faith."[14] Billy is vilified and Claggart sanctified. And as Melville ironically comments, this is the way it has stood "in human record" until his own reconstruction of the events. And such must be the result for the state to sustain itself. Usage, ritual, discipline, falsification, and literal adherence to political need and expediency then act in sharp contra-distinction to transcendental truth.

In the chapter on Vere's death, the mystery of Billy's character again hovers over the action. Vere's position in the narrative is ambivalent, and this ambivalence extends to his death. In terms of his native intelligence and imaginative insight, Captain Vere comes close to understanding Billy. But his habitual reliance on custom and usage finally inhibits his perception. The cause for which he fought, insofar as it was directed against the excesses of French revolutionary action, was a good cause. But in the need to preserve its own existence the state legislated away freedoms in the name of freedom, a contradiction which could only lead to tragedy for those enrolled in the service of the state. In his devotion to the state, as well as to the institutions the state elaborates for its own maintenance, Vere prepared the ground for his own untimely defeat. His capture of the *Athée* promises fulfillment of his ambition for greatness. But his mortal wound, his drugged lingering illness, and his death ashore all testify to a moral character cut short of conclusion. He realizes dimly that there was something he finally was unable to attain. His death is pathetic rather than tragic. He dies unenlightened, softly repeating Billy's name, like an invocation.[15]

Finally, in the reaction of the seamen to Billy's death, we have the most pathetic case of all because potentially there was great promise. Even though the seamen share in Billy's simplicity and to some extent in his innocence, they finally cannot comprehend his greatness. Chapter xxvii, which returns to events immediately following Billy's hanging, is heavy with tension, and much of the tone of the chapter on Billy's death is reestablished. In the silence following the hanging, there are only the flutter of the sail and the soft wash of the sea to be heard. Then gradually a mounting murmur is heard, much as in the night announcement of Billy's sentencing. The reaction of the officers is immediate. Once again the metallic peremptory whistles are blown, and once again the men yield to the "mechanism of discipline" and disperse. Later the men reassemble to witness Billy's burial, where the "croaked requiem" of the crying birds provokes an "uncertain movement"; immediately there is the drummed call to quarters to which the men respond instinctively. Finally, they are made to stand ritualistically by the guns they serve. During the long roll call, usage gradually removes the immediacy of Billy's death and burial, giving cogency to Captain Vere's observation that "measured forms are everything" in the control of men. Three times the crew had threatened to follow inner impulses. And three times they had yielded to the habit of discipline to which they had been conditioned by the state.

Yet, as we see in the last chapter, the seamen realize intuitively that Billy's death has some latent significance to them. Ignorant of the facts, they accept Billy's condemnation as the inevitable expression of naval authority. But they also know that he is guiltless. And so Billy becomes a sort of Christ figure to them. Billy, however, does not possess Christ's redemptive meaning in the ordinary sense. It is simply that Billy has exposed the magnificence of the primitive soul that has in it a touch of the divine, just as a touch of the divine may be in us all when not deformed by custom, usage, or austere discipline. The very simplicity of the seamen prevents them from coming to this elementary understanding. They lack the ability to link imagination with intelligence, which after all must be combined for superior understanding. Their dim perception of Billy's nobility is gradually modified into a ritualistic and fetishistic worship of pieces of wood. Such is always the case. Great men like Christ and Billy always transcend measured forms. The rest of mankind, lacking the capacity for true comprehension, progressively downgrade such greatness until it is neutralized within the folds of ordinary thurification.

These last chapters give us an ironic vision that over two-thirds of a century of living had confirmed in Melville. No one in the novel is finally able to ascertain who Billy really is. Billy's character remains enigmatic. The symbolic roles he plays as Adam, as Isaac, as Christ, become at last meaningless and futile. To the extent that we deny the existence of constituent elements in human nature and see man as simply a bundle of social habits, we impose limits to man's perception. Culture becomes simply a pattern of response. Thinking thus, it is no great step for the state to "engineer" habitual action toward some desired end. In the process, men lose their individual capacity to realize the ultimate moment of transcendental awareness.

And yet there is at the same time something more to Melville's novel. For whatever ease it might give one, the tone of that last chapter indicates that a modicum of comfort is better than none, acceptance preferable to despair. *Moby Dick* is in many ways an angry, anguished outcry against evil and an unsuccessful exploration of its origins. *Billy Budd* accepts evil as part and parcel of the universe within which we live. This acceptance establishes a tone of wintry serenity mixed with an ironic regret that provides much of the fascination of the novel. The ballad ending is essential to Melville's purpose. "Billy in the Darbies" is the only real imaginative extension of an experience that obviously had meaning to the "artless poetic temperament" of Billy's fellow seamen. However crude in insight, it is preferable to the coldly impersonal account of Billy's death in the "authorized" naval chronicle of the time. What Melville seems to be saying is that as social creatures we fail to properly understand our saints. Our insight is clogged by forms and conventions. But fortunately for some of us our individuality is not completely buried. Our perceptions are dimmed and our aspirations limited, which is pathetic, yet occasionally we can be stirred to a muted awareness of our humanity.

Notes

1. Herman Melville, *Billy Budd, Sailor (An Inside Narrative)*, edited by Harrison Hayford and Merton M. Sealts, Jr. (Chicago, 1962). Subsequent references to this edition will be in the body of the article.

2. The relevant passages (pp. 101–102) seem to indicate that the surgeon and the other officers are simply inclined to postpone action in a difficult case. The surgeon, whose doubts are given at some length, is a "prudent," politic man who thinks confinement of Billy should be conducted as "dictated by usage." The whole passage, however, as Hayford and Sealts point out, is ambiguous. See their comments, pp. 9–11, 35.

3. A useful interpretation of the latitude given Captain Vere in employing the Mutiny Acts is in C. B. Ives, *"Billy Budd* and the Articles of War," *American Literature*, XXXIV (March, 1962), 31–39.

4. This parallels Captain Vere's own sense of right when Claggart makes his accusation before Vere too falls back on usage.

5. As I will indicate at various points in the article, whistles serve as a remarkable means to recall men to their habituated sense of duty and custom.

6. Cf. Karl Zink, "Herman Melville and the Forms — Irony and Social Criticism in *Billy Budd*, *Accent*, XII (Summer, 1952), 136, for an effective comment on this passage. As will

shortly appear, however, Mr. Zink and I disagree on the interpretation of Captain Vere's character.

7. The attitude is persistent in Melville's writings, as Hayford and Sealts point out, pp. 185–86.

8. The context for the following paragraphs is the conflict between two concepts of government: the divine rights of kings and the Christian Commonwealth. I would argue that Melville's novel is sympathetic to the ideas of the Christian Commonwealth, which was far more liberal and far more cognizant (in theory) of the welfare of its citizens. Social and economic inequities would obviously abide in any temporal social structure, but such inequities would be held to a minimum by the Commonwealth itself as it sought to administer God's justice. With the advent of the divine right theory, the correspondence of divine and temporal justice declines, and as a matter of fact comes to be sharply discriminated. These points are admirably documented in the book of William Appleman Williams, *The Contours of American History* (New York, 1961), in the initial chapters.

9. Hayford and Sealts take a somewhat different tack in suggesting that "the opposing positions of [Paine and Burke] concerning the doctrine of abstract natural rights lie behind the dialectic of *Billy Budd*" (p. 138). Cf. also William Bysshe Stein's article on the role of history in the novel: "*Billy Budd*: The Nightmare of History," *Criticism*, III (Summer, 1961), 237–250. Stein is probably too harsh on Captain Vere, and he does not see the central significance of the Abraham-Isaac analogy which I discuss later in this article.

10. Cf. William Braswell, "Melville's *Billy Budd* as " 'An Inside Narrative,' " *American Literature*, XXIX (May, 1957), 133–134: "The King is a symbol of the Deity: he does not physically appear in the story, but he is the supreme authority under whose law the ship operates."

11. Hayford and Sealts correctly see Billy, Claggart, and Vere as three types of men who act out of the necessity of their inner natures to affect the circumstances and action of the novel (p. 167). It seems odd, then, that they should suggest that the "theme of moral accountability and responsibility . . . is of major importance in *Billy Budd*" (p. 166). Billy, Claggart, and Vere act as they must act, and Melville does not seem so much disposed to attributed blame as to lament men's lack of perception of what actually occurs in this world. Interesting comment from a theological point of view is in James Smylie, "*Billy Budd*: The Work of Christ in Melville," *Religion in Life* (Spring, 1964), 286–296.

12. I think this is the only view of Vere consistent with the tone and imagery of the novel. It is a point of mediation between the position of James E. Miller, Jr., that Vere is a "Hero of Humanity" ("*Billy Budd*: The Catastrophe of Innocence," *MLN*, LXXIII [1958], 168–176) and the position of Phil Withim, who argues that Vere represents all that Melville means to attack ("*Billy Budd*: Testament of Resistance," *MLQ*, XX [June, 1959], 115–127.

13. Hayford and Sealts note a "pattern of . . . antitheses" may be found in the novel and illustrate their point by reference to three incidents (p. 162). But they also say (p. 194) that "the deliberate juxtaposition of contrasting attitudes" in the last chapters argues against any attempt to find Melville's intent. I think precisely the opposite can be maintained. The strange sense of unreality in the last chapters is persuasive evidence for my general thesis — that social convention so clouds men's perception that imaginative insight into truth is almost totally impossible.

14. There is a difficulty here resulting from Melville's incomplete revisions. Vere's death would likely have been reported as well as Billy's and Claggart's. Cf. Hayford and Sealts (p. 8).

15. The fact that Vere's character is developed late in the manuscript revisions (designated, X, E, F, G by Hayford and Sealts) seems to confirm the idea that Melville, as he worked out his ideas and organization, came to see Vere as a dramatic example of how even the most "exceptional" man can be so altered by habits of perception as to fail to escape their bondage.

Nelson and Vere: Hero and Victim in *Billy Budd, Sailor*

Ralph W. Willett*

Emerson's faith in the historic role of the hero did not prevent him from evaluating Nelson morally as a man without principle.[1] Unfortunately, he failed to make his criticism specific; only the grouping of Nelson with Napoleon offers a clue to the origin of Emerson's disapproval. Hawthorne and Melville were more well-disposed in their appreciations, which resemble each other in extravagance of sentiment. Whereas Hawthorne's treatment takes the form of an essay, Melville incorporates Nelson into his short novel, *Billy Budd, Sailor*,[2] and puts to his own uses what Hawthorne called, in *Our Old Home*, the "symbolic poetry" (i, 275) of Nelson's life.

Why Melville, in his last prose work, should have chosen to create a perfect hero in the figure of Nelson requires some elucidation. It is no accident that Chapters iv and v, in which Nelson appears most prominently, precede the introduction and description of Captain Vere. The historical personage and the fictional character are surely juxtaposed for the purposes of comparison. The differences between Nelson and Vere have been adequately rehearsed by various critics,[3] particularly those who see Vere as an inferior version of Nelson. The English admiral represents, for Melville, the ideal version of the governing principle; not only does Nelson help to defeat the revolutionary, anarchic ideas of the French, but he also demonstrates his ability to manage effectively any crew with traces of recalcitrance, "not indeed to terrorize the crew into base subjection, but to win them, by force of his mere presence and heroic personality, back to . . . allegiance."[4] Vere, on the other hand, is unable to emulate this ideal; he is an illustration of Melville's contention that man, at any level below that of the hero, is the victim of his own ambiguities and inconsistencies, and of history.

The temporal context of the story is the era of the Napoleonic Wars and of the Nore Mutiny, and it is against this background that Vere's conduct has to be judged. It is the historical situation which is responsible for Vere's obsession with mutiny and which exposes his human frailty. An awareness of the possibility of mutiny at this time, a few months after the Nore incident, is, says Melville guardedly, "not unreasonable," but he also points out that such a possibility is in no way suggested by the behavior of the *Bellipotent*'s crew. These circumstances, in conjunction with Claggart's machinations, Vere's temperament, and Billy's simplicity, produce the catastrophe.

Insufficient importance has been attached to Vere's irascibility, which

*From *PMLA* 82 (1967):370–76. © 1967 by *PMLA*. Reprinted by permission of the Modern Language Association of America.

Melville makes no attempt to hide. Normally Vere controls this instantly, but the fact remains that Claggart's accusation against Billy Budd and his frequent references to mutiny are delivered at a time when Vere is emotionally agitated. His refusal to be unduly alarmed by Claggart's "revelations" might have been sustained had his response not been followed soon afterwards by the shocking violence in his cabin. His reaction this time, excited and febrile, with a startling religious flavor, precludes any attempt at self-control. Billy is prejudged, as the drumhead court comes to realize (p. 108), and Vere's fear of mutiny serves to rationalize the prejudgment.

This should indicate that it is dangerous to regard Nelson and Vere as schematically arranged symbols of recklessness and prudence. Since these modes of behavior are available to both men, the difference between them narrows down to the question of the appropriate attitude for the occasion. Nelson dies glamorously, boldly, a self-sacrificing priest absolving his crew, yet he can also be circumspect, as he is when he leads the fleet up the channel to Copenhagen. Vere's background is academic and, as Melville suggests, such a training may be responsible for an ignorance of human nature. Vere is excessively cautious in discounting his intuitive knowledge of Billy Budd and Claggart,[5] and it is his generally prudent approach which, in a sense, causes his strange behavior after Billy Budd kills Claggart. Accustomed to controlling emotion as soon as it manifests itself, Vere's powers of cerebration are temporarily impaired when he is overtaken by an irresistible emotional response. Consequently, his arguments as they stand in the text are not even *a priori* reasoning, but are rationalizations of a hasty decision: "Yet the angel must hang!" (p. 101).

Vere's rashness is emphasized by Melville through two pertinent metaphors: when a ship encounters fog, "speed is put on at the hazard of running somebody down" (p. 114); the *Bellipotent's* captain is also likened to a migratory fowl which fails to notice when it crosses a frontier. But Melville's attitude toward Vere's behavior is not simply condemnatory; in Chapter xiv of *The Confidence-Man*, he argues that novelists are justified in creating inconsistent characters since life itself contains so many inconsistencies. Melville also points out in *Billy Budd, Sailor* that it is easy to be wise after the event. Irrespective of our motives, we cannot guarantee what the results of our actions will be. A superseded passage neatly illustrates this view: "the prudent method adopted by Captain Vere to obviate publicity and trouble having resulted in an event that necessitated the former and under existing circumstances in the navy indefinitely magnified the latter."[6] As retained passages suggest, the world is unpredictable and ironic. Violence and disorder sometimes lead to progress, as the Nore mutiny and the French Revolution testify; conversely, Vere's soothing words to Billy Budd have a result which is "contrary to the effect intended" (p. 99). The most clearly ironic example begins with Vere's attempt to forestall mutiny by making an example of Billy Budd; this only serves to stimulate discontent among the crew and to make Billy a martyr. And the irony is deeper yet: Vere's reputation as a seaman and fighter is, among the officers, as high as Nelson's, yet it is through Vere that Billy Budd joins Nelson in the realm of naval myth and naval hagiology, a more enduring sort of fame.

Only the responsible hero can be relied upon to impose harmony and to neutralize the effects of chance, and a clearer idea of Melville's conception of a great man can be obtained by an examination of Carlyle's *Lectures on Heroes, Hero-Worship and the Heroic in History* (1841–46). This work, when drawn into critical service, illuminates both Lord Nelson and, to a lesser extent, Captain Vere, for these figures grow in solidity as the resemblances between Carlyle's theory and Melville's fictional actuality are observed.

In Carlyle's dogmatic eulogies we find the conception of the hero which was to inform Melville's book in the shape of Lord Nelson. What is almost Carlyle's first observation brings Nelson and the British Navy to mind: "We cannot look, however imperfectly, upon a great man, without gaining something by him. He is the living light-fountain, which is good and pleasing to be near."[7] This surely is Melville's view of Nelson, a glowing figure in "the jewelled vouchers of his own shining deeds" (p. 58), inspiring his men at Trafalgar and elsewhere. (The definition of character in terms of light also occurs in *The Confidence-Man*, where the original character is described as being "like a revolving Drummond light, raying away from itself all around it — everything is lit by it, everything starts from it.")[8] Moreover, Nelson seeks and achieves a hero's end: "Difficulty, abnegation, martyrdom, death" (p. 64) — these, says Carlyle, are allurements to the heart of the heroic man. Thus it is with Nelson, "a reckless declarer of his person in fight," unafraid to face death and to become a martyr.

Yet Melville, like Carlyle, does not consider the hero merely in abstract conceptual terms; for both writers, great men form part of their interpretation of history and of their political ideologies. Carlyle indicates the decay and ruin that result from rebellion but at the same time optimistically points to the hero as "the one fixed point in revolutionary history," a cornerstone standing firm amidst the maelstrom of social chaos. For Melville also, the hero represented by Nelson is a stabilizing figure, well equipped to suppress and control insurrections. As Melville's story reveals, Nelson was transferred to the *Theseus*, a ship which had taken part in the Nore mutiny, in order to win over the crew by means of his magnetic personality. The occasion, it seems, calls forth the man whether it be one of Carlyle's heroes, Cromwell, at the time of the English Civil War, or Melville's Nelson at the time of the Napoleonic wars.

However, these heroes are not just examples of historical concatenations. What the hero is and what he does are morally and socially desirable. Carlyle is able to affirm that "society is founded on hero-worship" (p. 11), and his reasons are not difficult to find: "every Great Man . . . is by the nature of him a son of Order not of Disorder. . . . He is the missionary of Order. Is not all work of man in this world a *making of order?*" (p. 185). Thus he articulates the ideas which concerned Melville increasingly during the latter part of his life.

Nelson, who emerges as a result of Melville's lifelong concern with order, fits neatly into Carlyle's last category, the hero as King, that is, "the Commander over men." This type of hero, in Carlyle's view, is "practically the summary for us of *all* the various figures of Heroism; Priest, Teacher . . . to *command* over us . . . to tell us for the day and hour what we are to *do*" (p. 178). Carlyle had earlier referred to "the wayfaring and battling priest," and Melville explicitly sees Nelson in these terms, a man of "priestly motive" and one of the moving forces in the "plenary absolution" the English sailors received through the battle of Trafalgar. (By this token, Billy Budd, too, has traces of the heroic, for he is a "fighting peacemaker" and is compared to a Catholic priest.)

Yet it is not only the positive qualities of men in high positions which find their way from Carlyle's pages to Melville's. "A man is right and invincible, virtuous . . . when he joins himself to the great deep Law of the World, in spite of all superficial laws, temporary appearances, profit-and-loss calculations" (p. 51), says Carlyle, and the violation of this precept is clearly enacted by Captain Vere, who chooses to embrace man-made laws and to reject God's law: "At the Last Assizes it [the officer of marines' plea] shall acquit. But how here? We proceed under the law of the Mutiny Act."[9]

In other ways, too, Vere is the negation of Carlyle's and Melville's "Great Man." He lacks the spontaneity that characterizes Carlyle's hero, being rather a man of prudence, the naval counterpart of the Benthamite utilitarians who evoke the scorn of both writers. In addition, he is, unlike the hero, a creature of his time, a captain whose emotional balance and patterns of thought are dictated by historical pressures.

Amidst the correspondences of accepted values, one sharp difference stands out. Carlyle is heartened by his great men in the very process of describing them and their abilities. His treatment of revolutions and disintegration, though relevant, is brief, and he looks forward to an Emersonian world in which every man achieves his own kind of greatness. For Melville, on the other hand, the hero is a rarity, a kind of biological sport; much more common is the imperfect leader or unheroic administrator. Vere partakes of the work of man as defined by Carlyle, but cannot impose order through the exhibition of a heroic personality. This is his tragedy and by implication the world's.

The interesting parallels between Carlyle's and Melville's ideas of the hero-type are but one kind of evidence, and the importance of that evidence would be negligible were it not buttressed by similar indications in the text itself. Consequently, an examination of the stages of development in the novella, and of Melville's revisions, is not without relevance to the Nelson-Vere relationship.

Chapters iii to v in *Billy Budd, Sailor*, which are the chief "Nelson" sections, reveal a figure who fulfils two roles, those of peacemaker and of reckless hero. Both these functions are put in the narrative at an early stage (Bb),[10] but whereas the transfer in Chapter v of Nelson to a ship with an intractable crew receives no later addition or elaboration, Nelson's foolhardy heroism in Chapter iv is later augmented at stage G during the period when Melville decided tentatively to restore that chapter. His hesitancy over the inclusion of Chapter iv, which was only reintroduced during the post-D stage, and even then was kept in a separate folder, should not lead the reader to doubt the author's intention, since there remains sufficient material to link Nelson and Vere. Indeed, the fact that the Nelson chapter (iv) and one of the Vere chapters (vii) were kept separately would seem to indicate that they were connected in Melville's scheme. Moreover, we have Hayford's evidence that Melville revised the scene between Vere and the surgeon shortly after revising the Nelson chapter: he used the verso of superseded Bb leaf 16^5 for the new leaf 41 (post-G pencil), in the revised Vere-surgeon scene.[11]

The restoration stage comes after the extensive additions to the characterization of Vere in Chapters vi and vii, and the sharpening of the contrast between "martial glory" and prudence in Chapter iv obviously refers to Vere's undemonstrative appearance and his avoidance of injudiciously intrepid behavior. Melville leaves no doubt when, in the final pencil stage, Vere's lack of brilliancy is emphasized.

Whereas both Billy Budd and Nelson are presented as peacemakers at stage Bb, the development of Vere in this role proceeds piecemeal during the later stages. At E, his concern for the men's welfare is made part of the narrative, and at F his ideas of peace and, more especially, discipline are stated. It is at this stage too, however, that Melville begins to show how limited is Vere's success in keeping the peace, a result further emphasized at stage G. Three times ominous murmurs emanate from the crew, accompanied on one occasion by a restless movement. The crew is still governed by rigid discipline, but ironically there is more real need for strictness now. Indeed, Vere's knowledge of and the men's adherence to usage, and references by both Vere and Melville to the crew's unquestioning obedience (pp. 87, 112, 127), show how ill-founded is one, at least, of Vere's reasons for executing Billy Budd. But the chief additions at stage G both clarify Vere's dilemma sympathetically and criticize his actions (insofar as the other officers are sceptical). Thus Melville increases the ambiguity and attempts to preclude a simplistic view of Vere as a melodramatic villain.

Revisions of the text by Melville substantiate the interpretation already outlined. Wrestling with language in an attempt to convey his horror of disorder, Melville found his needed tool in the word "mutiny."

Not only is it frequently used in original drafts, but "two outbreaks" become "the two mutinies," and "naval insurrection" is changed to "the Great Mutiny" (pp. 307–308). (In a pencil revision, Nelson, a queller of mutiny, is capitalized as "the Great Sailor" somewhat earlier in the text.) Melville's fondness for the word is not unrelated to his characterization of Captain Vere, who uses the Mutiny Act as justification when he advocates the execution of Billy Budd. In a superseded passage he affirms that "the blow itself, setting aside its consequence, was mutiny" and as such was "a capital crime" (p. 391). All this was true under Article xxii of the Articles of War; Billy Budd was indictable and punishable by death for striking a superior officer during time of war.[12] It is strange then that Vere should refer continually to the Mutiny Act, which was a military, not a naval statute, but his confusion can be understood in the light of his excessive fear of mutiny, and as a projection of Melville's own sentiments. Moreover, the change in the text which Melville makes on page 396 ("Mutiny Act" becomes "Articles of War") suggests Melville was hoping to convey the confusion and agitation Vere was experiencing.

Although Melville describes and comments on Vere's actions and their consequences in such a way that they cannot be evaluated superficially, he did augment the criticism levelled at Vere in late stages and revisions. These shifts of perspective are worth noting, but they should be related to the full and ambiguous context. What can at least be affirmed is that Melville's revisions do prevent the reader from seeing Vere as another Nelson.

The captain is originally described as "distinguished even in the time of naval heroes," but Vere is no hero, so "naval heroes" is reduced to "renowned seamen" (p. 309). Moreover, the comparison with Peter the Barbarian, implementing criticism of Vere's secrecy, originally read "Peter the Great, chiefly Great by his crimes" (p. 384). This was softened and the irony of Vere's "barbarism," seen in contrast to Billy Budd's innocent barbarism, is artistically more satisfying, though the previous harshness does show the direction Melville's thoughts were taking at that stage (Ga). It was at the same stage that Melville introduced the discussion of sanity and insanity, after the surgeon questions Vere's mental condition, and it is significant that Melville's final comments on Claggart (in the late pencil stage) concentrate on lunacy, at a time, of course, when Vere was very much in his mind. The references on pages 336–337 to secrecy, to the seeming rationality of insane actions and to the occasional nature of such actions (for they are "evoked by some special object") would not be out of place in the passage after the Vere-surgeon scene.

Significant revisions of the characterization of Nelson are few, but, as one would expect, they tend to increase his stature. The fleet becomes his fleet, and Trafalgar becomes great not merely in "naval annals" but also in "human annals" (p. 302). (Also the phrase "unique hero" was considered before "the Great Sailor" was restored — p. 305.) Of greater importance is Melville's pencilled notation at the bottom of Leaf 61 (p. 304): "XX the mark on the deck where he fell." In the next leaf, the mark becomes a star, but Melville's term of reference here is metaphorical since the mark is in fact a silver plate.[13] Melville, in using the word "star," would seem to be indicating ironically the connection between Nelson and "Starry Vere," who lacked any brilliant qualities.

Nelson, then, is the modern counterpart of the "pagan gentleman" in "The Age of the Antonines" (1877), a poem in which Melville's post-Civil War fear of social turbulence takes the form of a wistful glance at an era when "Orders and ranks they kept degree," and "the Emperor" was "The foremost of men the best."[14]

. . . Critics who chart the pattern of Melville's social thought usually detect an important shift [late in his career] and suggest that Melville finally achieved a serenity, a reconciliation to life in *Billy Budd, Sailor*.[15] This bland interpretation neglects the role of Nelson as the rare ideal commander, for his presence in the story would seem to suggest, not that Vere is also a hero — this would be too unequivocal for a writer of Melville's literary propensities — but that Vere is a victim of the historical situation and of his own suppressed emotions. Only by seeing Vere in this way can we fully appreciate the ironies of the tale. First, the process of Billy Budd's crime and of the judgment of that crime takes the same form, a sudden, unexpected outburst. Secondly, Vere's rationalization of the action that he recommends to the court is an attack on the emotionalism he himself experienced after the killing (the language describing Vere is quite unambiguous: "excited," "passionate," "vehemently" — pp. 100–101). Lastly, attention should be drawn to the picture of the naval band playing a sacred tune to suppress the men, a scene which suggests the incongruity of religion and war. But it also provides, not a further illustration of, but rather an ironic contrast to the emblem of Orpheus taming the beasts of the wood with his lyre.

A prey to ironies, Vere is one of Melville's "isolatoes," a pedant among practical men, a "civilian" among sailors. Richard Chase's appraisal of Captain Delano is equally applicable to the captain of the *Bellipotent*: "he has a fatal limitation of personality which separates him from other men and renders his dealings with them imperfect and his future dark."[16] Stylistically, too, he is an alien, for while Claggart, Billy Budd, and Nelson belong to the world of romance, Vere's all too human agonies do not belong in that convention. Small wonder that Melville, in his last years, should have shown compassion and understanding for a character who illustrates the complexity of human hopes and behavior in a tense and uncertain world.

Notes

1. *The Journals and Miscellaneous Notebooks of Ralph Waldo Emerson*, Vol. II, 1822–26, ed. William H. Gilman, Alfred R. Ferguson, Merrell R. Davis (Cambridge, Mass., 1961), p. 90.

2. References are to the definitive edition: Herman Melville, *Billy Budd, Sailor (An Inside Narrative)*, ed. Harrison Hayford and Merton M. Sealts, Jr. (Chicago, 1962) — hereafter cited as *Billy Budd, Sailor*. I am deeply indebted to Professor Sealts and Professor Lyon Richardson for reading this paper and offering suggestions.

3. See, e.g., Wendell Glick, "Expediency and Absolute Morality in *Billy Budd*," *PMLA*. LXVIII (March 1953), 103–110, and Phil Withim, "*Billy Budd*: Testament of Resistance," *MLQ*, XX (June 1959), 115–127.

4. *Billy Budd, Sailor*, p. 59.

5. Vere is so impressed by Billy Budd that he thinks of promoting him; conversely he is suspicious of Claggart's "patriotism."

6. *Billy Budd, Sailor*, p. 377, Leaf 229 c.

7. Thomas Carlyle, *Lectures on Heroes, Hero-Worship and the Heroic in History*, ed. P. C. Parr (Oxford, 1925), p. 1.

8. Herman Melville, *The Confidence-Man: His Masquerade* (New York, 1961), p. 278.

9. *Billy Budd, Sailor*, p. 111.

10. For a full description of the stages, see the definitive edition, *Billy Budd, Sailor*, pp. 236–239.

11. Ibid., p. 246.

12. See John McArthur, *Principles and Practice of Naval and Military Courts Martial*, 4th ed., 2 vols. (London, 1813), I, 333.

13. See Herman Melville, *Moby-Dick* (New York, 1950), p. 39.

14. "The Age of the Antonines," ll. 21, 25–28, in *Collected Poems*, ed. Howard P. Vincent (Chicago, 1947), pp. 235–236.

15. See, e.g., Henry Bamford Parkes, *The American Experience* (New York, 1959), p. 213, and A. N. Kaul, *The American Vision* (New Haven and London, 1963), p. 277.

16. *Herman Melville* (New York, 1949), p. 158.

The Definitive *Billy Budd:* "But Aren't It All Sham?"

Paul Brodtkorb, Jr.*

There is a sentence in the preface to the Harrison Hayford-Merton Sealts version of *Billy Budd*[1] that has been quoted before and will be quoted again. It is the one in which the editors hope that their "comprehensive scholarly edition will narrow the ground of disagreement and widen that of understanding." It is doomed to repetition because it allows any critic who cites it a ready-made rhetorical stance: with its sanction he can assume the posture of the reasonable reader and humbly offer himself

*From *PMLA* 82 (1967):602–12. © 1967 by *PMLA*. Reprinted by permission of the Modern Language Association of America.

as mediator between the various opposing critical armies. Then, having established himself as a man of good will and peacemaker, he can do his best to annihilate at least one of the armies, the views of which it somehow turns out he rabidly despises. . . .

Where does all this leave the unbiased reader? Unfortunately, with a series of critical opinions, some less interesting than others, all unprovable, finally. I would therefore seek to promote peace between the irrationally warring critical armies of the ironists and the plain speakers (thus narrowing the ground of disagreement and widening that of understanding) by saying that virtually anything goes, everything is demonstrable, and there can be no end to interpretive disagreement even within the framework of one set of categories and controlling assumptions. Such is the dismal ground that peace and understanding may have eventually to occupy; and what I have to offer here is dim enough illumination of that ground — a reading that by my own tenets can be only "one more reading of *Billy Budd*," a reading that differs from other published readings chiefly in its attempt to respect the story's incompletion: first, by concerning itself with the implications of one dramatic action present in the narrative at all stages of composition, and, second, by avoiding commitment on the more notoriously debatable points of interpretation, tone, and allusion. To do this latter may be to omit too much; yet, at least, if mine is an incomplete interpretation, it is so necessarily, because what it addresses is incomplete: it is an attempt to deal with the problematic interpretation of an "unfinished" book that the new Hayford-Sealts text throws into relief.

The central dramatic action I have in mind is present first of all in the narrator's relation to his material. Whether the narrator is to be understood as a simple fictive surrogate for the elderly Melville come to his conservative Christian senses at last, or an ironic persona intended to strike us as occasionally a pompous ass, the narrator is a kind of amateur historian. He is a man trying with all the resources at his command to give an accurate account of what really happened, an "inside narrative." He is aware that history as it appears in books is much less elusive than it seems as its events happen *to* us: "The era appears measurably clear to us who look back at it, and but read of it. But to the grandfathers of us graybeards, the more thoughtful of them, the genius of it presented an aspect like that of Camoëns' Spirit of the Cape, an eclipsing menace mysterious and prodigious" (p. 66). If our narrator here were Ishmael, he would further imply that historians achieve their clarity at the expense of simplifying what happened; that historians even sometimes deliberately lie. But this narrator does not say that about his own efforts. He plainly believes in the possibility of history. He thinks there are good and bad historians and he tries to be a good one. He wishes to be judicious in his appraisals, balanced in his analyses. When he speculates or guesses, he usually admits it by phrases like "more than probable" and "more likely" (pp. 77, 49). Taking as many alternative hypotheses as occur to him into at least passing account, he tries to help us understand his characters.

But he seems at least half aware that he must ultimately fail in this, given the sort of exceptional characters that he is trying to understand. Shrewdly, he comments that "something more, or rather something else than mere shrewdness is perhaps needful for the due understanding of such a character as Billy Budd's" (p. 90). About Claggart, he writes: "His portrait I essay, but shall never hit it" (p. 64), and part way through his admittedly inaccurate portrait of Claggart he feels the need of quoting "an honest scholar" on the necessity for *a priori* metaphysical systems to assist in the comprehension of difficult personalities: "You are aware that I am the adherent of no organized religion, much less of any philosophy built into a system [says the honest scholar]. Well, for all that, I think that to try and get into X——, enter his labyrinth and get out again, without a clue derived from some source other than what is known as 'knowledge of the world' — that were hardly possible, at least for me" (p. 74). And so the narrator resorts to Plato on natural depravity to buttress his intimations of Claggart, just as many critics resort to Freud on homosexuality to buttress theirs. But in doing this, the narrator is not aware that his text, which he amusingly refers to as *the* "authentic translation of Plato,"[2] was apparently tampered with by Christian redactors and so could not be authentic as text let alone as translation, while his splendidly circular definition of natural depravity ("Natural Depravity: a depravity according to nature") *explains* nothing about the shadowy and devious Claggart. Even Captain Vere, the most articulate and self-revealing of the lot, eludes full or certain comprehension in the end: "The spirit that 'spite its philosophic austerity may yet have indulged in the most secret of all passions, ambition, never attained to the fullness of fame" (p. 129).

In short, the narrator is engaged throughout in trying to understand his characters; in trying, that is, to get at the always problematic nature of the *other*. This act of understanding is, I think, close to the book's dramatic heart. At any rate, the narrator's attempt is paralleled by all the characters, and repeatedly so. The book's turning point, when Billy, Claggart, and Vere come together, is a fatal encounter of "mutually confronting visages" (p. 98) unable to understand one another, but as such it is merely the climactic one of a series of confrontations all involving Billy Budd, who is the common denominator of each such recognition scene wherein very little is recognized. Billy is the human mystery which virtually all the characters must solve in their own way; and Billy, in his turn, must solve the mysteries of others. But as far as the reader is concerned, each character ends up as merely *given*, never solved.

Billy, we are told, is innocent, simpleminded, a man taught little by experience, who has no "intuitive knowledge of the bad" (p. 86) to help his ignorance of the world. His "pristine and unadulterate" virtues seem out of keeping with "custom or convention . . . as if . . . exceptionally transmitted from a period prior to Cain's city and citified man" (p. 53). Part of what all this suggests is that Billy has somehow escaped *time*, and the educative experience that life in time normally brings. He is a "child-man," neither quite one nor the other.

Yet my first assertion, about his escape from time, is not *quite* true: Billy does have his famous stutter, evidence of his contamination by original sin, the legacy of "the envious marplot of Eden" (p. 53) and the beginning of Judaeo-Christian time. Perhaps what Billy has escaped may more accurately be called "history." He has no understanding of or involvement with the intense social issues of the day: impressment affects him not at all, a flogging merely horrifies him into the resolve that "never through remissness would he make himself liable to such a visitation" (p. 68). Further, he belongs to no contemporary social caste: he is both high-born (the "pretty silk-lined basket," p. 51) but, as a seaman, lower class. He has no real place in society, as he has none in history.

In several ways, he seems cut off from normal humanity. Other men have "kith and kin," while Billy does not know his parents (p. 50). Physically, he suggests the "heroic strong man, Hercules" (p. 51), but certain of his features are rather delicate, and these, along with his almost feminine "purity of natural complexion" (p. 50), suggest something that was apt to provoke "an ambiguous smile in one or two harder faces among the bluejackets" (p. 51); Billy, in other words, seems *both* masculine and feminine. He is not so much cut off from humanity as from normal categories of classifying it.

Finally, "of self-consciousness he seemed to have little or none" (p. 52). Thus he is unaware of himself as an existent in the world, and his actions characterize him as pre-reflective, spontaneous. Spontaneity is not predictable: it has no history, no antecedents; it can not, therefore, be understood as anything other than itself.

One analogue to Billy in Melville is, in a curious way, the white whale. It also eludes categories of time and space, is not to be apprehended, is merely *given*. At least one commentator, Vern Wagner,[3] has noticed this and drawn from it the Ahabian conclusion that Billy is "an object 'terrible in itself' " whose whiteness "veiled a blacker beyond," while Claggart, who looks at times like the "man of sorrows," is a kind of tragic hero. Though such conclusions are more than debatable, the fact that they were drawn at all does suggest something central about the story: most people in going along with the narrator tend to conceptualize Billy, who in his non-understandability invites this, as Natural Good; they allegorize Billy onto the static level of the moral abstract. Faced with a mystery, we pin a tag on it according to whether it attracts or repels us in the light of our nature, insight, and moral beliefs; to do this is a primary way of understanding, and it is done at various heights of sophistication, as, in fact, it is done by the characters of Melville's story.

Billy's first extended encounter with another being defines this pattern of understanding. It is reported to us by Captain Graveling (the shipmaster of the *Rights of Man*) in his conversation with the *Bellipotent*'s Lieutenant Ratcliffe. Billy, the Captain says, has been a peacemaker. All the men liked him, except the "buffer" (that is, fighter), a man then characterized only in terms appropriate *to* a fighter. The buffer taunted Billy, and finally provoked him into a fight in which Billy "gave the burly fool a terrible drubbing" (p. 47); as a result of the fight, the burly fool now loves Billy.

Why? The buffer *alone* had been disturbed by the new man's forbearance, his peacefulness; by, given the buffer's characterization, what can only be called Billy's radical difference *from* him. When the buffer is beaten by Billy on his own "moral" terms, those in which only might is right, he can suddenly understand this previously alien being: Billy is now enough like himself to pass muster, Billy's mystery has been cleared up, Billy's existence is no longer an elusive threat to his own existence. From the buffer's point of view, Billy is now a good man because he fits comfortably into the buffer's limited world of physical strength.

If Billy's act of violence has defined his nature for the buffer, who can then accept him in illusory understanding, the encounter is the simplest, most direct one in the book. In the "more knowing world of a great warship" (p. 50), Billy's encounters will become more complex, but the pattern of static mystery solved by action will hold true, even out to the most complex action of all, the narrator's act of writing the story to get at the characters.

Aboard the *Bellipotent*, Billy's spontaneity is absorbed into the "more knowing world," the more sophisticated world. The captain of this world has "a marked leaning toward everything intellectual" (p. 62). The man assigned the practical details of running this world on a day to day basis, Claggart, has a brow indicating "more than average intellect" (p. 64), and is, in fact, a schemer. The Dansker is a man of "eccentric, unsentimental old sapience" (p. 70). The surgeon and the purser, each undoubtedly limited in intellect, nevertheless discuss the abstruse question of "euthanasia" as an intellectual problem (pp. 124–125). In short, there seems to be some kind of polarity set up between Billy's spontaneity and self-conscious *mind*.

As soon as it is looked at, however, the polarity becomes a different relationship. Claggart's nature is "surcharged with" *energy* (p. 78), and his conscience is merely the lawyer to his irrational *will* (p. 80); whatever his motives in relation to Billy, they are based on a *passion* of some sort (p. 77), itself not quite reasonable, for which his intellect later finds justification. Vere, the apparently disinterested intellectual, nevertheless has "settled convictions" (p. 62) about order in the world which define him and which form the basis for his spontaneous judgment of Billy's crime. The Dansker's imagination is "primitive in its kind" (p. 70), instinctive in its understanding. The surgeon and the purser get nowhere in their discussion of euthanasia; each merely takes a line of argument that expresses his own nature. In short, intellection in the book is not polar to spontaneity, but based on it. Because this is so, intellection might even be called rationalization, if the pejorative overtones of the latter could be removed. Vere, for example, cannot be condemned merely because he intuitively prejudges Billy, if that is what everyone does.

In any case, intellection is beyond Billy because his kind of spontaneity does not extend into its dimensions, and in the more knowing world of the *Bellipotent* he faces Claggart at a disadvantage, for Claggart's reaction to him is the buffer's in a much more sophisticated form. How can one be "nothing more than innocent" (p. 78) and live in the same world as that of Claggart, wonders the master-at-arms; and yet, such an existence and such a world seem attractive to him. It is as if Billy puts all of Claggart's values in radical doubt.[4] Claggart resolves his discomfort by attributing to Billy one half of his own ambivalence, and chooses to believe that Billy has deliberately affronted him by spilling some soup at his feet. This evidence of antipathy allows Claggart's conscience to act as lawyer to his will, and he plots to get even with Billy. His solution, though more Machiavellian than the buffer's, has quite the same goal: to annihilate what disturbs him.

Claggart's plot then manifests itself in ways incomprehensible to Billy; and Vere faces the scheming Claggart with "strong suspicions clogged by strange dubieties" (p. 96). When to resolve his doubts Vere brings the two men together, Billy stands "like one impaled and gagged" (p. 98), totally unable to fathom either Claggart or the situation. Ordered to defend himself by Vere, Billy at last resolves his intellectual paralysis by action, translating his dilemma into physical gesture more primitive than speech; but as if it *were* in the medium of speech, the translation involved turns the mystery into simple moral terms (natural antipathy to evil) and resolves it by an action aimed at annihilating the absolute mystery of the other that here quite literally has put the self in jeopardy. Billy's spontaneous reaction is Claggart's intended one, with the bogus paraphernalia of deliberation removed; and both are types of the buffer's.

To the mystery of Billy's act, Vere reacts as spontaneously as Billy has done with his prejudgment that is founded on everything his own nature has up to that point become.[5] "Fated boy" (p. 99), he says to Billy in the very moment of Claggart's death; but what has fated Billy is *Vere's* existence in the mode of political conservatism: his position of authority as Captain, all his self-ratifying reading in "realistic" philosophers and historians. Vere's full decision follows as a virtually automatic expression of his very being. His reasoning afterward proceeds from his instinctive "decision" and exists to justify it legalistically; but the decision itself expresses deeper elements than reason. Which is why the surgeon, entering just after Billy's removal, is faced with Vere's "excited manner" which "he had never before observed in the *Bellipotent*'s captain" (p. 100). Vere's "passionate interjections" understandably baffle the surgeon, and he reacts by accommodating this new, mysterious, "passionate" Vere to his own professional experience by conjecturing about Vere's sanity.

Thus far, each major character has tried to give form and thereby meaning to the incomprehensible by translating it into something else, something morally conceptualizable, something that he can understand and act upon. The trial itself provides the next major instance of the action. The members of the court see before them a difficult, ethical dilemma. When Billy leaves the courtroom, Vere tries to shift the unwieldy ethical terms into simpler ones more easily dealt with. He does not succeed until he dissolves the issues into a spectre of the chaotic future, a "forethought" of "the practical consequences to discipline" if they let Billy go. This is the dilemma in such different moral terms that "their instinct as sea officers" (p. 113) needs no more; the court votes to hang Billy, and thereby votes with Vere to dispose of all the problems he represents, all the problems that might bring into question their world, and Vere's. Their verdict is the instinct of self-preservation in the guise of reason.

Told of the verdict, and baffled by it and its antecedents, the crew of the *Bellipotent* react with "a confused murmur" (p. 117) that might presage disorder, or might not. Before the confused emotions of the crew can resolve themselves into moral terms and negative action, positive action is commanded and the crew obeys.

Mystery is present next in Billy's execution, as he dies peacefully, by violent means. Although the surgeon cannot explain this paradox by the word "euthanasia," evidently Billy does will his death to the extent at least of not in any way resisting it. Therefore he is "gone, and in a measure mysteriously gone" (p. 131). His death is an enigma, just as his birth, and, indeed, his whole existence have been. The watching crew experiences at least part of the mystery in Billy's death by noting first "the prodigy of repose in the form suspended in air" and then the strange behavior of "certain larger seafowl" that haunt the area where Billy's body was dropped, "circling it low down with the moving shadow of their out-stretched wings and the croaked requiem of their cries" (p. 127). Experiencing this mystery in which nature now seems to share, the crew again murmurs inarticulately in a way that might presage disorder; but, once more, before the confusion can resolve into possible revolt, the murmur is "met by a strategic command" that directs the tension, and the crew automatically obeys.

Billy Budd ends with its two contrasting reports bearing witness to the events aboard the *Bellipotent*. One is from "a naval chronicle of the time" (p. 130), and is written in the sententiously patriotic and abstractly remote rhetoric of the military establishment. It is the "authorized" (p. 130) version of events. Naturally, it is completely wrong. The second witness is a poem, spoken as if by Billy; it is perhaps more nearly "right" in its intense human intimacy with Billy, but also finally "wrong" in the sort of personality it attributes to its speaker, allowing him puns like "O, 'tis me, not the sentence they'll suspend, / Ay, ay, all is up; and I must up, too" (p. 132), ironical puns that "deal in double meanings . . . quite foreign" to everything we know of Billy's previous speech and character, which were "by no means of a satirical turn" (p. 49). One report by diminishing him says Billy is a villain; the other by magnifying him implies he is a hero. Each does so in its own kind of language, a subject I should like now to consider, following out a train of thought suggested by a footnote in the Hayford and Sealts edition about the various particularized vocabularies in the narrative.[6]

When analyzing Claggart, the narrator had avoided a "lexicon" in any way reflecting "Holy Writ" (p. 75) in order to "turn to some authority not liable to the charge of being tinctured with the biblical element." The new lexicon purports to be Plato's, and it provides in its tautological (and biblically tinctured) definition of natural depravity a means to capture the essence of Claggart's murky character, but does so only to leave Claggart as mysterious as before. The ship's surgeon, faced with the unprecedented serenity of Billy's death, rejects the purser's explanatory phrase "will power" because it is "not yet included in the lexicon of science" (p. 125), although he cannot, with his "present knowledge," pretend to account for the manner of Billy's death at all (p. 125), because it eludes *his* scientific lexicon also. The digression on Lord Nelson contrasts the discourse of "martial utilitarians" with "each more heroic line in the great epics and dramas" (pp. 57, 58), and the contrasting vocabularies yield opposed estimates of Nelson's worth; just as, at the end, the self-serving rhetoric of patriotic bombast is set against the concrete drama of a ballad, and two opposed Billy Budds emerge.

In each case, language is proved inadequate to formulate experience, though each "lexicon" satisfies and expresses its user as it implies his values and world. Part of the point being reached for, I think, is that language is intimately related to the way we bring our worlds into existence. In a very direct manner, one's habitual vocabulary and syntax connect with who one is and what one's world is; for, just as each individual consciousness is constitutive of its own "reality," so it is that the common fund of intersubjective meanings—that is to say, language—constitutes a *public* world.[7] As one of the British analytic philosophers has put it, "Language . . . contributes to the foundation and participates in the constitution of a fact."[8] A way of stating this negatively might be to say that different languages may very well involve differing experiences of the world; and something like this seems to be implicit in *Billy Budd*, where the various vocabularies out of various lexicons debate with each other and seem to reflect various experiences of particular phenomena in the story.

These vocabularies perform very much in the way that opposing critical camps in the "actual" world construe the supposed facts of the story, each position stated in its own characteristic rhetoric and each position reflecting a genuinely different experience of the story's events, characters, and implications. Perhaps because *Billy Budd* with all its digressions quickly extends itself into important historical areas of political experience and value, the critical rhetorics tend to divide into liberal and conservative, supporting, respectively, the positions of the ironists and the plain speakers. But what such critical rhetorics disagree over is a story which is itself indecisive, though to some extent at least — in the narrator's qualifications, speculations, and hesitancies as well as in the narrative's contrasting "lexicons" — the story knows some of its own indecisions. If its central action concerns the repeated translation of mystery into something else, then that translation must after all involve language; and if language may be said to participate in the constitution of "world," then the particular lexicon used for the translation will be basic and crucial for the character and interpretation of the translated mystery.

In *Billy Budd*, it is Vere's language which is superficially the most sophisticated, flexible, and knowing; and it is the language that sets the moral issues before us. But as language it is also abstract and pedantic — Phil Withim, one of the best of the ironist critics of the story,[9] has cited many examples that sound suspiciously like patriotic and moral cant (to Withim, at least; the alternative to his reading from his liberal viewpoint would be that Melville himself had become canting in his old age). Whether or not Vere is given to high-sounding platitudes, he does speak above the heads of his associates, as passage after passage testifies. Indeed, as Withim also points out, part of Vere's difficulty in convincing the members of his court is that they do not quite understand what he says. Perhaps Starry Vere's kind of sophisticated language suggests that he may be understood as knowing more than his subordinates, but what he knows and the words in which he knows it indicates that his world and its values are by no means identical with theirs, and may be rather radically different from the worlds of some of the involuntary sharers of his (i.e., the impressed sailors in his command). At Billy's trial Vere can find words to express or give form to the jury's thoughts about Billy — he can, to that extent, enter its world — but he is relatively isolated from the full force of other and different world views since he reads chiefly books that tend to confirm his own ideas (p. 62) and tends to be unable to communicate with his men at the level of ideas (p. 63). It is also to be noted that despite his breadth of abstract vocabulary and flexibility of diction he uses his more complex language, like his habitual reading, to circumscribe meanings and issues. This may show his narrow-minded bigotry, as critics like Withim judge it ethically to be, but it may *not* show that, for Vere is at least aware of alternatives and consciously rejects them: his choice may be reductive but he knows that it is. His choice is in effect a choice of weapons, a way to live in the world that he sees before him and reconstitutes in his kind of formalized language. From the standpoint of *his* wisdom, Vere argues that such reduction is necessary, though tragic, because "with mankind . . . forms, measured forms, are everything" (p. 128).

What Vere means by this, as his use of the Orpheus story says, is little more than that the human beast can only be tamed by harmonious order imposed from without. But what Melville might mean by it is not necessarily the same. If Vere's formula is read with emphasis on the "everything," we get an irony: with mankind, *forms are all there are.* Societal forms, like that of a trial, do not have the ethical content normal language presupposes to be there—in this instance, justice—because beneath the quasi-ethical deliberation of the characters lies that uncaused spontaneity not wholly translatable into ethical terms. Human personality is a kind of potential chaos, which, even when it seems harmonious, always carries the incipient stutter that presages the eruption of the anarchic. This is, in fact, probably quite close to Vere's view of mankind, and Billy confirms him in it. The consequently reductive moral choice is for Vere a tragic one: he knows Billy to be a desirable ideal of human grace, beauty, strength, and innocence, and he knows that Billy is not really humanly judgeable, but that he must be judged because circumstances demand it; he knows Billy is "good," but that Billy did, after all, kill a man. Vere guides Billy's trial as he does as a kind of conscious acceptance of all the moral responsibility for his individual prejudgment of the specific issues, and for all the consciously reductive moral choices that preceded it. But the further moral problem is that neither Billy's goodness nor badness seems much more than an accident resulting from spontaneity interacting with circumstances. . . .

Vere's language is one more vocabulary that tries to deal with man. If all vocabularies are reductive by categorizing their elusive referents, Vere can at best be only relatively right. Vere is as direct in his use of a moral Occam's razor as he is in talking over the heads of his subordinates, and *perhaps* a warning is to be understood when his "directness" is characterized as "sometimes far-reaching like that of a migratory fowl that in its flight never heeds when it crosses a frontier" (p. 63). Yet men are not birds, and frontiers are man-made and concern men as they do not concern birds, and Captain Veres are the very men who make frontiers and should heed them. The surgeon wonders professionally whether Vere is sane or not, but the surgeon is a limited man and it is probable that in the public, professional sense he means insanity, Vere is quite sane; there is, however, an unprofessional sense of insanity that the surgeon could not mean but that the story might: Vere is sane if normality and common sense are sane—if the king's law is sane, a law which cuts through frontier boundaries and distinctions quite as directly as Vere does; because the more knowing world of the *Bellipotent,* captained by Vere, is finally a legalistic world based on linguistic simplifications clearly drawn. It is preeminently the world of "measured forms" that are there to protect against disorder: the chaos of war and revolution is the background against which the *Bellipotent* imposes its massive rule; and to prevent subversion of the ship's ability to protect efficiently against outward disorder, the inner life aboard the *Bellipotent* is itself a set of forms. . . .

Is Vere, then, "right" or "wrong"? Society's measured forms are all that exist; they are empty of ethical content because individual, human, measured forms (the judicious moral estimates we make of others, the discrete characters of others as we read them) have no content in *time* beyond spontaneous energy finding unpredictable expression. This condition need not demand that Vere should not have judged Billy: to be able to act at all in such circumstances requires judgment, and society requires that we act, therefore that we judge. But Vere may well be wrong in his *particular* judgment; this, however, we as critics can argue over eternally; for the story is not clear on the specific implications of alternative judgments, providing, as it does, merely the "boggy ground" of various might-have-beens (p. 57) to build conclusions on. Insulated as Vere's language and reading show his temperament to be, insulated as that temperament must therefore finally be from what is going on in the unread, unintelligent (but feeling, and possibly plotting) minds of the lower ranks, Vere has no way of knowing the outcome of various alternative judgments. Nor in fact do we. Because neither he nor we can predict the further acts of the muttering sailors, we cannot escape subjectivity: both he and we must choose in darkness, then rationalize our choice. And neither he nor we can coerce by force of personality the acceptance of our best choices, as Nelson, or Ahab, could: the old heroes are gone with the old ships. *Any* particular pragmatic choice must therefore be wrong in that better possibilities will soon rankle in the mind to sour it; and the only "right" choice, the ideal one of clemency for Billy, would, so far as Vere or we can know, become *fully* right solely by the accident of enough of the elements potentially there for once coming together in harmony, but to make this morally more adequate choice would be to leave everything in the lap of the absent, on inattentive, gods. Vere's choice "says" man can not escape responsibility for his acts even when he is not responsible; beyond that, it might very well be wrong.

I would say, then, that *Billy Budd* implies that virtue and vice are relative even when they seem, as at first they do in Billy and Claggart, nearly absolute. They are relative because they reveal themselves to us only in the fluid dimensions of time, not the static eternity suitable to such moral abstractions; they reveal themselves in the accidental circumstances of historical context, in the temporal events that bring virtue and vice into problematic collision. As Pierre once said to Isabel: "Look: a nothing is the substance, it casts one shadow one way, and another the other way; and these two shadows cast from one nothing—these, it seems to me, are

Virtue and Vice."[10] Or, as in the ballad Billy asks, "But aren't it all sham?" I would argue that the story escapes advocating either conservative or liberal moral choices, eludes liberal or conservative critical rhetoric, and retreats onto a twilit ground where few important human actions are rationally choosable.

If it does, then about Vere's particular choice, as about Vere's (and perhaps society's) ultimate sanity, "every one must determine for himself" in the very dubious light the narrative affords; and "who in the rainbow" *can* "draw the line where the violet tint ends and the orange tint begins?" (p. 102). The plain fact is that no one can, for what the story provides is mystery that is almost but not quite solvable. The moral forms we impose on it do not, in the end, fit well; which may help to explain why, despite all the story's Christian imagery and allusiveness, the archetype of the crucifixion applies only unsatisfactorily and up to a point; and to explain, also, why Billy, though of heroic physical mold and admired by many of his fellow seamen and evoking from the narrator comparison with so many legendary heroes, is finally "not presented as a conventional hero" (p. 53); and why art's "symmetry of form" is incompatible with the "ragged edges" of "truth uncompromisingly told" (p. 128). *Billy Budd* is architecturally unfinished because it explicitly tries to deal with "fact" (p. 128), but, as Vere, for one, knows, while artistic conventions will neatly organize the world of facts, they do so in human temporality only by simplifying and, therefore, by falsifying our full sense of that world. *Being*, here, no less than in *Moby-Dick*, is tinged with the white hue of nothingness. Because it is, interpretational warfare has followed. The story impresses us as an allegorical fable of some sort, and fables have often to do with moral events to which we can respond with some moral precision. To help us so respond, we have, as critics, given the story clearly measured forms, Aristotelian or Christian or Freudian or Jungian; we have, like the narrator, invoked authorities and clarified terms. Because, like the narrator, and even like his characters, we prefer definable moral issues, and justified action, and judicial murder, and war, to suspension of what we think we fundamentally believe about the world: in belief resides identity.

Therefore we stake ourselves on what we see in books, just as on what we see in life. This book, more than most, invites our either/or interpretational response: it presents us with basic enigmas, begins to structure them in alternative moral terms, then, in part because that is the way we habitually understand things, asks us to choose. . . .

Possibly, though, if there is any sort of a "final" attitude in the story it is to be found in a viewpoint that from time to time breaks through over the shoulder of its narrator, a viewpoint that, though always focussed on humanity in *this* world, is secretly located in the void of eternity far from the false perspectives and lexicons of history and historians and even poets. What the story watches is the wrangles of men, at once so momentous and so petty, made up as they are of death and spilled soup. But what the story silently records is Melville's last and dogged making up of his mind (as he once prematurely told Hawthorne that he had "pretty much" done[11]) to be annihilated. If this is the story's inmost "inside narrative," it explains why one's overall impression of *Billy Budd* is of something like patience, directed at passion. The serenity of Melville's "acceptance," it seems to me, is real enough as *serenity*; though it is not like the serenity of Nirvana or Christian resignation, but more like that of an infinite and in the end gentle despair accepted by a man about to leave the merely human world of time.

Notes

1. All references in the text of this paper, which is a revised version of an address given before the Melville Society in Chicago in Dec. 1965, are to Melville's *Billy Budd, Sailor (An Inside Narrative)*, ed. Harrison Hayford and Merton M. Sealts, Jr. (Chicago, 1962). Edited from Melville's manuscript, this edition differs in several substantive ways from preceding ones, as I must assume my readers know.

2. Translations of Plato later than the one Melville apparently used (see Hayford and Sealts, p. 162, n. to leaf 130) omit the definitions as apocryphal. Whether or not Melville knew this was a Christianized Plato (see Erich Auerbach's splendid essay "Figura" in *Scenes from the Drama of European Literature*, New York, 1959, for an account of why Christian redactors indulged in this sort of thing) is of course not verifiable. But evidently, at least, he found the definition comic, for he changed and shortened his original to emphasize and clarify only its absurd circularity. His reaction is further evidenced by the way he has his narrator refer to the text as "the authentic" translation of Plato: who would have the "authority" to dub a translation "authentic" except the anachronistically bilingual ghost of Plato himself? Possibly Melville's use of the phrase is an indication that the narrator is ironically presented, at least at certain points, for what sort of a man would speak honorifically of the authentic translation of anyone, except where pirated editions of living foreign authors might be involved? The narrator is either obtuse and humorless here or Melville is pulling our leg, though I can see no contextual evidence of the latter.

3. "Billy Budd as Moby Dick: An Alternate Reading," in *Studies in Honor of John Wilcox*, ed. A. Dayle Wallace and Woodburn O. Ross (Detroit, Mich., 1958), pp. 157–174.

4. I base my account here on Kierkegaard's famous definition of *Angst* as a "sympathetic antipathy." Anxiety underlies all the important human encounters in the text.

5. "Spontaneity" may seem to some readers too elastic a term to fit Billy's instinctual naïveté as well as Claggart's calculation and Vere's political assumptions sifted through reflection and reading. Ordinary denotative language is here perhaps not adequate; one wants a phenomenological description of Vere and Claggart that would, unfortunately, be both inappropriate and too long for the scope of this paper. But, to simplify: my argument above and below is that the personalities of Claggart and Vere express their values, which directly reflect (and are "caused" by) their psychological essences. As characters, they are primarily *given*, not explained. In Vere's case, the value-determining essence appears structured by experience and reading and reflective thought, and thus Vere is further from primal spontaneity than Billy is. But Vere's experience, reading, and thought have tended to ratify, not modify, what he was born as. His reasoning, like that of Claggart, is self-justifying and a priori even when it believes itself a posteriori; in Sartrean terms, such reasoning is always in bad faith. Therefore, Melville typically gives us Claggart's and Vere's apparently decisive acts as defensive reactions to primitive and unrepressible manifestations of psycholog-

ical essence called up by disturbing events that seem to Claggart or Vere to jeopardize some of either character's reasoned, structured, but actually quite arbitrary values and ideas about the world, values and ideas that always express their projectors before they reflect actuality. To call such defensive upsurges of primal being "spontaneous" may be to beg psychological questions, but in this area the story offers as alternatives only tautology or infinite regress.

6. P. 162, n. to leaves 129–130.

7. The formulation is taken from Richard Schmitt, "In Search of Phenomenology," *Review of Metaphysics*, xv (Mar. 1962), 450–479. Schmitt notes that this idea is part of the common ground between European phenomenology and the philosophy of the British analytic school. Many American critics will be familiar with versions of this idea from the poetry of Wallace Stevens, or the essays in linguistics of Benjamin Lee Whorf. George Orwell's "Politics and the English Language" makes polemical use of the basic notion. It is crucial to Hannah Arendt's *Eichmann in Jerusalem* (New York, 1963).

8. Anthony Flew, ed. *Language and Logic*, First Ser. (New York, 1951), p. 151; quoted in Schmitt, p. 471.

9. "*Billy Budd*: Testament of Resistance," MLQ, xx (June 1959), 115–127.

10. *Pierre* (New York, 1949), Bk. 19, xx, p. 322.

11. See Hawthorne's journal entry for Nov. 1856, quoted in Jay Leyda, *The Melville Log* (New York, 1951), II, 529.

The Tragedy of Justice in
Billy Budd
Charles A. Reich*

To read *Billy Budd* is to feel an intense and indelible sense of helplessness and agony. A youthful sailor, loved by his shipmates for his natural goodness, is put to death for the sake of seemingly formalistic, insensate law. In this final work of Melville's, law and society are portrayed in fundamental opposition to natural man.

The confrontation takes place in a stark and somber shipboard drama. Billy, the Handsome Sailor, is falsely and maliciously accused of mutiny by Claggart, the master-at-arms. Momentarily losing the power of speech while trying to answer, Billy strikes out at Claggart, and the blow kills. Captain Vere, who witnesses the act and must judge it, is caught in "a moral dilemma involving aught of the tragic." Knowing full well Billy's goodness, and that he did not intend to kill, Vere sees no choice but to apply the inflexible law of military ship in time of war. Billy is hanged.

The problem of *Billy Budd* has produced much argument. Some critics have considered it Melville's "testament of acceptance," a peaceful, resigned coming-into-port after a stormy lifetime. Some have thought that Billy, though dead, triumphs because his sacrifice restores goodness to the world. Others have found the novel a bitter and ironic criticism of society. Most recently and persuasively, it has been called a Sophoclean tragedy, a

*From *The Yale Review* 56 (Spring 1967):368–89. © 1967 Yale University. Reprinted by permission.

contemplation of life's warring values. All of these views have merit. But there is still more to be seen in *Billy Budd*.

Melville's last book seems clearly to be different from his earlier works. It is true that Billy and Claggart are archetypal Melville figures. But in *Billy Budd* neither of these characters is developed or explained; each remains static. Instead, the focus is upon a new kind of character — the civilized, intellectual Captain Vere. He is the only character whose feelings we are permitted to see, and his is the only consciousness which seems to grow during the action. In addition, the book's focus is upon a new situation: not the old clash of good and evil, but an encounter of these natural forces, on the one hand, with society and law on the other. Significantly, Vere, and the dilemma of this encounter, were the last elements to be added when Melville was writing, as if he had started out to repeat an old drama but ended up with something new and unexpected. *Billy Budd* is also different in that the central theme is presented through the medium of a problem in law. And "law" is used not merely in the general sense of order as opposed to chaos. Instead, we are given a carefully defined issue. This issue receives an extraordinarily full treatment which, together with its crucial position in the story, makes it the major focus of action and conflict.

In approaching *Billy Budd* almost all critics, whatever their ultimate conclusions, have started with the assumption that Billy is innocent, and that the issue is an encounter between innocence and formalistic society. But to say that Billy is innocent is a misleading start, for it invites a basic confusion and oversimplification. By what standard is he innocent? Is it by law deriving from nature, from God, or from man? And to what is the concept of innocence applied — to Billy's act or to Billy himself? Billy is innocent in that he lacks experience, like Adam before the Fall, but he is not necessarily innocent in that he is not guilty of a crime. The problem of justice in the book is a profoundly difficult one; its possibilities are far richer than is generally recognized. In turn, such recognition affects the reader's view of Vere and, ultimately, the understanding of the novel as a whole.

There are at least three basic issues in *Billy Budd*. First, how and by what standards should Billy, or Billy's act, be judged? Second, how does Vere, the man committed to society, perceive the problem and respond? And third, how adequate are the standards which society has adopted? The structure of the novel is such that these problems are presented in three overlapping, climactic scenes: the discussion of the law, Vere's actions and feelings, and the execution, at which society is present and takes its final action.

In 1884, close to the time when Melville wrote *Billy Budd*, there came before the courts of England in a great and famous case a true-life sea tragedy, one which also presented a dilemma for the law. Three English seamen, Dudley, Stephens, and Brooks, and Richard Parker, an

English boy of seventeen or eighteen, were cast away in an open boat 1600 miles from the Cape of Good Hope. For eighteen days they drifted, with no fresh water except occasional rain caught in their oilskin capes, and nothing to eat but two tins of turnips and a small turtle which they caught and which was entirely consumed by the twelfth day. On the eighteenth day, when they had been seven days without food and five without water, Dudley and Stephens spoke of their having families, and resolved, if no help arrived by the next day, to kill the boy, who was lying helpless and near death in the bottom of the boat. On the twentieth day, no ship appearing, Dudley and Stephens, offering a prayer for God's forgiveness, told the boy his time was come, and put a knife into his throat, and the three men fed upon his body and blood. On the fourth day after the act they were rescued, in the lowest state of prostration. The three survivors were carried to Falmouth, and Dudley and Stephens were committed for trial on a charge of murder.

The decision of the case was rendered, for the Queen's Bench, by the Chief Justice of England, Lord Coleridge. It had been found that at the time of the killing there was no reasonable prospect of help, that had the men not fed upon the boy they would probably all have died before the rescue, and that the boy would probably have died first. In these circumstances, it was argued, the killing was not murder. In an elaborate and scholarly opinion which drew on the views of philosophers and legal authorities from the time of Henry III forward, Lord Coleridge rejected this defense. He found that no writer except one considered necessity a justification for killing, except in the case of self-defense, which differs because there it is the victim, and not some external element, who actively threatens the killer's life. The defense of necessity must be rejected, said the Lord Chief Justice, because law cannot follow nature's principle of self-preservation. "Though law and morality are not the same, and many things may be immoral which are not necessarily illegal, yet the absolute divorce of law from morality would be of fatal consequence. . . ." Contrasting that morality with the law of nature, Lord Coleridge said:

> To preserve one's life is generally speaking a duty, but it may be the plainest and highest duty to sacrifice it. War is full of instances in which it is man's duty not to live, but to die. The duty, in case of a shipwreck, of a captain to his crew, of the crew to the passengers, of soldiers to women and children, as in the noble case of the *Birkenhead;* these duties impose on men the moral necessity, not of the preservation, but of the sacrifice of their lives for others, from which in no country, least of all, it is to be hoped, in England, will men never shrink, as, indeed, they have not shrunk. . . . It is not needful to point out the awful danger of admitting the principle which has been contended for. Who is to be the judge of this sort of necessity? By what measure is the comparative value of lives to be measured? Is it to be strength, or intellect, or what? . . . Such a principle once admitted might be made the legal cloak for

unbridled passion and atrocious crime. There is no safe path for judges to tread but to ascertain the law to the best of their ability and to declare it according to their judgment; and if in any case the law appears too severe on individuals, to leave it to the Sovereign to exercise that prerogative of mercy which the Constitution has intrusted to the hands fittest to dispense it.

It must not be supposed that in refusing to admit temptation to be an excuse for crime it is forgotten how terrible the temptation was; how awful the suffering; how hard in such trials to keep the judgment straight and the conduct pure. We are often compelled to set up standards we cannot reach ourselves, and to lay down rules which we could not ourselves satisfy. But a man has no right to declare temptation to be an excuse, though he might himself have yielded to it, nor allow compassion for the criminal to change or weaken in any manner the legal definition of the crime.

Dudley and Stephens were sentenced to death. But the history does not end there. After an appeal for mercy, the Queen commuted their sentence to six months' imprisonment.

There are striking similarities between the history of Dudley and Stephens and the tale of *Billy Budd*. Billy, falsely accused before the Captain by Claggart, and unable to defend himself verbally because at the critical moment he cannot utter a word, responds to pure nature, and to the dictates of necessity. He is overwhelmed by circumstance, placed in the greatest extremity of his life. He stands "like one impaled and gagged," "straining forward in an agony . . . to speak and defend himself"; his face assumes "an expression which was as a crucifixion to behold." Suddenly he strikes a blow at the master-at-arms, and the blow kills. "I had to say something, and I could only say it with a blow, God help me!" Billy testifies later.

Captain Vere renders his judgment in much the same words as Lord Coleridge. He says "In natural justice is nothing but the prisoner's overt act to be considered?" Budd purposed neither mutiny nor homicide, Vere acknowledges. "And before a court less arbitrary and more merciful than a martial one that plea would largely extenuate. At the Last Assizes it shall acquit." But under the law, Billy's blow was a capital offense; the Mutiny Act made no exceptions for palliating circumstances. The officers' responsibility is to adhere to it and administer it. The exceptional in the matter moves the heart and the conscience, but it cannot move the upright judge.

In the discussion of the law that takes place aboard the *Bellipotent* among the members of the drumhead court, the first argument for Billy's innocence is based upon what is natural in the circumstances. Billy's act took place under the most extreme provocation. And it is described as almost automatic or instinctual, the unbearable tension of Billy's violent thwarted efforts at utterance suddenly finding outlet in a blow. If Billy is innocent for these reasons, it must be because of what Captain Vere calls "natural justice." Such justice, so Vere implies, looks to circumstances like self-defense, extreme provocation, or dire necessity. Natural justice exonerates, presumably, when the crime was forced upon the killer; when he did not kill by his own free choice. Billy was overcome by forces beyond his control. From the moment he was taken off the merchant ship *Rights-of-Man* and impressed into the King's service, until on the last night he lay prone in irons between two cannons upon the deck, Billy was "as nipped in the vice of fate." At the crucial moment when he was beset by Claggart's evil, society was not able to protect him; his separation from civilization is symbolized by the sea: in Vere's words, "the ocean, which is inviolate Nature primeval . . . the element where we move and have our being as sailors." The mood of the drama is all inevitability; against the impersonal movement of events Billy is but "Baby Budd." No wonder Vere whispers "Fated boy, what have you done!"

Billy, moreover, is presented less as a rational being than as a child of Nature. Illiterate, unselfconscious, "one to whom not yet has been proffered the questionable apple of knowledge," Billy was "little more than a sort of upright barbarian," one standing "nearer to unadulterate Nature." "Like the animals . . . he was . . . practically a fatalist." And although Claggart has the surface appearance of reason, he is as natural as Billy underneath. Like Heathcliff in *Wuthering Heights*, he personifies a nonhuman force. Although he has some very human qualities, the force that moves him is "Natural Depravity: a depravity according to nature," "born with him and innate." Like a storm or tidal wave, he represents "an unreciprocated malice." Billy's "mere aspect" calls up in Claggart "an antipathy spontaneous and profound." Thus their clash is as unavoidable as that of natural forces like fire and water.

The opinion of Lord Coleridge speaks to Billy's case as well as that of Dudley and Stephens. Like Billy, they found themselves in an extremity of circumstances, overwhelmed by forces beyond their control. Like Billy, they were called upon to act in the isolated universe of the sea and a boat, far removed from the protective influence of civilization. Like Billy, they acted as natural men.

Indeed, if Billy is innocent, why not Claggart? Is it just to blame Claggart for evil that was not his choice but was innate and inborn? His nature, "for which the Creator alone is responsible," must "act out to the end the part allotted to it." His antipathy was no more within his control than Billy's fist was under Billy's control. Billy's very existence and nearness was an excruciating, unbearable provocation to Claggart, as D. H. Lawrence's young soldier is to his superior in *The Prussian Officer*. In Lawrence's story, a striking parallel to the Claggart-Billy aspect of *Billy Budd*, a cold and haughty officer is assigned a youthful orderly, "an unhampered young animal" whose presence was "like a warm flame upon the older man's tense, rigid body." Something about the boy so disturbs and enrages the officer that he goads and torments the orderly until the boy, seized by a flaming, nearly suffocating instinct, breaks the officer's neck with his bare hands, then dazedly awaits his own death. In yielding to a similar provocation Claggart only shows the same inability to control his nature that Billy and, for that matter, Dudley and Stephens (who could not control the primal drive of hunger) have shown.

Nature contains both Billy's goodness and Claggart's evil. But in times of stress and extremity, the law of nature offers no support to goodness, and no check to evil. It interposes no objection when Dudley and Stephens kill the weak boy. And it allows Billy to kill a weaker man who was not immediately threatening his life. Human law must set a higher standard. To do so, it must look beyond the immediate theatre of action. Harsh though this may be, we must be judged by a universe wider than the one in which our actions are played out. The actions of Dudley and Stephens must be judged from England, and not from within the narrow universe of a lifeboat in the open sea. The act of Billy must be judged from outside his desperate "struggle against suffocation," and from beyond "the inner life of one particular ship."

In addition, man's law must posit a free will, an ability to choose. Not because free will always exists — or ever exists — but because law must rest on the assumption that man can control his own conduct, so that he may strive to raise himself above his natural state. Even psychiatry and psychoanalysis, the sciences which most strongly support a deterministic view of human nature, insist that an area of choice exists, and that the patient can change his course. Even the psychotic makes some response to rules or law. Man must reject the concept of determinism if he is to live in and adapt to the society of others, whether that society is our complex twentieth-century world or the primitive groupings of four beings in an open boat. Not only Vere and Coleridge, but all men, wear the buttons of the King.

Natural justice, as the drumhead court sees it, has a second aspect: the guilt or innocence of the mind. Billy did not intend to kill. He testifies, "there was no malice between us . . . I am sorry that he is dead. I did not mean to kill him." Moreover, Billy's whole character shows an innocent mind. The sailors all loved him. His virtues were "pristine and unadulterate." He was the Handsome Sailor, blessed with strength and beauty, of a lineage "favored by Love and the Graces," with a moral nature not "out of keeping with the physical make," "happily endowed with the gaiety of high health, youth, and a free heart." Vere calls him "a fellow creature innocent before God." The chaplain recognizes "the young sailor's essential innocence." Even Claggart feels that Billy's nature "had in its simplicity never willed malice."

Of course Billy cannot escape all responsibility for the consequences of his blow. He intended to hit Claggart, although possibly not full on the forehead. Intending the blow, Billy took upon himself the responsibility for the possible consequences. But should not his responsibility be limited because this was an unintended killing? At first thought, we agree. The law does not punish children; it does not punish the insane. An accidental killing is not murder. The law recognizes the difference between premeditated killing and killing in hot blood, or by provocation, or in fear. Should not Billy's innocent mind be considered in extenuation? But although modern law is more flexible than the Mutiny Act, its basic approach is similar; primarily it judges the action and not the man or his state of mind. The law stands at a distance from the crime and the criminal, and judges "objectively." And while such an approach may not satisfy the demands of divine justice, it is the only possible basis for human law. Justice Holmes, in *The Common Law*, says:

> When we are dealing with that part of the law which aims more directly than any other at establishing standards of conduct, we should expect there more than elsewhere to find that the tests of liability are external, and independent of the degree of evil in the particular person's motives or intentions. The conclusion follows directly from the nature of the standards to which conformity is required. These are not only external, as was shown above, but they are of general application. They do not merely require that every man should get as near as he can to the best conduct possible for him. They require him at his own peril to come up to a certain height. They take no account of incapacities, unless the weakness is so marked as to fall into well-known exceptions, such as infancy or madness. They assume that every man is as able as every other to behave as they command. If they fall on any one class harder than on another, it is on the weakest. For it is precisely to those who are most likely to err by temperament, ignorance or folly, that the threats of the law are the most dangerous.

The problem of subjectivity is shown by the case of Dudley and Stephens. They were, for aught that appears, the most upright and God-fearing of men, perhaps even the real-life equivalents of Billy. Possibly their motives were wholly altruistic. Maybe they would actually have preferred death to eating the flesh of the boy, but felt responsibility to wives and children. The necessity for their killing was far greater than the need which directed Billy's arm. Perhaps they, too, were men incapable of malice.

The divine law of the Last Assizes, a law that judges the totality of man, is beyond human ability to administer; more, it is beyond human ability to *imagine*. Such justice must ever remain unknowable to humans. When Claggart, the lying Ananias, is killed, Vere exclaims, "Struck dead by an angel of God! Yet the angel must hang!" But this is no paradox. Men cannot enforce divine judgments.

Human law must accept the fact that the mind is largely unknowable; that motives can seldom be ascertained. How are we to judge a man who kills because he *thought* the other was threatening his life, or because he *thought* the other had killed his child, or because he *thought* God had commanded him to do the act? In such cases, the law ordinarily resorts to some objective test of the supposed state of mind. In a case of self-defense, we do not simply ask the killer what he thought at the time. We seek to determine on an objective basis whether the victim was actually approaching with a weapon in circumstances where the killer had no reasonable opportunity to escape. Provocation must likewise be determined not only by reference to the state of mind of the person provoked (he may be hypersensitive, or even paranoid) but by an objective look at the nature of the provocation. To some extent all law, and even more so the military law, "looks but to the frontage, the appearance." In sum, human law looks primarily to men's actions, the one objective reality that is presented. Human law says that men are *defined* by their acts; they are the sum total of their actions, and no more.

In this light, the initial conflict in *Billy Budd* can be reassessed. Billy is not innocent in the sense in which that term is used in resolving issues of justice. Billy is innocent in what he is, not what he does. The opposite of his Miltonic type of innocence is not guilt, but experience. The conflict is not a "catastrophe of innocence"; it is a conflict between society and Nature that contains — even in Billy's case — both good and evil. It is a "catastrophe of Nature." His inability to adapt to society is the inability of nature to be civilized. Billy is incapable of acquiring experience. And the failing that leads to his execution is his incapacity to use the civilized man's weapon of speech. In society, natural forces cannot fight out their battles; Billy cannot use his physical strength to strike back at Claggart. The novel, then, is not an analysis of Billy or of Claggart. Instead, it asks the question *how did it fare* with Billy in the year of the Great Mutiny? With this question framed, our interest turns to the responses that are made to this encounter.

The chief agent of the law is Captain Vere. It is his decision that dooms Billy, and many critics have blamed him: they have suggested that Vere is everything from a conscientious but rigid military disciplinarian to an unprincipled autocrat — that the summoning of a drumhead court was unnecessary or illegal; that Vere acted impulsively; that Vere's approach to the law, and to the possibility of mitigation, was either expedient or rigid and unimaginative; that Vere may even have been temporarily affected in his mind (as the surgeon suggests). But not only is this blame misplaced, it obscures the drama that takes place in Vere's consciousness — a drama that is crucial to the novel's development.

At the outset, it is vital to note that Melville allows Vere no choice within the terms of the law itself; if the law is obeyed, Billy must hang. It is quite true that criminal law can be far more flexible than the Mutiny Act. Under modern law Billy would not receive a death penalty; he would probably get a relatively short prison sentence. But that is not the kind of law that Melville gives us. We are told that under the Mutiny Act a mere blow to a superior, regardless of its effect, is a capital offense, and the law provides no exceptions for palliating circumstances. "Budd's intent or non-intent is nothing to the purpose." Could Vere have mitigated the penalty? While the question is not wholly free from doubt, the answer seems to be no. Vere begins his answer to this question, addressed to him by the lieutenant, by saying "were that clearly lawful for us under the circumstances," the implication clearly being that it is not. The efforts at compromise must therefore be rejected. The court must "condemn or let go."

Vere did have the option of holding the case for the admiral, instead of summoning his own drumhead court. Vere, we are told, "fain would" have submitted the case to the admiral. But as a true military officer he kept to his vows of allegiance to martial duty; and here the urgency of preventing any slumbering embers of the Nore Mutiny from igniting among the crew overruled for him every other consideration. By hindsight, we can surmise that the danger did not exist. But are we entitled to judge the actions of a military commander in wartime by hindsight? The narrator's answer is unequivocal. He argues that forty years after the event we cannot reason how a battle should have been fought, nor second-guess other emergencies when it was imperative promptly to act. "Little ween the snug cardplayers in the cabin of the responsibilities of the sleepless man on the bridge." We may perhaps criticize the law, but not the officer whose "vowed responsibility" is to "adhere to it and administer it."

Moreover, the Mutiny Act, however unreasonable it may seem today, was accepted as the norm by those aboard the *Bellipotent*. Vere says:

> The people [meaning the ship's company] have native sense; most of them are familiar with our naval usage and tradition, and how would they take it? Even could you explain to them — which our official position forbids — they, long molded by arbitrary discipline, have not that kind of intelligent responsiveness that might qualify them to comprehend and discriminate. No, to the people the foretopman's deed, however it be worded in the announcement, will be plain homicide committed in a flagrant act of mutiny.

Clearly, then, *Billy Budd* is designed to give us a case where compromise is impossible, and where Vere, and we, are forced to confront the imperatives of law. As Melville presents the case, there is no escape for Vere. It is in this light that we must appreciate Vere's reactions.

Vere, as he is described to us, is no deranged zealot or unfeeling automaton, but a very superior and very human man. Although a man of settled convictions, his objection to novel ideas was not due to moral blindness — rather "because they seemed to him insusceptible of embodiment in lasting institutions, but at war with the peace of the world and the true welfare of mankind." More than this, Vere was a man of unusual sensitivity, one who, unlike many judges, could imaginatively perceive the truth about Billy's nature and state of mind. When Billy and Claggart confront each other, and Billy cannot answer or defend himself, Vere immediately divines Billy's liability to vocal impediment. Later, when Billy is asked by the court to explain why Claggart so maliciously lied, Vere understands that Billy lacks the sophistication to explain. And when Billy declares, "I have eaten the King's bread and I am true to the King," Vere exclaims "I believe you, my man." Far from being a military ramrod, "something exceptional in the moral quality of Captain Vere made him, in earnest encounter with a fellow man, a veritable touchstone of that man's essential nature." The reader may, in fact, surmise that Vere realizes as well as we do how hard is the role he is fated to play.

Moreover, Vere is from the first deeply affected by Billy. The narrator states of Vere: "Though in general not very demonstrative to his officers, he had congratulated Lieutenant Ratcliffe upon his good fortune in lighting upon such a fine specimen of the genus homo, who in the nude might have posed for a statue of young Adam before the Fall." Is the description of Billy in this sentence an intrusion of the author, or is it what it seems to be — a statement of Vere's own feelings? We are reminded of the feelings of Billy's other captain, the master of the *Rights-of-Man*, when Billy was taken away from him: " 'Ay, Lieutenant, you are going to take away the jewel of 'em; you are going to take away my peacemaker!' And with that the good soul had really some ado in checking a rising sob." But in Vere there is something deeper. Billy is some ways a son to the childless Captain. Several times, in his dealings with Billy, Vere is described as fatherly, and this aspect of Vere is recognized by the orphan Billy, "doubtless touching Billy's heart to the quick."

How does Vere react to the encounter between Billy and the law? As we first meet Vere, he is a man of "settled convictions," who doubtless accepts law quite unthinkingly; he is also a man whose humanity is closely confined: "the most undemonstrative of men." But from the moment that Billy strikes his fateful blow, we see Vere changing. When Vere first realizes what the consequences of Billy's act must be, Vere becomes so excited and convulsed that the self-poised surgeon, who has never before seen the Captain like this, is himself "profoundly discomposed." The surgeon almost supposes Vere to have lost his reason. Later, when Billy testifies that he has been true to the King, Vere exclaims that he believes Billy, Vere's "voice indicating a suppressed emotion not otherwise betrayed." Soon after, Vere interrupts the testimony in such a way as "to augment a mental disturbance previously evident enough." And at one point in his argument to the court, Vere implies his own inner state when he says, "To steady us a bit, let us recur to the facts." After the decision, Vere himself communicates the judgment to Billy. The narrator surmises that Vere, in his last interview with Billy, may have developed a passion latent under his stoical exterior, and finally caught Billy to his heart, "letting himself melt back into what remains primeval in our formalized humanity." When Vere emerges, his face is "expressive of the agony of the strong," and the narrator suggests that "the condemned one suffered less than he who mainly had effected the condemnation." When, at the penultimate moment, Billy cries out, "God bless Captain Vere," "Vere, either through stoic self-control or a sort of momentary paralysis induced by emotional shock, stood erectly rigid as a musket in the ship-armorer's rack." Vere has been condemned for being a ramrod, but quite plainly he stands like a musket in order to control the feelings within him. Vere's death comes not long after Billy's. And just as Billy dies with Vere's name on his lips, so Vere's last recorded words are "Billy Budd, Billy Budd."

We see two things at work here. First is the growth of Vere's consciousness and humanity, all the more notable for the fact that Vere is the only character in the book who visibly changes. It is not the pedantic Vere of the opening who finally embraces Billy. Second, Vere comes to recognize that there are values beyond those which the law embodies. It is not that Vere ever gets so far as to question the law itself; clearly he does not. But he does learn — and this is the vital point — that if the law is to be followed, other values must be sacrificed; in this case, the life of "a fellow creature innocent before God." It is for this reason that he calls the law pitiless, and that he finally realizes that to obey the law he must reject not only the urgings of his heart, "but also the conscience, the private conscience." Private conscience, he says, "must yield to the imperial one."

Thus Captain Vere is shown not as the protagonist of the law, but as a man faced with an awful choice. Because he is a man in and of society, because he occupies a position of duty and responsibility, he chooses the law, however inadequate it may be. Echoing the words of Lord Coleridge, he says: "But the exceptional in the matter moves the hearts within you. Even so too mine is moved. But let not warm hearts betray heads that should be cool. Ashore in a criminal case, will an upright judge allow himself off the bench to be waylaid by some tender kinswoman of the accused seeking to touch him with her tearful plea? Well, the heart here, sometimes the feminine in man, is as that piteous woman, and hard though it be, she must here be ruled out."

Although this complex and subtle portrait of Vere is essential to *Billy Budd*, it is not in itself the central concern of the novel. It is, rather, a means to bring us to the central problem. Melville has shown us a law whose logic is impeccable, and yet made us feel that the law has terrible shortcomings. What is wrong with the law? What is wrong with society, the law's progenitor? It is these questions that the novel ultimately asks.

However deep Vere's feelings may be, his vision is sharply circumscribed, for he is not privileged to observe events at a distance but must act. And after we have glimpsed his humanity, we are reminded that his understanding is limited; his last comments are that "forms, measured forms, are everything," and this is the only lesson he draws from "the story of Orpheus with his lyre spellbinding the wild denizens of the wood." We, however, are allowed to witness events through the eyes of observers, and as observers ourselves, and thus we are invited to look beyond Vere's range of vision.

After the judging of Billy and the dilemma of the judge comes the climax—the execution. It is a truly extraordinary scene, a formal, solemn act of society which every onlooker regrets. It is as if society has become a will separate from the will of all of its members. Vere himself stands in a state of shock. The members of the court other than Vere are deeply troubled. The surgeon is full of misgiving. The chaplain is certain that Billy belongs in heaven. As for the crew, they receive the announcement of Billy's crime and forthcoming punishment "in a dumbness like that of a seated congregation of believers in hell listening to the clergyman's announcement of his Calvinistic text." At the execution, after a moment of silence, an inarticulate murmur passes through the men like a fresh torrent advancing through precipitous woods, a wordless sound of pouring mountain showers.

Nor does the narrator accept the execution without implicit protest. Although he describes himself as an old man and affects a mood of meditative distance from the events he relates, he frequently makes comments that suggest his feelings are not so serene as his manner. To cite one of many examples, he says that the chaplain is lending "the sanction of the religion of the meek to that which practically is the abrogation of everything but brute force." Even stronger feelings are implied by the narrator's many descriptions of Billy. Far from being a purely symbolic character, Billy is made very alive and very human. The narrator needs only a few swift brush strokes to bring Billy to life: Billy's cheerful salute to his old ship ("And goodbye to you too, old *Rights-of-Man*"), his affectionate and humorous respect for the salty old Dansker, his impulsive thanks to Captain Vere. Despite a pose as philosophical observer, the narrator betrays a passionate intensity of feeling when he speaks of the Handsome Sailor. In contrast to the Dansker, who regards Billy with "a certain grim internal merriment," the narrator is obviously deeply moved by the rare goodness of the young sailor.

Moreover, the execution scene presents its own elements that question the law, for in the end the scene is one of transcendence. The sky is "shot through with a soft glory as of the fleece of the lamb of God seen in mystical vision"; Billy ascends; his body does not struggle but by some prodigy reposes while suspended in the air; his form takes the full rose of the dawn. The sailors make a legend of Billy, and it is their ballad about him, "Billy in the Darbies," which ends the book.

How are we to understand this scene? It does not challenge the law that forbids one man to kill another; as to this commandment a mood of acceptance seems to prevail. What the scene does challenge is how society enforces this rule. Because Billy has unintentionally killed, must he be utterly destroyed? The focus of our anguish in *Billy Budd* is not Billy's innocence but the rejection of human values symbolized by his punishment.

Seeing Billy hanged, we are compelled to question whether Billy's punishment accomplishes any purpose at all. Certainly nothing is accomplished with respect to Billy; fear of punishment did not deter him, and even if the sentence were not capital, it is difficult to see what he could be expected to learn. Nor is the punishment useful in curbing mutinous tendencies among the crew; as we are shown, Billy's execution is far more likely to cause mutiny than to quell it.

The problem of punishment brings us back to the case of Dudley and Stephens. It is a commonplace assumption that punishment is necessary to make people obey. But Dudley and Stephens knew very well that murder was punishable by death under the law of England, and perhaps they believed in divine punishment as well, for they asked God's forgiveness. Nevertheless, they killed. No punishment, no matter how severe, can possibly deter men from eating one another if this offers their only chance of survival. Nor is punishment likely to reform or rehabilitate in such circumstances; until starvation forced them to crime there is nothing we know of in Dudley and Stephens that required reform or rehabilitation, and their experience is not one which they would have been likely to want to repeat. At first glance the case of Dudley and Stephens seems to present a unique situation. But the more that we know about the causes of criminal behavior, the more the predicament of Dudley and Stephens seems to be the predicament of most criminals. Crime stems from family background and upbringing, environment (especially slum environment), character disorder, mental illness, overwhelming circumstances, and the like. The individual who commits a crime is responding to the forces of a separate universe. For one person that universe may be an unbearable family situation leading to violence, for another, a subculture in which criminal behavior is the norm rather than the exception, as shown in Claude Brown's *Manchild in the Promised Land,* and in Oscar Lewis's *The Children of Sanchez.* More often than not, the universe from which the crime derives is isolated from the influence of society as a whole, precisely as in the Dudley and Stephens case. That case, rather than being unique, is virtually a paradigm of the criminal situation. It is exceptional, however, because in its unique circumstances we can clearly see the forces that made criminals out of ordinary men, while in the usual case we cannot or will not see them. And it was doubtless because of this special clarity that even the government of Queen Victoria was able for once to see the uselessness of execution and to commute the sentences.

The law forbids acts, while punishment destroys the whole man. But, as Melville shows, in human beings, as in nature, we cannot expect perfection. Early in his story, the narrator tells us that "Billy was a striking instance that the arch interferer, the envious marplot of Eden, still has more or less to do with every human consignment to this planet of Earth. In every case, one way or another he is sure to slip in his little card, as much as to remind us—I too have a hand here." But society has not learned how to deal with man as a flawed creature. Like the Benthamites, it is narrowly "scientific" or rational, and thus makes a profound error. Society, in its morality and in its laws, insists upon a black and white dichotomy. Men are either good or evil; the law must "condemn or let go."

It is this limited and inadequate view of human nature which is exposed by the most brilliant turn of the story: the ironic reversal of roles between Billy and Claggart. By presenting a man whose character is almost perfectly good, and another who is almost pure evil, the story forces upon our sensibilities the inadequacy of society's formal understanding of man.

> In the jugglery of circumstances preceding and attending the event on board the *Bellipotent* and in the light of that martial code whereby it was formally to be judged, innocence and guilt personified in Claggart and Budd in effect changed places. . . . Yet more. The essential right and wrong involved in the matter, the clearer that might be, so much the worse for the responsibility of a loyal sea commander, inasmuch as he was not authorized to determine the matter on that primitive basis.

In Billy's case, the law is unable to distinguish the human being from his act. The act is a guilty one, but does that mean that an individual whose life as been the purest goodness must be cast out forever? Billy is treated by the law as if he were no longer human, as if it is necessary for all others to distance themselves from him. But the onlookers retain their knowledge of Billy's humanity, and for them — and for us — the spectacle of his destruction is all but impossible to bear. Billy's execution is thus an image of society's failure to make its actions fit its understanding. Society's spiritual knowledge of man is far in advance of its laws. Time after time in the novel compassion and understanding struggle to break through the forms. The onlookers know what Billy is—even the sailors feel that he is morally incapable of malice. But the onlookers do not know how else to deal with his transgression. Hence they permit and participate in an action that destroys a fellow man and dehumanizes them all. This disparity of knowledge and action is perfectly embodied in the chaplain: he accepts all of society's forms, but when taking leave of the condemned fellow, "he kissed on the fair cheek his fellow man."

Indeed, from the moment of Billy's impulsive blow we feel caught in a process of insane logic that, once under way, proceeds to its final conclusion despite the better judgment of all concerned. The logic is faultless within its own terms, but the terms fall short. The law's insanity is like that earlier attributed to Claggart: although apparently subject to reason, it is deeply irrational. "Toward the accomplishment of an aim which in wantonness of malignity would seem to partake of the insane, he will direct a cool judgment sagacious and sound." Such madness "is to the average mind not distinguishable from sanity, and for the reason above suggested: that, whatever its aims may be—and the aim is never declared—the method and outward proceeding are always perfectly rational." The law, designed to be the protector of man's highest aspirations against the savagery of nature, has become instead the irrational destroyer of man.

Billy Budd is directly concerned with the law, but its broader concern is with society as a whole. Melville's novel shows how little the formal actions of society are adapted to the compound of good and evil which we know to be the essence of man's humanity. Civilization, in fact, is equated with blindness. "Nay, in an average man of the world, his constant rubbing with it blunts that finer spiritual insight indispensable to the understanding of the essential in certain exceptional characters, whether evil ones or good." Law, we are told, hardly sheds "so much light into obscure spiritual places as the Hebrew prophets." This blindness is illustrated by society's picture of Billy as shown by the newspaper account: a depraved criminal. The newspaper article grotesquely mimics the way in which the law views Billy and deals with him, and in the book it perfectly represents society's inability to comprehend or to accept natural man.

Throughout the novel Melville sets off the Natural against the formal artificiality of intellect and civilization. There is, for example, the symbolic but vital matter of speech versus gesture. All of the characters are at their most human when they gesture rather than speak: Vere when he embraces Billy, the sailors when they murmur wordlessly at the execution, the chaplain accompanying Billy, "the genuine gospel . . . less on his tongue than in his aspect and manner toward him." Billy, illiterate and subject to an infirmity of speech, is wholly natural.

The theme of the richness of humanity versus narrow utilitarianism is also the point of the much debated passage on Lord Nelson early in the book. The passage contrasts steel with firearms, knightly valor with ungallant modern warfare, and the oldtime ships, grand, picturesque, and poetic, with the unsightly ironclads. As for Nelson himself, that gloriously un-utilitarian sailor, he is a heroic counterpart of Billy. Like Billy, Nelson dies because of the natural qualities in him, his reckless valor and display, qualities disparaged by the narrow-minded "martial utilitarians," those "Benthamites of war." As Melville said in his poem, "A Utilitarian View of the Monitor's Fight":

> No passion; all went on by crank,
>   Pivot and screw,
>   And calculations of caloric. . . .
> War yet shall be, but warriors
> Are now but operatives. . . .

This theme is sounded with a soaring affirmation of the grandeur of natural man in contrast to the utilitarian rationality of society. Billy, the natural man, is not only good, he is regal. The Handsome Sailor receives the homage and love of his shipmates; he is young Alexander, "A superb figure, tossed up . . . against the thunderous sky." Here Melville seems to return at the end of his life to the romance of his youth, to *Typee* and *Omoo* and the full life of nature. In contrast, society is a poor and artificial thing.

> The character marked by such qualities has to an unvitiated taste an untampered-with flavor like that of berries, while the man thoroughly civilized even in a fair specimen of the breed has to the same moral palate a questionable smack as of a compounded wine.

> The sailor is frankness, the landsman is finesse. Life is not a game with the sailor, demanding the long head — no intricate game of chess where few moves are made in straightforwardness and ends are attained by indirection, an oblique, tedious, barren game hardly worth that poor candle burnt out in playing it.

Billy indeed is, ironically, the true civilizer. For while the war in which the *Bellipotent* fights is the product of what passes for civilization, Billy is the maker of peace. "Billy came and it was like a Catholic priest striking peace in an Irish shindy . . . a virtue went out of him, sugaring the sour ones . . . they all love him . . . and it's the happy family here."

"Billy in the Darbies," a picture of Billy dreaming and awaiting death in the iron fetters of the law, is not only the ending of the novel, it was also its beginning, for Melville first wrote the poem, and then the novel. In essence, the poem is a question: Why is Billy to be hanged from the yardarm-end; why is he to be dropped "Fathoms down, fathoms down"? And just as the poem is a question, so the entire book is a question. In telling Billy's story Melville is asking about the fate of the natural in man. There are some who have found in Melville's book a mood of peace, and they are right, for Melville seemingly had made peace with the old warring elements of good and evil in nature that obsessed him in *Moby Dick*. It is as if Melville has finally accepted the antinomies of good and evil as being essential parts of fully realized life. But the overall mood of *Billy Budd* is not peaceful, for Melville at the end of his life is wondering whether youth, feeling, and love can survive into the drabness of a civilization dominated by material and organizational values. It is like the question he asked obliquely in "Bartleby the Scrivener," where civilization isolates the man of perverse but genuine independence. It is the same question he asked in the Civil War poem, "On the Slain Collegians," where civilization's single-minded cold logic sends its ardent boys to death: "Like plants that flower ere comes the leaf — / Which storms lay low in kindly doom, / And kill them in their flush of bloom."

Billy Budd is an intensely modern novel. It is concerned with the coming of a materialist, commercial civilization, rational and scientific, in which society grows ever more distant from the rich overflowing of human experience. Billy harks back to a more adventurous and youthful America which, with the frontier and the whaleship, was already passing in Melville's lifetime. Billy's type comes from "the time before steamships," the significant words with which the novel opens.

Melville's last book is a pessimistic view of America's destiny. But the novel does not have a conclusion. As Melville himself says, it lacks an "architectural finial." It looks ahead. Just as Billy, in death, transcends the limitations of the ship's world, so the novel, through the medium of art, transcends the world of Melville's day. For us in this day, the novel is a reminder of the indispensable importance of the artistic vision in the structuring of society — an expression of the need for society to accept the natural in man. Law, as a *creation* of man, needs the imagination and the insight of art so that it is not drawn in such a way as to imprison the human spirit. Law and society need the help of the artist, to the end that we do not forget man's natural humanity, which is embodied, timelessly and unforgettably, in "the fresh young image of the Handsome Sailor."

The Politics of Melville's Poetry   Milton R. Stern*

Billy Budd arose from the poetry that Melville was working on during his last, retrospective years. The short novel began as one of many poems whose burden was the recollection of friends and times past. Among the many attitudes that can be isolated in the poems, of which "Billy in the Darbies" was one, two major recurrences are a sorrow — indeed, a resentment — occasioned by change, and a nostalgic joy in the celebration of the common sailor as a carefree child who gallantly does his duty. The first attitude is central in the psychology of conservatism — an insistence upon the past for the establishment of values by which the present may be guided. It is an insistence upon history, law, and precedent. But the second attitude, nostalgic joy in recalling the carefree sailor, also enters into Melville's political stance, as we shall see, and it is best to discuss the two attitudes one at a time.

Melville's attitude toward the past and change was not something that came to him in his last years only, for his Civil War poems return again and again to the themes of law versus anarchy, of order versus rebellion, and of art versus chaos. Even this last theme is one in which art becomes a metaphor for the ordered control of human affairs (Captain

*From Introduction to *Billy Budd, Sailor (An Inside Narrative)* by Herman Melville (Indianapolis: Bobbs-Merrill, 1975), xiv–xxxiv. Reprinted by permission of the author.

Vere's "forms, measured forms"), synonymous with law. The creation of measured forms became for Melville the highest expression of the human spirit in its struggle with the overwhelming, dark forces of an incomprehensible universe both inside and outside man — the unconquerable, double vastness he indicated in *Moby-Dick* and *Pierre*. There was something protoexistentialist about Melville, as about so many preexistentialist writers who wrestled with similar problems. He seemed to see the universe as enormously beyond a single unifying shape, meaning, or purpose, at least for the uses of human comprehension. Whatever ordered meaning, whatever formal shape, whatever moral purpose man saw in his existence, man put there. Man's fate, man's identity become what men make of themselves, and the making of man is in the terrible struggle of that weak, limited, mortal, animal creature to create out of raw existence the meaningful forms that are expressions of his own spirit. . . .

. . . It is the terrible agony, so vain and so necessary, that the artist, the former, the shaper, the maker, the orderer transforms his own small and personal mortality into a demigod apotheosis that is the glory of the entire race. Melville's poems are constant testimonials to the crucial importance of art as order. His Civil War poems constantly place the rebellion in the role, consequently, of the forces of chaos and anarchic change and the Union in the role of preserver, conserver, orderer. The temperamental antipathy to change, the nostalgia, in the late poems is prefigured in the metaphysics of Melville's political allegiances in the Civil War poems. Ironically, he opposed the South because of a conservative temperament. This is not to say that he did not care about slavery, human rights, and brotherhood — the driving democracy of Melville's mind was very much alive to moral ideologies involved in the war. What I am saying is that philosophically and temperamentally the mind behind *Moby-Dick* had shifted some of its priorities of belief and that Melville's political allegiance to the Union was essentially conservative. His support of formal order and art in his support of the Union is expressed in many of the war poems, most explicitly in "Dupont's Round Fight," a celebration of the victory of Commodore Samuel Dupont over the Confederate forts at Port Royal, South Carolina. Dupont's ships steamed around in a circle, first destroying the forts on one side of the sound and then on the other.

> In time and measure perfect moves
>   All Art whose aim is sure;
> Evolving rhymes and stars divine
>   Have rules, and they endure.
>
> Nor less the Fleet that warred for Right,
>   And, warring so, prevailed,
> In geometric beauty curved,
>   And in an orbit sailed.

> The rebel at Port Royal felt
> The Unity overawe,
> And rued the spell. A type was here,
> And victory of LAW.

The overtones of the war in heaven leave no doubts as to who is in the Royal right. As I will try to indicate, Melville recreated that "type" again in Captain Vere in different and more complex and more agonized circumstances.

The essentially conservative nature of Melville's poetry generally has been ignored. First of all, the man who wrote the books preceding the Civil War poems certainly did not appear to be primarily conservative. *Omoo* is, in part, an attack on established and institutionalized Christianity and evangelism. *White-Jacket* is a rebellious exposé of the mistreatment of sailors in the naval service of the United States government. *Redburn* is a continuing cry against the established forces of power, wealth, and privilege. An iconoclastically democratic spirit is everywhere seen in *Moby-Dick*. Yet, as Melville completed his "prose years" (*Typee*, 1846; *Omoo*, 1847; *Mardi*, 1849; *Redburn*, 1849; *White-Jacket*, 1850; *Moby-Dick*, 1851; *Pierre*, 1852; *Israel Potter*, 1855 [serialized in 1854]; *The Piazza Tales*, 1856 [which were tales and sketches he published in periodicals, 1853–1856]; and *The Confidence-Man*, 1857), his rebellious attitudes diminished — although his anger didn't — and his doubts about human progress and the nobility of the common man had increased considerably. The light in his books became dimmer as his view of man's fate became darker. . . .

It has often been noted that *Billy Budd* is concerned with political choices, but few commentators have seen the true focus, the major dimension of the tale: in essence it is a political fiction. . . .

. . . When we talk about people's politics, we really talk about their ways of seeing the meanings of human experience. We are really talking about deep attitudes and visions, often unspoken and even unformulated, concerning the nature of human possibility and, therefore, the nature and possibility and desirability of liberation and, therefore again, the nature and function of the state, the very concept of government. It is the underlying visions that I refer to when I say that *Billy Budd* is a political fiction and when I refer to politics as universal in human affairs. And even though obviously I cannot undertake here a definition of political philosophies, there are some useful general observations to be utilized within the context I suggest.

When divisions and subdivisions of social and political theory are categorized, they seem to indicate always two major and opposed definitions — consciously or unconsciously assumed — of the human being and human potential. In topical terms one may classify these tendencies as the "left" and the "right." But these terms, like "conservative" and "radical," like "revolutionary" or "reactionary," become necessarily less useful as they must be redefined in terms of particular people, and particular issues at particular times. Perhaps the most useful terms have been supplied by a "conservative"—to use the traditional term for the moment—T. E. Hulme. In his famous and influential essay, "Romanticism and Classicism," Hulme defines the romantic impulse as a belief in inexhaustible human potential and, therefore, in individual liberty and in endless and perfectibilitarian change. He defines the classicist impulse as a belief in the limited nature of human potential and the fallen nature of man and, therefore, in control and decorum and in the illusory quality of change and perfectibility. It seems to me that when all is said and done these opposing tendencies define the continuing dialectic between left and right, between radical and conservative, and inform the topical allegiances of particular people in particular issues at particular times most deeply, beneath the considerable and vastly important particularities of selfish and private involvements.

Both positions surround profound truths, or at least profound recognitions of some of the most central meanings of human experience and necessity. The need for aspiration beyond the values and expediencies of the moment, the need to break old bonds and chart new possibilities, the hopeful sense of progressively new identity (particularly held by the young)—in short, the existential sense of the libertarian possibility of freeing man into a new essence—these become the center of one set of ageless human realities and needs. On the other hand, the recognition that history sees "revolution" become the same old struggle all over again (*"plus ça change plus c'est la même chose"*), that the limited human animal is capable of and constantly expresses the most fallen and depraved behavior and therefore is in constant need of control and enforced rules of some kind or other if any kind of sane society is to be possible—in short the sense of limitation, precedence, and law—these become the center of another set of ageless human realities and needs. In the most extreme, visible, and oversimplified opposition of these views, the conflict between the two has been historically one of anarchy on the one hand and the police state on the other.

In *Billy Budd*, Melville, in the classicism of his old age, directly confronts the opposition of revolution and order. He creates in Billy an unwitting type of all the possibilities of human goodness. The imagery creating his physical and moral natures and the imagery creating his death scene recall prelapsarian Adam and even Christ. He is associated with grace, redemption, resurrection, and almost unlimited perfection. Almost. He is, withal, mortal (his stutter is the sign of his limitation) and he is susceptible to that other creation of Melville, Claggart, a type of the hideousness of the human beast, the endless "mystery of iniquity." The imagery creating Claggart's physical and moral natures and the imagery creating his death scene recall fallen man and even Satan. He is associated with mortal sin, pride, hell and damnation. Animal imagery is applied to both Billy and Claggart, but the animals are as different as the St. Bernard and the serpent. Close scrutiny of incidents and imagery will reveal that Melville draws on the literary conventions of the fair character and the dark character to create two opposing categories. Within the literary traditions Melville draws on, the good and fair man is also the creature of spontaneous instincts and generous heart, as Billy is; he is the noble savage, the natural and innocent animal, the sunny creature of magnificent and warm body, the unspoiled Adam ("Angles" look like "angels") who is first toward heaven (the foretop), the redeeming Prince of Peace ("my Peacemaker"); he is the representative of the Sermon on the Mount. The dark man is "citified man" ("Cain's city"), the man of strong and devious intellect, of sallow, pale complexion and high forehead, an underworld creature (the bowels of the ship), the vengeful creature of "ire, envy, and despair," the fallen man, the Prince of Lies (his death is the judgment on Ananias); he is the representative of the Articles of War. Associated with Billy is an English identity; associated with Claggart is the faint hint of French origins (ironically reversed in the "official" version of the affair on the *Bellipotent*).

Between these two views of human identity, between Christ and Satan, if you will, Melville places Captain Vere, a governor who must impose his power on society on the basis of which type most closely characterizes the actual world he governs. Both types, both Billy and Claggart, die. But both are deathless. As the spar that Billy hung from is hunted by the crew as though a piece of it were a piece of the true cross, and as the last line of "Billy in the Darbies" tells you that the voice is still living in the depths of the sea, and as Billy in death mysteriously was not subject to the spasms of ordinary mortals, so too everything Claggart represents is continued by the erroneous version of the affair given in the naval chronicle's "News from the Mediterranean." Claggart's underworld in a man-of-war continues, the world of the gun continues, the history of depravity continues. Both human aspiration to heavenly goodness and human degradation in bestial history continue as opposing sets of yearnings and necessities, both of which lay heavy claim on the human spirit.

Ideally, a choice between the two would be easy. But Melville does not allow for such a simple choice between Christ and Satan. He makes history an amalgam of man's devilish nature and man's yearning for heaven. In a world of mixed necessities and mixed desires, how do you govern the ship? What is operative? What is not? The French Revolution, a monstrous and threatful presence like Camoens' Spirit of the Cape, becomes Melville's major metaphor for the mixed and bitter facts of history. It is a revolution that perhaps has effected good all along the lines for Europeans and yet it also results in a continuation of all the wrongs created by the upstart kings. England is the "sole free conservative Power," and yet it engages in impressment practices that reflect the brutality of war as much as does the Revolution. Welkin-eyed Baby is "homeward bound" on the "Rights of Man" on the "Narrow Seas." But always this heavenly babe, whose mother was eminently favored by "Love and the Graces" and whose father only "God knows, Sir," is nipped in the budd and never does go home through the straight and narrow gate. Mortal man, grave-ling, captains a ship of only temporary peace from which the peacemaking "jewel" of the crew is taken by the ship of war, eventually to be framed and crucified. The ship of the State is not a peace-ship but is a "fighting peace-maker."

The loyalties of the crew of the state's ship are torn between the laws of command and the promptings of the human heart. Summing up the agony of the crew and the officers in deeper feeling than anyone else's, the captain, who is responsible for the safety of the ship in which everyone sails, must activate his vision of man within the "art of the possible." In his speech to the court martial, Vere, whose very name suggests "truth," makes it clear that he recognizes the categories in which Billy and Claggart each belong and that he recognizes the anguish with which heaven must be postponed as an operative principle within the hellish immediacies of history. Yet what he knows — he is a student of history and biography and an honest man of independent mind — is lost in his death. Just as Nelson's dying injunction was overruled by a less experienced officer, so Vere's dying knowledge is reversed in the "official" version of the affair in the naval chronicle. Always new Veres must go through the same crucifixions all over again. There is no end to the identity of Vere as there is no end to the identities of Billy and Claggart. All are mortal and all must die, and in the endlessness of their deaths and the continuation of their identities is the deathlessness of mortal necessity that is prefigured in the myth of Sisyphus. No generation can ever really give its experience to another; no final plateau is reached on the ultimate heights in which the human race can say, "There! we've made it! We have accomplished heaven!" The world is never Billy Budd's. Yet man keeps trying and the Veres keep struggling in agony, so the world is never wholly Claggart's, either. But our human experience will always be marked by struggle, and the devil's calling card will announce forever that our purest ideals in all their beauty will always go a-stuttering.

Is history, after all, an endless repetition of man's crucifixions of his loveliest hopes? Will the helplessness of innocence and unaided goodness condemn us always to the paradox of using the gun to put an end to the use of the gun? Has there already been a second coming and a third and a fourth and will there be an infinite series of them? Is there ever an escape from history, or must the wise and tortured ruler ever have to try to adjust Christ and Satan to human actualities within history rather than beyond it? In the complex and profound problems and contradictions and counter-contradictions that spin off these central questions, Melville created a most deeply political novel and expressed his conservative point of view.

When I identify Mellville as a conservative in his classicism, I do not mean that automatically all leftists are romanticists and that all rightists are classicists. When we consider the particularities of people, issues, and times, history presents us with endless examples of betrayals of self-labelled positions and with exotic hybrids, from the "revolutionary" commissar who is an extreme exponent of repressive law and order to the "ultraconservative" who seems to believe in the unlimited possibilities of the unusual, determined, and elite individual. Moreover, people are conservative in some issues, radical in others, and Melville was no exception. Generally, however, by the time Melville entered his "poetry years" (*Battle-Pieces*, 1866; *Clarel*, 1876; *John Marr and Other Sailors*, 1888; *Timoleon*, 1891 — poems from the "Burgundy Club" group and from his projected volume, *Weeds and Wildings*, were given occasional publication after his death), the classicism implicit in "Dupont's Round Fight" predominated and was to do so all through the "poetry years," including the years of *Billy Budd*, to the end of Melville's life.

Another war poem, "The House-Top," helps to illustrate the distance between the politics of his poetry and the politics of his earlier prose.[1] When Melville considered the tension between invested power and the masses, between men as corporate and men as individuals at variance with the state, he championed the common man and democracy rather than kings and robes in his earlier prose. He emphasized the individual, the honest primitive, and the worker rather than the requirements of power. Perhaps his most famous statement of his romanticist point of view is in the exalted prose of the familiar passages from the first "Knights and Squires" chapter (XXVI) in *Moby-Dick*. . . .

Yet, in "The House-Top," when Melville considers the opposition of the common masses to the state — the specific subject is the New York draft riots of July 1863 — his attitudes have changed considerably. Here the sound of the "commons" is "the Atheist roar of riot" and the lighting spread over this "most mournful" and "abased" group of "mariners, and renegades and castaways" is "red Arson." The self-expression of the masses in this poem becomes a dreadful recidivism, and the police power of the state, imposing law and order on the crowd, becomes necessary Draconian wisdom. Just as "Dupont's Round Fight" has little to do with topical particularities of person, issue, or times but has everything to with Melville's classicist view of rebellion, so "The House-Top" does not center on the political particulars of the draft riots. They were indeed terrible. Anti-draft mobs burned buildings indiscriminately and lynched all the Negroes they could lay their hands on. But like *Billy Budd*, which really gives almost no particulars of political history and offers very few specifics of Anglo-French antagonisms and concentrates instead on the deepest political *view* of those antagonisms, "The House-Top" does not concentrate on specific events of the riots but on the essentially classicist point of view from which those riots are seen. *Billy Budd, like the poetry it grew out of, does not offer a dramatization of political events but of a political perspective.* Melville is concerned less with the specifics of power manipulation than with his vision of limited human possibility. If in *Moby-Dick* the crew is a visible metaphor for both nobility and debasement, in *Billy Budd* the crew has become an indistinct background, a threatful presence that is a metaphor for potential chaos, like the mobs in Shakespeare's plays. In "The House-Top" what is clear is a dominant distrust of men, a sense of the limitations of fallen man, and a consequent need for formal imposition of law and order:

> No sleep. The sultriness pervades the air
> And binds the brain — a dense oppression, such
> As tawny tigers feel in matted shades,
> Vexing their blood and making apt for ravage.
> Beneath the stars the roofy desert spreads
> Vacant as Libya. All is hushed near by.
> Yet fitfully from far breaks a mixed surf
> Of muffled sound, the Atheist roar of riot.
> Yonder, where parching Sirius set in drought,
> Balefully glares red Arson — there — and there.
> The Town is taken by its rats — ship-rats
> And rats of the wharves. All civil charms
> And priestly spells which late held hearts in awe —
> Fear-bound, subjected to a better sway
> Than sway of self; these like a dream dissolve,
> And man rebounds whole aeons back in nature.
> Hail to the low dull rumble, dull and dead,
> And ponderous drag that jars the wall,
> Wise Draco comes, deep in the midnight roll
> Of black artillery; he comes, though late;
> In code corroborating Calvin's creed
> And cynic tyrannies of honest kings;
> He comes, nor parlies; and the Town, redeemed,
> Gives thanks devout; nor, being thankful, heeds
> The grimy slur on the Republic's faith implied,
> Which holds that Man is naturally good,
> And — more — is Nature's Roman, never to be scourged.

The angry, sarcastic bitterness of this poem and its explicit contrasts to "Knights and Squires" makes the point quite clear. And when one turns to *Billy Budd* itself, it is significant to note that when Melville presents the common sailor, the knights and squires of *Moby-Dick* are gone. The closest one comes to a visible crewmember is the portrait of the Dansker. What had been the magnanimous veteran sailor, who was strength, generosity, and the glory of the democratic ideal in the earlier prose, is now a tight old veteran who knows the score and will not stick his neck out. Although there is a shadowy crew around Billy, a sense of masses of sailors, the Handsome Sailor stands alone. There are "Squeaks" and other bought traitors, faceless and all but nameless companions, but there is no Queequeg who will dive down to the head of the whale to save a friend. The crew, the mass, is not a force from which salvation might come, in which romantically seen glory exists, but is a force from which sullen confusion and violent mutiny threaten to erupt at every moment.

And when we turn to the noble sailor in the late poems — to that other attitude of Melville, his joy in the common sailor as a carefree and courageously daring child who obediently does his duty — we again come up against a view in which the romanticist or revolutionary sense of man is gone. Melville's joy in the common sailor was evident from the very beginning. He expressed delight at the feats and childlikeness of his sea-chums and handsome sailors. But there is a considerable difference between the celebration of the sailor in the "prose years" and in the "poetry years." There are many ways to sum up that difference and perhaps this is as good as any: early in the "prose years," in *White-Jacket*, the hero witnesses a flogging and, struck with the horror of it, determines that if ever he is carried to the gratings he will rush the captain and take him overboard in a rebellious act of suicide and murder. Late in the "poetry years," in *Billy Budd*, the hero witnesses a flogging and, struck with the horror of it, determines to be so good that he shall never give occasion to be carried to the gratings.

There are, as *Moby-Dick* so richly indicates, populist overtones as well as potentially conservative ones in the early prose celebration of the sailor. There are no populist overtones in the later poems or in *Billy Budd*. The nostalgic poetry of *John Marr* celebrates the common sailor *not* as a romanticist's political entity but as an apolitical child of danger who is too innocent, loyal, and obedient a rakehell to have any inclination toward rebellious political thought or action. The glamorously daring but fatalistic sailor has been politically castrated. Like the conception of the "darky" in Shirley Temple movies, the good sailor is the child who lives cheerfully, zestfully, and essentially mindlessly and gratefully under the care and control of the master. The good sailor may be associated with high-spirited glee and larking sport, with danger and daring, but never with any threat to law, order, and established power. It is this aspect of Melville's nostalgic late poems that tends to make some of them merely sentimental — the good times and good chums they yearn for are sometimes too simple to be fitting objects for such yearning, undeniably felt though it be. What Billy longs for in the darbies, for instance, is a bit of biscuit and a bit of grog as he remembers his friends. John Marr, remembering back to other times, recollects the good friends as those who acquiesce, not those who rebel, those cheerful children of the waves who simply take what befalls them with fatalistic gallantry:

> Once, for all the darkling sea,
> You your voices raised how clearly,
> Striking in when tempest sung;
> Hoisting up the storm-sail cheerly,
> *Life is storm — let storm!* you rung.
> Taking things as fated merely,
> Child-like though the world ye spanned;
> Nor holding unto life too dearly,
> Ye who held your lives in hand —
> Skimmers, who on oceans four
> Petrels were, and larks ashore.

The handsome sailor is the quintessence of all that is best and that is so nostalgically longed for. And when he is celebrated, as in the poem "Jack Roy" ("King" Jack, a memory of Jack Chase, the handsome sailor Melville had known aboard the frigate *United States*), the magnanimously care-free, uncaring, ever-young man emerges once more as the eternal child obedient to his patriotic duty:

> But thou, manly king o' the old *Splendid's* crew,
> The ribbons o' thy hat still a-fluttering, should fly —
> A challenge, and forever, nor the bravery should rue.
> Only in a tussle for the starry flag high,
> When 't is piety to do, and privilege to die,
> Then, only then, would heaven think to lop
> Such a cedar as the captain o' the *Splendid's* main-top:
> A belted sea-gentleman; a gallant, off-hand
> Mercutio indifferent in life's gay command.
> Magnanimous in humor; when the splintering shot fell,
> "Tooth-picks-a-plenty, lads; thank 'em with a shell"
> ....
> Never relishing the knave, though allowing for the menial,
> Nor overmuch the king, Jack, nor prodigally genial.
> Ashore on liberty, he flashed in escapade,
> Vaulting over life in its levelness of grade,
> Like the dolphin off Africa in rainbow a-sweeping —
> Arch irridescent shot from seas languid sleeping.
>
> Larking with thy life, if a joy but a toy,
> Heroic in thy levity wert thou, Jack Roy.

The late poems make clear the origins of the characteristics that "belted Billy," that man-child, displays in his role of the handsome sailor. Also, it is not insignificant that the sea-poet recalled to Melville's mind as he developed the prose story of *Billy Budd* out of his "John Marr" kind of poems was Charles Dibdin . . . , whose patriotic sea songs were supposed to express the sentiments of His Majesty's navy's sailors. In Dibdin's songs the sailors are men of submission to authority, men of patriotic loyalty, men of childlike and courageous acceptance of their lot. When, in a reference reminiscent of "The House-Top," Melville in *Billy Budd* recalls the Great Mutiny as "the transmuting . . . of founded law and freedom defined into the enemy's red meteor of unbridled and unbounded revolt," he evokes Dibdin as "no mean auxiliary to the English Government at that European conjuncture," whose strains celebrate "among other things, the patriotic devotion of the British tar: " 'And as for my life, 'tis the King's!' " "The English Government at that European conjuncture" Melville defines as "a Power then all but the sole free conservative one of the Old World." It is a matter of stretching the tone considerably to insist that all these statements are ironically intended by Melville. One may stretch as one will, but when one considers the materials out of which *Billy Budd* grew, such stretching becomes less supportable.

Finally, the two attitudes I have been discussing merge into one in Melville's sense of a bleak present. Melville's celebration of the child of the sea is intimately connected in his nostalgia to his increasing dislike of change. The Jack Roys of the old wooden navies led a colorful life, "vaulting over life in its levelness of grade." With the departure of the sailor's old times, glee and vividness in life also departed. Melville's poems, both of the Civil War and of the later, "John Marr," variety, are consistently marked by an appraisal of the present as dull, mechanical, and monotonous, especially when held side by side with the old days of wooden-sided ships. The old man's certitude that life was better in the good old days (when the old man was a young man) psychologically intensified what had long been Melville's classicism. As he increasingly praised law, order, and measured form, and as he increasingly came to distrust change and assumptions of limitless human freedom and perfectibility, he reminisced more and more about the life and times of the Dibdin-sailor and saw the present as a gray, utilitarian, depersonalized era. In the prose headnote to "John Marr" the old sailor comes to realize what the difference is between his past and the present lives of the staid and practical working people among whom he now dwells: something had gone out of life and "that something was geniality, the flower of life springing from some sense of joy in it, more or less." In his earlier poem on the *Temeraire*, "that storied ship of the old English fleet," as he called it, Melville looked back to the glory of old ships in old sea-fights. His thoughts were those that might have been "suggested to an Englishman, of the old order by the fight of the Monitor and Merrimac," and the distinction between the iron-clad, steam-powered present and the golden, oaken-hearted past is made clear:

> O, Titan Temeraire,
>   Your stern-lights fade away;
> Your bulwarks to the years must yield,
>   And heart-of-oak decay.
> A pigmy steam-tug tows you,
>   Gigantic, to the shore—
> Dismantled of your guns and spars,
>   And sweeping wings of war.
> The rivets clinch the iron-clads,
>   Men learn a deadlier lore;
> But Fame has nailed your battle-flags—
>   Your ghost it sails before:
> O, the navies old and oaken,
>   O, the Temeraire no more!

As for the iron-clad present itself, "A Utilitarian View of the Monitor's Fight" leaves no question about the evaluation made by nostalgia:

> Hail to victory without the gaud
>   Of glory; zeal that needs no fans
> Of banners; plain mechanic power
> Plied cogently in War now placed—
>   Where War belongs—
> Among the trades and artisans.
> . . . .
>
> War yet shall be, and to the end;
>   But war-paint shows the streaks of weather;
> War yet shall be, but warriors
> Are now but operatives; War's made
>   Less grand than Peace.
> And a singe runs through lace and feather.

In *Billy Budd* itself the tone is unmistakable in the comparison of Present and Past.

> But as ashore knightly valor, though shorn of its blazonry, did not cease with the knights, neither on the seas [did it cease], though nowadays in encounters there a certain kind of displayed gallantry be fallen out of date as hardly applicable under changed circumstances. . . .
>   Nevertheless, to anybody who can hold the Present at its worth without being inappreciative of the Past, it may be forgiven, if to such a one the solitary old hulk at Portsmouth, Nelson's *Victory*, seems to float

there, not alone as the decaying monument of a fame incorruptible, but also as a poetic reproach, softened by its picturesqueness, to the *Monitors* and yet mightier hulls of the European ironclads. And this not altogether because such craft are unsightly, unavoidably lacking the symmetry and grand lines of the old battleships, but equally for other reasons.

But if times have changed, not so the fallen nature of man. "War shall yet be, and to the end." The present is less grand than the past, but sisyphean history never changes. This paradox, formed at the juncture of temperamental and political conservatism, remains constant in the poems. The changelessness of history and the human heart are perhaps most explicitly expressed in "The Conflict of Convictions," another Civil War poem about the state of the nation:

> Age after age shall be
> As age after age has been,
> (From man's changeless heart their way they win);
> And death be busy with all who strive—
> Death, with silent negative.
>
> YEA AND NAY—
> EACH HATH HIS SAY;
> BUT GOD HE KEEPS THE MIDDLE WAY.
> NONE WAS BY
> WHEN HE SPREAD THE SKY;
> WISDOM IS VAIN, AND PROPHESY.

In sum, the classicism of Melville's outlook at the time he wrote *Billy Budd*, a general conservatism made unmistakable in all the poetry which was the genesis of the narrative, makes it clear that if one is to take into account the mind of the writer when evaluating the written product, the conservative tone of the tale is to be taken not ironically but at face value. Seen from the perspective of Melville's classicism, Captain Vere becomes a sympathetic character.

Note

1. After I had completed the text and the introduction, I compiled the bibliography. One title in an annual bibliography caught my eye as possible corroboration of my idea about the poetry: Jane Donahue's essay, "Melville's Classicism: Law and Order in His Poetry" (1969). When I read the piece, I discovered that the idea, the language, and the conclusion were astonishingly close to my introduction—Miss Donahue even singles out "Dupont's Round Fight" and "The House-Top" as central poems in the revelation of Melville's classicism. There are a few differences between us: like many critics of *Billy Budd*, Miss Donahue is somewhat victimized by two decades (in American criticism that's enough time to create a tradition!) of articles about Vere as villain, so that she does not quite see the implications of

her article for *Billy Budd*: she remains content to characterize Melville's treatment of Vere as "ambiguous." However, Miss Donahue's emphasis is not upon *Billy Budd* but upon the poetry, and I am delighted to find in her statement about the poetry the rare joy of complete agreement with a colleague. Although I had not read Miss Donahue's essay before I completed this volume, I am happy to acknowledge her commentary as first in time and idea. The reader is urged to consult "Melville's Classicism" for a more detailed substantiation of the point I make about the political orientation of the materials out of which *Billy Budd* grew.

Billy Budd and Melville's Philosophy of War

Joyce Sparer Adler*

Billy Budd, Sailor concentrates Melville's philosophy of war and lifts it to its highest point of development.[1] Its themes are recapitulations and extensions of those he had many times developed, and its poetic conceptions are the offspring of earlier ones which had concretized his ideas concerning the "greatest of evils. . . ."[2]

The view of *Billy Budd* as the final stage in the development of Melville's philosophy of war embraces both the work's abhorrence of war and the war machine (the feeling ignored by those who, in the classical argument about *Billy Budd*, see it as a "testament of acceptance") and its genuinely affirmative, nonironic, and luminous aspects (the qualities set aside by those who see it in its totality as irony, rejection, or darkness alone). Along with Melville's continued rejection of the world of war there is in *Billy Budd* a new affirmation that within that world's most cruel contradictions lies the potentiality of its metamorphosis. . . .

By the time of his last work Melville was so experienced a poet and narrator that he could rely solely on poetic conceptions integrated into narrative to carry his ideas. For this reason it is possible to consider all main aspects of the work in the course of recalling the story.

What happens in *Billy Budd*, with the exception of what takes place within the psyche of the crew, is what Melville had all along demonstrated must necessarily happen—what is, in that sense, fated—in the "present civilization of the world."[3] Impressed from the English merchant ship *Rights-of-Man*[4] to serve the King on the battleship *Bellipotent* in 1797, the year of the Great Mutiny during the Napoleonic wars, Billy is *White-Jacket*'s sailor "shorn of all rights" (p. 301; Ch. lxxii). Young and of considerable physical and personal beauty, like Melville's typical "Handsome Sailor" in aspect though not like him a "spokesman" (p. 44; Ch. i),

*From *PMLA* 91 (1976):266–78. © 1976, *PMLA*. Reprinted by permission of the Modern Language Association of America. The essay also appears in Adler, *War in Melville's Imagination* (New York: New York University Press, 1981). The present abridgment was made by the author.

called "peace-maker" and "jewel" by the merchantman's captain (p. 47; Ch. i), and "flower of the flock" and a "beauty" by the lieutenant who carries him off (p. 48; Ch. i), he is from the first the symbol of the good and beauty "out of keeping" (p. 53; Ch. ii) and doomed in the world of war, as, in *White-Jacket*, are Jack Jewel (p. 70; Ch. xvi) and the blossoms which cannot survive on the *Neversink*. He is, at the same time, representative of sailors as a class, as the title *Billy Budd, Sailor* conveys. The words of John Marr describing seamen generally apply to him: "Taking things as fated merely, / Child-like through the world ye spanned; / Nor holding unto life too dearly, / . . . Barbarians of man's simpler nature, / Unworldly servers of the world."[5] He is shortly seen to represent also the jewel and flower of youth sacrificed to war, like the soldiers in *Battle-Pieces* "nipped like blossoms,"[6] willing children sent through fire as sacrifices to a false god, fated to die because an older generation has failed to rectify wrongs which lead to war. In either aspect — representative or outstanding — he embodies *White-Jacket*'s conception of a sailor as the "image of his Creator" (p. 142; Ch. xxxiv).

Billy accepts his impressment without complaint. Like the crew of the *Pequod* and all but a few sailors on the *Neversink* he is incapable of saying "no" to anyone in authority, or indeed of speaking at all when he most needs speech to defend himself. His "imperfection" is concretized in an actual "defect," a tongue-tie or "more or less of a stutter or even worse" (p. 53; Ch. ii). The reverse of this "organic hesitancy" — the ability to speak up to authority — is possessed by no one in *Billy Budd*, but the dedication to Jack Chase, whose outstanding quality in *White-Jacket* is his willingness to be a spokesman, points up the contrast. There is no one resembling him on the *Bellipotent* — a rereading of the dedication after the novel is read will remind one — no independent spirit to speak up firmly for Billy.

The day after Billy's impressment the *Bellipotent*'s crew must witness an admonitory flogging.[7] The young sailor, now a foretopman, vows never to do anything to bring down on himself such a punishment or even a reproof. But while he never does, and while his simple virtue, friendliness, and good looks make him well-liked by the crew, these very qualities arouse a "peculiar" (p. 73; Ch. x) hostility in Claggart, the master-at-arms, a functionary peculiar to battleships. Billy's goodness calls forth a natural antipathy in Claggart; the devil, associated in Melville's imagination with war and inevitably hostile to all good, resides in Claggart, as once before in Bland, the master-at-arms in *White-Jacket*. What Melville stresses in both masters-at-arms is their function. The diabolical power of each derives from his position, given him by the war machine. Claggart's "place" puts "converging wires of underground influence" under his control (p. 67; Ch. viii). The navy "charges" him with his police duties so that he can preserve its "order" (p. 64; Ch. viii). He lives in "official seclusion" from the light (p. 64; Ch. viii). The words *function* and *funtionary* are regularly used in relation to him. Since his qualities are what the navy needs in a master-at-arms, Claggart has advanced rapidly to his post, and, as with Bland, the navy defends him, posthumously, even when his evil is exposed. His mystery, which is something to be probed, is social in its significance and consequences, not so emptily abstract and supernatural that one must abandon all attempts to understand it. As Melville had said in *White-Jacket*: "Ourselves are Fate"; man fashions or chooses his own gods to rule him (pp. 320–321; Ch. lxxv); there are "no mysteries out of ourselves" (p. 398; "The End"). The depravity Claggart stands for is encouraged by the values that dominate the world: "Civilization, especially if of the austerer sort is auspicious to it. It folds itself in the mantle of respectability" (p. 75; Ch. xi).

Melville accents the mutually exclusive character of the values of war and peace, for which Claggart and Billy stand, in an unusual spatial way, in terms of "the juxtaposition of dissimilar personalities" (p. 74; Ch. xi); the "mutually confronting visages" of the master-at-arms and the young sailor (p. 98; Ch. xix); and their eventual assignment to "opposite" compartments (p. 101; Ch. xix). Billy is associated with the sunlight, the master-at-arms with the contrasting space, the shade. They are "essential right and wrong," which in the "jugglery of circumstances" attending war are interchanged (p. 103; Ch. xxi). For what is evil for man is war's good; what is good for mankind is what war has no place for.

An old Danish sailor's thoughts present the question to which the book responds. Seeing in Billy—Baby as he calls him—something "in contrast" with the warship's "environment" and "oddly incongruous" with it, he wonders what will befall such a nature in such a world (p. 70; Ch. ix). He warns Billy that Claggart is down on him, but just as Claggart is powerless to contain any good, so Billy is unable to take in the evil of the master-at-arms.

At a moment when the *Bellipotent* is on detached service from the fleet, Claggart seeks an interview with Captain Vere. He accuses Billy of plotting mutiny, a charge well calculated to create fear at that moment, but one which Vere cannot credit in the case of the young sailor. Called in to face the accusation, Billy is speechless with horror, his "impotence" noted by the captain (p. 99; Ch. xix). Claggart's eyes as he confronts Billy lose their human expression. His first glance is that of a serpent, his last that of a torpedo fish, Melville again associating the devil, as represented by the serpent, with war, as implied by the torpedo. Unable to use his tongue, Billy can express himself against Claggart only with a blow, which strikes the master-at-arms in the forehead and kills him.

Vere's instantaneous utterance, "Fated boy" (p. 99; Ch. xix), unconsciously pronounces Billy's doom. His response is the result of conditioning so strong that his verdict has the force of an instinct. The moment sets forth dramatically what was put forward as exposition in *White-Jacket* in regard to the power which a man-of-war captain's long-instilled prejudices and training have over his thought (p. 232; Ch. lv). So thoroughly has Vere been dedicated to the ritual of war that to him it seems Fate. He covers and then uncovers his face, the "father in him, manifested towards Billy thus far in the scene . . . replaced by the military disciplinarian" (p. 100; Ch. xix). This is a gentler version, but an imaginatively related version, nonetheless, of the two faces of the *Neversink*'s captain, a fatherly one for special occasions and an uncompromising judge's face when he condemns a man to be flogged. The two faces cannot coincide. The face of the military disciplinarian in Vere must take the place of that of the father.

Vere must at this point make his conscious choice between God's will and that of Mars. He is not in any degree unclear about the nature of that choice; in his mind Claggart has been struck dead by an "angel of God." But neither is he for a moment undecided about his verdict: "Yet the angel must hang" (p. 101; Ch. xix). For, as Melville will make increasingly clear, the god whom Vere has been trained to worship is Mars; his religion is war; his thoughts and acts are conditioned by the ritual patterns of warmaking. So he silences that part of himself that recognizes God in Billy; he is, in effect, knowingly striking at God when he decides to sacrifice God's angel. Melville shows him self-alienated to the extreme. Vere does feel sympathy, even deep love for Billy, but "a true military officer is in one particular like a true monk. Not with more of self-abnegation will the latter keep his vows of monastic obedience than the former his allegiance to martial duty" (p. 104; Ch. xxi). The comparison extrapolates the one in *Clarel* in which an imagined warship is a grim abbey afloat on the ocean, its discipline cenobite and dumb, its deep galleries "cloisters of the god of war."[8] Indeed, as far back as *White-Jacket*, officers were "priests of Mars" (p. 209, Ch. xlix), and an English fighting frigate's tall mainmast had terminated "like a steepled cathedral, in the bannered cross of the religion of peace" (p. 268; Ch. lxv). Throughout *Billy Budd* the contrast between the religion of war and "the religion of Peace" is evoked, largely by church images — an altar, a place of sanctuary, confessionals or side-chapels, sacraments, covenants, and ceremonial forms — until the *Bellipotent* becomes, in effect, a cathedral dedicated to War. Billy is an offering Vere makes to Mars, an offering not demanded by law or ethics or even military necessity (Melville plainly eliminating these as Vere's felt motivations) but by his own obsession.

Vere's inner compulsion, like Ahab's, drives him so "steadfastly" on (p. 113; Ch. xxi) that he cannot delay. As he prepares to make his sacrifice, he is so strangely excited that the surgeon who has been called in to attend to the corpse wonders whether he is sane (p. 101; Ch. xx). The question thus raised about Vere's sanity is a symbolic one, the concrete poetic expression of Melville's long conception of war as the "madness" in men. A significant subsidiary question is presented as well: does Vere's strange behavior indicate a sudden aberration, a "transient excitement" brought about by the unusual circumstances? Vere's devotion to war — his "madness" — is not sudden; it is his constant state of mind. But the peculiar circumstances of Billy's killing of Claggart bring his obsession into sharper focus.

Instead of waiting to submit Billy's case to the admiral when they rejoin the fleet, as the other officers think should be done, Vere sets up the form, though not the substance, of a trial, carefully selecting the members of his court. He conducts the proceedings in extreme secrecy. The naval court-martial which *White-Jacket* condemns as a "Star Chamber indeed!" and compares to the Spanish Inquisition (p. 302; Ch. lxxii) here resembles those palace tragedies which occurred in the capital founded by the czar of Russia, "Peter the Barbarian" (p. 103; Ch. xxi).

The first part of the trial, which establishes the facts and at which Billy is present, presents in dramatic form ideas set forth in *White-Jacket*, Billy being the representative "plebian topman, without a jury . . . judicially naked at the bar" (p. 303; Ch. lxxii) and Vere the captain clothed with unlimited, arbitrary powers. To Billy, who cannot say "no" to anyone in authority, a foundling child who wants to be liked and who fears to call forth even a reproof, Vere, the king's aristocratic "envoy" (p. 60; Ch. vi), is someone he could certainly never gainsay. His statement, "I have eaten the King's bread and I am true to the King" (p. 106; Ch. xxi), recalls the unquestioning obedience exacted in return for food in *Moby-Dick*'s cabin-table scene. . . . One realizes at this point why Melville had earlier made Vere refer to Billy, in "naval parlance," as a "King's bargain" (p. 95; Ch. xviii).

Although Billy symbolizes what is essentially good, he has the weakness of the sailors he represents: his silence gives consent to war's demands. When he grasps what Vere has in mind for him, he acquiesces to the decision as to Fate. His silence — like that of all the others on the *Bellipotent*, including the silence of Vere's humane part — is an accessory of war, partaking of its evil. Thus an earlier remark about Billy, unexplained at the time, is clarified; namely, that his vocal flaw shows that "the arch interferer, the envious marplot of Eden, still has more or less to do with every human consignment to this planet of Earth" (p. 53; Ch. ii).

The second part of the trial, the arrival at a joint verdict (pp. 109-14; Ch. xxi), begins just after Billy is sent back to the compartment opposite the one where Claggart's body lies. Vere asks the question he knows to be in the officers' minds: "How can we adjudge to summary and shameful death a fellow creature innocent before God, and whom we feel to be so? — Does that state it aright? You sign sad assent. Well, I too feel that, the full force of that. It is Nature." But he urges the court to remember that their allegiance has been sworn to the King, not to Nature. And now, as in his most subtle earlier fiction, Melville speaks through another, saying in part what that character says but in essence and in total intention something far different; it is the technique used with especial artistry in the case of Captain Delano in *Benito Cereno* and of Judge Hall in *The*

Confidence-Man. Speaking through Vere, Melville espouses the reverse of the religion for which Vere proselytizes. The captain addresses to the court what could stand alone in another context as an eloquent speech against war. He does not intend it so; Melville, however, does, conveying obliquely that war itself is the "Great Mutiny" against God, striking at "essential right." It is Vere, not Melville, who rules out "moral scruple" in favor of that strength in war, that bellipotence, which to him is "paramount." Through Vere's speech to the court Melville reveals the absence of morality in war and shows himself prophetically sensitive to a question whose centrality would not be generally clear until well into the twentieth century, the question of individual conscience and responsibility in time of war. Vere asks: ". . . suppose condemnation to follow these present proceedings. Would it be so much we ourselves that would condemn as it would be martial law operating through us? For that law and the rigor of it, we are not responsible. Our vowed responsibility is in this: That however pitilessly that law may operate in any instances, we nevertheless adhere to it and administer it," (pp. 110–11; Ch. xxi). He urges that warm hearts not betray heads that should be cool, that in war the heart, "the feminine in man," must be ruled out. . . . The Mutiny Act is, in the words of *White-Jacket* about the Articles of War, his "gospel" (p. 292; Ch. lxx).

To guarantee their going along with his "prejudgment" (p. 108; Ch. xxi), Vere concludes with an appeal to the officers' sense of fear, his argument being that the crew, learning of Billy's deed and seeing him continue alive, will believe the *Bellipotent*'s officers weak and may mutiny against them. . . . Billy is sentenced to be hanged at the yardarm at dawn. Vere takes upon himself the burden of telling him privately "the finding of the court" (p. 114; Ch. xxii), knowing Billy will feel for him (p. 113; Ch. xxi).

The narrator gives no account of the interview, only a conjecture that Vere in the end may have developed the passion sometimes "latent" under a stoical exterior: "The austere devotee of military duty, letting himself melt back into what remains primeval in our formalized humanity, may in end have caught Billy to his heart, even as Abraham may have caught young Isaac on the brink of resolutely offering him up in obedience to the exacting behest" (p. 115; Ch. xxii). The narrator sees a resemblance between the two situations, the one biblical, the other military, in order that Melville may accent the contrast between the God who created man and the god of war who would destroy him. For God in the story of Isaac and Abraham does not in the end exact the sacrifice. In the history of the ancient Jews, as told by those who composed the Old Testament, the Abraham-Isaac story signifies the first recorded repudiation of the tradition of human sacrifice. It is God's final behest that Isaac should live and that Abraham's seed should multiply through him. But Vere's internal behest condemns Billy, and the tradition of human sacrifice on the altar of war goes on.

Nevertheless, Vere does suffer, and intensely; it is one of the most important ideas in the work that all suffer from war. . . . His is the agony of a martyr to an inhumane religion. Vere turning from Billy, as Ahab from Pip, turns from his own humanity, sacrificing to war his capacity for love, for "fatherhood." All that will seem to remain of him from this moment on is his military function. He has adhered to his choice between the values represented by Claggart and by Billy, sacrificing Billy and what he represents and, in effect, upholding what Claggart stands for. And suddenly we know why it was said earlier of Claggart's depravity that civilization, "especially if of the austerer sort" (which denies its heart), is auspicious to it (p. 75; Ch. xi).

Underlining the reversal of human values in war, Melville has Claggart prepared for burial "with every funeral honor properly belonging to his naval grade" (p. 117; Ch. xxiii), while Billy lies on the upper deck awaiting an ignominious death. Billy's significance as the good and beauty sacrificed to war is represented as if in a painting. Since all of *Billy Budd* is only some eighty pages, the two-page painting (pp. 118–20; Ch. xxiv) of the young sailor in a bay formed by the regular spacing of the guns must have been of extreme symbolic importance to Melville.[9] Billy lies between two guns "as nipped in the vice of fate. . . . " "In contrast with the funereal hue of these surroundings," Billy lies in his soiled white sailor's apparel which glimmers in the obscure light. "In effect he is already in his shroud." Worked into the painting is the basic contrast between the ignored values of Christianity and the values actually held sacred in modern civilization.

> Over him but scarce illuminating him, two battle lanterns swing from two massive beams of the deck above. Fed with the oil supplied by the war contractors (whose gains, honest or otherwise, are in every land an anticipated portion of the harvest of death), with flickering splashes of dirty yellow light they pollute the pale moonshine all but ineffectually struggling in obstructed flecks through the open ports from which the tampioned cannon protrude. Other lanterns at intervals serve but to bring out somewhat the obscurer bays which, like small confessionals or side-chapels in a cathedral, branch from the long dim-vistaed broad aisle between the two batteries of that covered tier.
> (p. 119; Ch. xxiv)

. . . The chaplain who comes to talk to Billy finds him asleep in a peace that transcends any consolation he has to offer. This chaplain, as an accessory of war, is gentler than the one in *White-Jacket* (Ch. xxxviii), but his role, in essence, is the same . . . :

> Bluntly put, a chaplain is the minister of the Prince of Peace serving in the host of the God of War—Mars. As such, he is as incongruous as a musket would be on the altar at Christmas. Why, then, is he there? Because he indirectly subserves the purpose attested by the cannon;

because too he lends the sanction of the religion of the meek to that
which practically is the abrogation of everything but brute Force.
(pp. 121–22; Ch. xxiv)

The luminous moonlit night passes away, but "like the prophet in the
chariot disappearing in heaven and dropping his mantle to Elisha," it
transfers its pale robe "to the breaking day" and a faint light rises slowly in
the East (p. 122; Ch. xxv). With this association with Elijah and the
transfer of his mantle to suggest a progression to a brighter future day, the
early phrase, "the mantle of respectability" to signify the cloak which
civilization lends to Claggart-like depravity (p. 75; Ch. xi), seems to have
been meticulously worded to light the difference when this moment would
appear. For the transfer of Elijah's mantle to Elisha and the slowly rising
light in the East imply an advance to a day when men will no longer
worship false gods (the baals from whose designation the name Beelzebub
for the devil derives) and will fulfill their latent "God-given" humanity.[10]
This prophecy, with the believable reality upon which Melville will base
it, is the source of the luminescence that, despite the painful events to
come, will irradiate the remainder of the work.

At four in the morning silver whistles summon all hands on deck to
witness punishment. The crew's silence, like Billy's, gives consent. Only at
the moment of his death does Billy's frozen speech become fluid, touching
something deep within the crew. But the greater eloquence is Melville's as
he speaks through the young sailor and through the scene of his execution
(pp. 123–24; Ch. xxv and pp. 125–28; Ch. xxvii). His art makes the
spectacle "admonitory" for the reader, as for the crew, in another sense
entirely from the one Vere intends. Billy stands facing aft.

> At the penultimate moment, his words, his only ones, words wholly
> unobstructed in the utterance, were these: "God bless Captain Vere!"
> Syllables so unanticipated coming from one with the ignominious hemp
> about his neck—a conventional felon's benediction directed aft towards
> the quarters of honor; syllables too delivered in the clear melody of a
> singing bird on the point of launching from the twig—had a phenome-
> nal effect, not unenhanced by the rare personal beauty of the young
> sailor, spiritualized now through late experiences so poignantly pro-
> found.
>   Without volition, as it were, as if indeed the ship's populace were
> but the vehicles of some vocal current electric, with one voice from alow
> and aloft came a resonant sympathetic echo: "God bless Captain Vere!"
> And yet at that instant Billy alone must have been in their hearts, even
> as in their eyes.
>   At the pronounced words and the spontaneous echo that volumi-
> nously rebounded them, Captain Vere, either through stoic self-control
> or a sort of momentary paralysis induced by emotional shock, stood
> erectly rigid as a musket in the ship-armorer's rack.
> (pp. 123–24; Ch. xxv)

Imbued with the meaning and suggesting the shape of the whole book, and appearing at the climax of the narrative development, this moment fuses poetic concepts from earlier works and through their union gives birth to something new.

The poetic concepts that carry over involve both imagery and method. The association of Billy with the singing bird about to launch from the twig, confirming him as a symbol of harmony and as a captive in the world-of-war, has its forerunner in *White-Jacket* when, as the body of Shenly slides into the sea, Jack Chase calls a solitary bird overhead the spirit of the dead man-of-war's man and all the crew gaze upward and watch it sail into the sky (p. 342; Ch. lxxxi). The use of sound and silence to convey the responses of the crew also has its precedent in *White-Jacket*, as has often been remarked, but here the direction is not from sound to silence but from silence to sound. The creation of a memorable, intensely visualizable scene to pictorialize the form and significance of a social institution is also a tested Melville method, most fully developed in *Benito Cereno*. Vividly signified in this scene are the war machine's concentration of power, its sacrifice of what is beautiful and good, and its "abrogation of everything but brute Force." It uncovers the ironies and contradictions of the situation: Vere in whom power is centered suffers the most; his humanity is seen to be totally repressed as he stands "erectly rigid as a musket in the ship-armorer's rack." At the very moment that the humanity in the crew is touched and they react in harmony with Billy, Vere becomes a thing of war whose sole function it is to mete out death, as Ahab at the end is no more than an extension of his weapon. Death-in-life in Vere stands in contrast with Life-in-death in Billy. The benediction, "God bless Captain Vere," gives voice to the feeling shared by Billy and Melville that Vere is the one on the *Bellipotent* most in need of blessing.

The way in which sight and sound are combined in this scene constitutes the new technique Melville's imagination brings forth in this crucial "penultimate moment" on the edge of both death and dawn. What is visual and what is aural join in a strange counterpoint wherein one element is held motionless while the other moves, each working simultaneously both with and against the other, to convey at one and the same moment the seemingly forever fixed picture of the present civilization of the world and movement stirring within it. It is as if in a film the action were to be arrested and the sound continued. The tableau including Billy, the crew, and Vere impresses on the mind a picture that strikingly exhibits the established pattern of the world. It is the picture Vere wishes the admonitory spectacle to impress. But the aural accompaniment flows forward carrying first Billy's benediction and then the sympathetic, swelling echo from the sailors in whose hearts he is. While what the mind's eye sees is frozen and motionless, the moving sound suggests that the frozen structure may thaw. Something in the heart of the crew, long asleep but intact, has been stirred. The tension between sight and sound, between the apparently immutable form and the growth of feeling within, will continue to the point at which the idea that a seed of change is germinating inside the rigid form will take the ascendancy, giving the work its positive tone. The unusual use of sight and sound in this climactic scene seems to grow out of Melville's desire, newly born in the course of the composition of *Billy Budd*, to explore how the seemingly eternal world of war might begin to be transformed to that fluid, life-giving world of peace so suddenly and startlingly pictured — without any gradual transition to it — in the "Epilogue" to *Moby-Dick*.

As the signal for the hanging is given, a . . . cloud of vapor low in the East is "shot through with a soft glory as of the fleece of the Lamb of God seen in mystical vision, and simultaneously therewith, watched by a wedged mass of upturned faces, Billy ascended; and, ascending, took the full rose of the dawn" (p. 124; Ch. xxv), his spirit welcomed back into heaven. The climax of the exemplary spectacle the crew has been forced to witness turns out to be one to inspire, one to move the heart and work as a dynamic in the imagination.

The short chapter culminating in the execution closes: "In the pinioned figure arrived at the yard-end, to the wonder of all no motion was apparent, none save that created by the slow roll of the hull in moderate weather, so majestic in a ship ponderously cannoned" (p. 124; Ch. xxv). The sentence makes "visible an earlier statement concerning the ordinary sailor: "Accustomed to obey orders without debating them," he lives a life "externally ruled for him" (p. 87, Ch. xvi). Billy's "impotence," noted earlier by Vere when the young sailor could not speak up against Claggart, is now realized by the lack of any motion originating within his own body which is externally ruled by the "majestic" motion of His Majesty's Ship *Bellipotent*. His impotence is in sharpest contrast with the omnipotence of the captain who now stands erect as a musket, symbol of civilization's ultimate Force. And yet, the world of war, as *White-Jacket* notes near the end, is "full of strange contradictions" (p. 390; Ch. xci). Billy does have power. Though impotent to save himself, he has power to invoke the future. His death, illuminating the nature of the world represented by the *Bellipotent*, will quicken the imagination of the crew and in that respect be a good death. But Vere, the King's all-powerful representative, is, in a sense, the impotent victim of the ultimate power concentrated in him. While Billy has the miraculous ability to inspire love for a peaceful way of living, to be in that sense a savior, Vere's potency is only for death. Like Lot's wife, as Melville saw her in *White-Jacket*, he stands "crystallized in the act of looking backward, and forever incapable of looking before" (p. 150; Ch. xxxvi). Hence Melville's execution scene is symbolic of both the polarization of power in the world of war and the contradictions at the heart of such a world, contradictions that must eventually bring a metamorphosis. They have already caused a crack in the rigid mold; the silence, the aural equivalent of the frozen form, has been broken. Eventually, music (the ballad) will issue through the fissure in the seemingly unbreakable form.

Moments after the execution the silence is "gradually disturbed by a sound not easily to be verbally rendered." (The italics in the quotations to follow will all be mine except where the emphasis is stated to be Melville's.) The sound is an omen of a growth of feeling in the crew. "Whoever has heard *the freshet-wave of a torrent suddenly swelled* by pouring showers in tropical mountains, showers not shared by the plain; whoever has heard the *first muffled murmur of its sloping advance through precipitous woods* may form some conception of the sound now heard. The seeming remoteness of its source was because of its murmurous indistinctness, since it came from close by, even from the men massed on the ship's open deck" (p. 126; Ch. xxvii). Only seemingly remote, the source is deep within the men. The murmur is indistinct, but there has been some expression, though wordless, of a feeling going back to man's remote origin, and still latent within him. Then, like the "shriek of the sea hawk, the silver whistles of the boatswain and his mates pierced that *ominous low sound*, dissipating it" (p. 126; Ch. xxvii). . . .

But, again, as the closing "formality" consigns Billy's body to the ocean "a *second* strange human murmur" is heard from the sailors as vultures fly screaming to circle the spot (p. 127; Ch. xxvii). To the crew the action of the vultures "though dictated by mere animal greed for prey" is "big with no prosaic significance," a phrase that earlier in the growth of the manuscript had read, "big with imaginative import of bale" (p. 416). Though no elaboration follows, the unprosaic significance seems to involve human, as opposed to "mere animal," greed for prey and hints at an awakening of poetic sensibility to the meaning behind the sacrifice of Billy.

An uncertain movement begins among the men, to be counteracted by a drumbeat to quarters not customary at that hour. Vere intends the ensuing ritual to reinforce a strict pattern of conditioned response: "With mankind," he would say, "forms, measured forms, are everything; and that is the import couched in the story of Orpheus with his lyre spellbinding the wild denizens of the wood" (p. 128; Ch. xxvii). The crew's unresisting participation in the formalities seems to bear out his theory. . . . But while the day which has followed the rosy dawn brings the firm reimposition of the military forms, "the circumambient air in the clearness of its serenity" is "like smooth white marble in the polished block not yet removed from the marble-dealer's yard" (p. 128; Ch. xxvii); the uncut marble of future time contains the possibility of being shaped into something different from the static form visible on the deck of the *Bellipotent*.

This introduction of the idea of a freer, more dynamic form is followed at once by a passage about form which bridges the now completed account of "How it fared with the Handsome Sailor during the year of the Great Mutiny" (p. 128; Ch. xxviii) and the three remaining chapters, "in way of sequel," which will concretize Melville's creative concept of form and its meaning for him, the writer: "The symmetry of form attainable in pure fiction cannot so readily be achieved in a narration essentially having less to do with fable than with fact. Truth uncompromisingly told will always have its ragged edges; hence the conclusion of such a narration is apt to be less finished than an architectural finial" (p. 128; Ch. xxviii). The counterposition of the two statements about form, Vere's and Melville's, accents the fundamental difference between the thinking of the artist and the man of war. To Vere men are beasts to be tamed, "wild denizens of the wood" who must be bound. Brutishness is their sole potentiality. Melville, whose narrative has just revealed the humanity latent in man, evidenced by the crew's intuitive response to Billy, and has shown the men moved (unbound), has had Vere, the military man, speak of Orpheus, the artist, and find in his music only something akin to that "subserving the discipline and purposes of war." While to Vere war is a sacred, fated form and the *Bellipotent* a place of worship whose architecture is complete, to Melville that architecture is neither holy nor final. Vere would bind man's consciousness; Melville would awaken it. The conclusion of *Billy Budd* will be "less finished than an architectural finial" because Melville's art strives to be an equation of life, and life to him has no final form—a main theme in *Moby-Dick*. It may seem immutable, but within its set and apparently eternal form there are grains at work. Vere's ideas are to Melville's as long-settled, measured, closed, and static form is to the fresh, open, living, growing shape into which the work is about to bloom. The realizations of this new shape is a creative act by Melville closely related to his breaking out of the rigid circle of the chase at the end of *Moby-Dick*. The concluding chapters—a "sequel" in the sense of a necessary consequence—burst out of the established pattern of conventional narration and in so doing convey the idea that the rigid form of the world which has been pictured can also be disturbed.

The first of the chapters relates Vere's death (pp. 128–29; Ch. xxviii). Last seen as a musket, he is himself struck by a musket ball. The incident occurs on the return voyage to rejoin the fleet, when the *Bellipotent* encounters the French battleship, the *Athée* (the *Atheist*), "the aptest name, if one consider it, ever given to a warship." . . . Like the dream of the admiral in "The Haglets," Vere's dreams of glory in war, if he had them (and one knows that early in the novel excessive love of glory was described as the first virtue in a military man), are not realized.

But the account of his death reveals that, even in Vere, humanity, though determinedly suppressed, is not dead: "Not long before death, while lying under the influence of that magical drug which, soothing the physical frame, *mysteriously operates on the subtler element in man*, he was heard to murmur words inexplicable to his attendant: 'Billy Budd, Billy Budd' (p. 129). The drug has freed the subconscious part of him from the silence he has imposed upon it, and his murmur unites with the "strange human murmur" of the crew. Surely, the passage implies, the silence of man's suppressed humanity can be breached if the heart of even this most austere monk of war speaks out. "Billy Budd, Billy Budd" is man's unconscious yearning for peace. It may be that the book's subtitle, *An Inside Narrative*, refers to what is occurring inside the heart of man in the critical modern era, continuing into Melville's day, which *Billy Budd* exemplifies.[11]

Vere's "Billy Budd, Billy Budd" is his exit line from the drama, and he will not be heard of again. Who, essentially, has he been? The contradictions carefully worked into his characterization — sometimes interpreted as evidence of carelessness or indecision on Melville's part — have been the source of opposite extremes of opinion among critics, all but a few of whom have been impressed by one side of him to the virtual exclusion of the other. But the contradiction within Vere is his very essence; the split in him is as central to his meaning as is the split in Ahab. He is the symbolic figure — not crudely, but finely and fairly, drawn — of civilized man: learned, but not sufficiently imaginative; not devoid of the ability to love, but not allowing his capacity to develop; sensitive to the difference between the good and evil signified by Billy and Claggart, but the puppet of the god he has been trained to think must rule in this world. His ultimate faith is in Force, not only against the enemy but in dealing with his own side — utilizing impressment, flogging, and hanging — and in dealing violently with his own heart. Exceptional among the officers on the *Bellipotent*, and even among captains, in his rigidity, he is the comprehensive figure of what is dominant in modern civilization. There are over a score of references to, or images of, this rigidity, a quality always so appalling to Melville. The contradiction within him is the contradiction within civilization, between war's values and the primeval and enduring needs of men. In Vere, as in civilization, there exist two potentials — the one symbolized by the devil of war operating through Claggart and the other signified by Billy as the peace-loving angel of God — God and the devil continuing to be, as elsewhere in Melville's writing, poetic concepts signifying human potentialities and values. It is the tragedy of civilized man, as of Vere — tragic in the sense that creative potentialities are wasted — that he has so far continued to uphold the values symbolized by Claggart[12] and to sacrifice those signified by Billy.

As if to underline the idea that the dream of glory in war is doomed, Vere's name is not mentioned in the "authorized" naval account of the *Bellipotent* events quoted in the chapter immediately following his death.[13] The report is Melville's final illustration of how good and evil are interchanged in the world of war and of how "authorized" history may pervert the truth or use it for its own purposes. . . .

With no reason to worship Mars, though they are forced to take part in war's rites, with no illusion that war can satisfy for them "the most secret of all passions, ambition," the crew, inspired by Billy and groping toward some understanding of the mystery surrounding his hanging, has had engraved in its memory the execution scene that Melville has impressed upon the reader's. From ship to ship their "knowledges" follow the spar from which Billy was hanged. "To them a chip of it was as a piece of the Cross." And on the gun decks of the *Bellipotent* their "general estimate of his nature . . . eventually found rude utterance from another foretopman, one of his own watch, gifted, as some sailors are, with an artless *poetic* temperament." (This emphasis, central to the all-embracing meaning of the work, is Melville's.) "The tarry hand made some lines which, after circulating among the shipboard crews for a while, finally got rudely printed at Portsmouth as a ballad. The title given to it was the sailor's." So the inarticulate crew has found its voice. Feelings which had been only a murmur have "found utterance" not only in words but in poetry, however rude. The sailor-poet speaks for the men, unlike the songwriter Dibdin described early in the book as "no mean auxiliary to the English government" (p. 55; Ch. iii). The sailor's lines are "finally" printed, as the feelings of the crew are "eventually" worded; a slow process is under way. And the ballad, "Billy in the Darbies," goes on to have a life of its own. In this way is Billy resurrected.

"Billy in the Darbies" (p. 132; Ch. xxx), with which the book ends, is not the ballad as Melville originally conceived of it, the one that had given rise to the narration which was at first intended only to provide necessary background in an explanatory headnote. Early in the development of the work an organic interaction between the poem and the prose came into being, and as the narrative's implications grew, changes took place in the ballad as well and in its role in the book. . . . As it now stands, so integrated are the ballad and the rest of the book that the awakening feeling of the crew, as voiced by the sailor-poet, and Melville's own growing sense of the possibilities implicit in the internal contradictions of the world of war burst simultaneously into flower in the ballad.

In its last stage and final context "Billy in the Darbies" is extraordinarily subtle and complex. Yet Melville is utterly honest with the reader when he calls the gift of the sailor-poet an artless one. For it is Melville's art — as he speaks indirectly through the sailor's artlessness — that is sophisticated in the extreme. To read the ballad as the sailor's creation is prerequisite to appreciating it as Melville's.

The sailor identifies with Billy on the eve of his execution. Like Billy, he feels that the chaplain is good to pray for someone lowly like him. He sees the moonlight; he experiences Billy's fear, his hunger for companionship and food, the pressure of the handcuffs. He intends no symbolism, no irony, no complicated double meanings, only a few childlike puns. Yet, there is the beginning of questioning: "But aren't it all sham?" There is a dawning of consciousness of the grim sacrifice war exacts and men accede to: "But — no! It is dead then I'll be, *come to think*." He sees a correspondence between Billy and another sailor whose cheek as he sank was also roseate, and feels the tie that unites them all. He has a growing sense of being constricted; the oozy weeds twist about his body and hold him, too, down. He has glimpsed the reality which *White-Jacket* says "forever slides along far under the surface" of the sea on which the man-of-war sails (p. 399; "The End").

Melville's imagination works through the sailor's; his voice sounds in the overtones with which the narrative has endowed the sailor's simple words. The sailor's descriptive title is Melville's symbolic one: Billy Budd, sailor, lies in the darbies of war, from which he and all other sailors need to be released. He is a pearl of great beauty about to be jettisoned by the man-of-war world and "all adrift to go" like the drifted treasure in "The Haglets."

. . . Suggestive plays upon words, as Melville speaks through the language of the sailor, develop main themes of the prose. The "dawning of Billy's last day" will bring also the dawn of consciousness to the crew. "Heaven knows," indeed, who is responsible for the running of Billy up. The sailor's wondering query, "But aren't it all sham?" is Melville's implied question to the reader: "Isn't it all—the whole religion practiced in the *Bellipotent* 'cathedral'—a grotesque perversion of the religion whose music and rites it exploits but whose God in effect it denies?" A "blur" has been in man's eyes, his vision obscured by war and false songs and stories of war. He has been a child "dreaming."

. . . By making the ballad the work of a sailor-poet speaking for the crew whose dormant spirit of harmony Billy has awakened, Melville suggests a coming transfiguration of men and the world. While Billy's body lies bound by the weeds fathoms down, pictorializing the subterranean reality of war as *White-Jacket* pictures it (p. 294; Ch. lxx), as well as the good submerged in man but still capable of resurrection, his memory prompts in the imagination of the crew a subconscious quest for the meaning of his death, an inquiry that may some day ascend to full consciousness. In contrast to Vere who at the trial had spoken of the "mystery of iniquity" but had turned away from probing it, disclaiming moral responsibility, Melville is engaged in fathoming both the mystery of iniquity in the world and the mysterious potency of good. Since good can inspire mankind, even after the death of one epitomizing it, the ballad about Billy's physical end is not an architectural finial, either of the book or of the world it portrays.

The hanging of Billy has been translated into art (by both the sailor-poet and Melville) which in its interaction with life may give rise to a conscious desire by man to change his mode of existence. The *Bellipotent* form is not an inescapable part of the human condition but the result of the failure so far of man's heart and imagination to attempt to understand its mystery and to seek out the transforming possibility within it. Melville's imagination, as it makes itself known in all his works, even the most bitter, does not see civilization's forms as static, complete, devoid of all potentiality for "promoted life."[14] It is incapable of "that unfeeling acceptance of destiny which is promulgated in the name of service or tradition."[15]

So Melville in *Billy Budd* has shown the world-of-war, which "fallen" man created and then worshipped, in all its contradictions and potentiality, and his final emphasis has been on the creative in man and on the power of language and art to explore new values and inspire a fresh conception of life. He has written not of original sin but of original good and its continued, though sleeping, existence in man, while evil — outstandingly exemplified in war — has been shown as a depravity in man, a fall from his inborn creative potentiality. As far back as the second chapter Melville had introduced this theme, but its deeper meaning for the work had not then been clear (pp. 52–53; Ch. ii). . . . What we have seen in Vere is that his human nature has been so tampered with that he believes he is "not authorized" to determine matters on the "primitive basis" of "essential right and wrong" (p. 103; Ch. xxi) and that he must fight against his most natural emotions, his "primitive instincts strong as the wind and the sea" (p. 109; Ch. xxi). On the other hand, primitive good, as symbolized by Billy, has been seen to be too childlike to be able to survive in the present civilization of the world. To transform the institutions of civilization so that good and beauty can thrive in an environment of peace, the members of the crew of man have to develop the desire to probe civilization's nature and articulate their needs and dreams. They must, in terms of the imagery relating to "Baby" Budd, attain manhood. *Billy Budd* implies that this may yet be.

Thus, in this narrative of man's silence transmuted into poetry Melville uses his art to try to break the spell holding human beings captive in the marble "form" of war, to break the tyranny of the "religion" of war over the minds and acts of potentially creative man. His illumination that a transformation of mankind and of the world is conceivable — may even already be germinating in man's imagination — is the source of the radiance that suffuses the work from Billy's "God bless Captain Vere" on. *Billy Budd* is Melville's most searching exploration of war, reaching back to the beginning of man and his fall into "Cain's city" and forward to a possible recreation of the world by humanity awakened.

Notes

1. Herman Melville, *Billy Budd, Sailor (An Inside Narrative)*, reading and genetic texts edited from the manuscript with introduction and notes by Harrison Hayford and Merton M. Sealts, Jr. (Chicago: Univ. of Chicago Press, 1962). All references to *Billy Budd* will be to this edition; chapter numbers do not correspond in every instance to those in other editions.

2. *Omoo* (Evanston: Northwestern Univ. Press and The Newberry Library, 1968), p. 108, n. (Ch. xxix).

3. *White-Jacket* (Evanston: Northwestern Univ. Press and The Newberry Library, 1970), p. 293 (Ch. lxx).

4. The abbreviation of this name to the *Rights* suggests that Melville had in mind not only those things to which men are entitled but also those things which are morally right, the rights which will be out of place in the environment to which Billy is to be transplanted. See Vere's discussion of their irrelevance, p. 110 (Ch. xxi).

5. *Collected Poems of Herman Melville*, ed. Howard P. Vincent (Chicago: Hendricks, 1947), p. 165. To be referred to in parentheses in the text as *CP*.

6. *Selected Poems of Herman Melville*, ed. Robert Penn Warren (New York: Random, 1970), p. 109.

7. *White-Jacket* had found both flogging and impressment to be against God. When a captain flogs a man, he is flogging the "image of his Creator" (p. 142, Ch. xxxiv), and impressment is "an iniquity outrageous and insulting to God and man" (p. 381, n; Ch. xc).

8. *Clarel* (New York: Hendricks, 1960), p. 427 (Pt. iv, Canto vii).

9. The fact that the passage is in the present tense strengthens the impression of this scene as a picture symbolic of what exists in the world, not just a picture of what Billy looked like at that particular past moment.

10. For a discussion of Elijah's role in the Old Testament and the New Testament as the eschatological forerunner of the coming Day of the Lord, see entry, "Elijah the Prophet," in *The Interpreter's Dictionary of the Bible* (Nashville, Tenn.: Abingdon, 1962), 2:88–90.

11. Because of the valid comments of many (including speakers at recent MLA Conventions) who are concerned with women's liberation from the chains of language, I feel impelled to explain that I use the words *man* and *mankind* rather than *humanity* as a rule in this article because they accord with Melville's imagery in *Billy Budd* and because I employ the word *humanity* for the most part in connection with what is human as distinguished from what is mechanical or merely animal in human beings' responses.

12. Despite their differences and the fact that Claggart is naturally distasteful to Vere, Melville subtly links them so that Claggart's warmaking can be seen as one side of present-day civilized man, the side to which he veers; the word *austere* is repeatedly used in relation to both, and only to them, and civilization, "especially if of the austerer sort," which Vere represents, is "auspicious" to Claggart-like depravity; both are "discreet"; secrecy is a way both pursue; neither is sociable. Like Vere, Claggart is "zealous in his function" (p. 79, Ch. xiii). Vere's final appeal to fear reminds the court of the dangers of mutiny, the very appeal Claggart had made to him. Claggart's wish for Billy's death is ultimately carried out by Vere. Claggart acts against good; Vere rules out moral considerations. Both know Billy to be innocent yet condemn him; as the devil operates through Claggart, so Mars operates through Vere.

13. Melville had at first made a pencil notation at this point in the book to speak, in the authorized report, of the death of Captain Vere, but he *canceled the notation* (pp. 269, 420).

14. *Selected Poems of Herman Melville*, ed. Cohen, p. 53.

15. Wilson Harris, *Tradition, the Writer and Society* (London: New Beacon, 1967), p. 26.

Billy Budd and the Context of Political Rule

James R. Hurtgen*

I

This essay argues that *Billy Budd* is best understood as Melville's statement on the nature of politics and its location amidst the polarities of the demonic and the divine realms. The novel depicts the political order as bereft of natural or divine support. This means that Melville adopts the position of many modern political philosophers, beginning with Machiavelli, who teach that civil society is merely conventional; that man is, in essence, asocial. Hobbes argued in *Leviathan:* "For by Art is created that great Leviathan called a commonwealth, or State, . . . which is but an artificial Man; though of greater stature and strength than the Natural, for whose protection and defence it was intended; and in which the Sovereignty is an artificial soul. . . ."[1]

However, though Melville endorses the modern view of politics stemming from Machiavelli, he refrains from doing so openly. He is compelled to keep a form of silence lest the awareness of its radically conventional basis undermine the continued existence of the political order.[2] I believe that it was Melville's position that the unambiguous treatment of the conventional basis of politics seemed to him, to paraphrase Vere, "insusceptible of embodiment in lasting institutions, but at war with the peace of the world and the true welfare of mankind."[3] Thus Melville's obscurity, his use of a *rhetoric of concealment*, stems from a need to keep silent.

It is the argument of this study that Melville's intention in *Billy Budd* is deliberately obscure. This is not the view that informed the early criticism of the work. Initial studies focused on the element of tragedy in the novel by emphasizing the destruction of innocence in this man-of-war world. Many critics were persuaded that the novel expressed Melville's anguished acceptance of Vere's position, namely, that the law must be served, however harsh and pitiless it may seem.[4] Beginning in the late 1940s, this interpretation came under attack by a number of critics who concluded that Melville was *not* reconciled to the need for Budd's death, that the novel is in fact his final *testament of resistance* to an unjust world. Later critics interpreted the hanging of Budd as a tragedy precisely because it was avoidable and unnecessary, not the contrary, as the initial literature held.[5]

How could such opposed interpretations arise? Let me offer a few

*From *The Artist and Political Vision*, ed. Benjamin R. Barber and Michael J. Gargas McGrath (New Brunswick, N.J.: Transaction Books, 1982), 245–65. © 1982 Transaction, Inc. Reprinted by permission of the publisher. This present version was edited by the author.

observations to suggest the difficulties in determining Melville's intention. First, the narrator is silent or elliptical at key points. In the scene immediately following the confrontation between Budd and Claggart, the ship's surgeon is called in by Vere to verify the master-at-arms's death (*BB*, pp. 100–101). At this point the captain is described by the narrator as agitated and excited. We see Vere "convulsively grabbing the surgeon's arm while exclaiming, 'It is the divine judgment on Ananias! Look!' " (*BB*, p. 100). Shortly thereafter the narrator remarks that the surgeon was "profoundly discomposed" by Vere's "passionate interjections." Later we learn that Vere's decision to hold a secret drumhead court to decide Budd's fate is also greatly disturbing to the surgeon. It is his view that Budd should be confined until the ship can be reunited with the squadron, at which juncture the admiral could determine the outcome. So unusual does the surgeon consider Vere's decision and manner that he fears that the Captain may have been "temporarily unhinged" by the occurrence in his stateroom (*BB*, p. 102). In concluding the point, the narrator then tells us he will not judge between the captain and the surgeon; we must judge for ourselves "by such light as the narrative may afford" whether or not Vere was temporarily unhinged by Budd's action. The problem is that the narrative provides light to draw either conclusion depending upon the reader's prior disposition to accept or reject the need for Budd's trial and subsequent hanging.

There is another occasion on which the narrator leaves the reader ambivalent about events aboard the *Bellipotent*. During the trial scene Budd's act is compared in part to a mutiny aboard the American vessel *Somers* in 1842, which resulted in the hanging of three sailors. The mutiny and executions aboard the *Somers* immediately created a stir in the American press. The affair was revived in the press in the early 1880s, not long before Melville started *Billy Budd*. Again, note the narrator's obliquity in his comment on the events. The executions were "carried out though in time of peace and within not many days' sail of home. An act vindicated by a naval court of inquiry subsequently convened ashore. *History, and here cited without comment.* True, the circumstances on board the *Somers* were different from those on board the *Bellipotent*. But the urgency felt, *well-warranted or otherwise,* was much the same" (*BB*, 114; my italics).

However, the narrator's ambiguity is not uniform. He expresses himself unequivocally on the significance of the Great Mutiny in the British navy: "It was indeed a demonstration more menacing to England than the contemporary manifestoes and conquering and proselytizing armies of the French Directory" (*BB*, p. 54). And a bit later: "Reasonable discontent growing out of practical grievances in the fleet had been ignited into irrational combustion as by live cinders blown across the Channel from France in flames" (*BB*, p. 114).

A second source of difficulty in determining Melville's intention centers upon the ambiguities surrounding the characterization of Vere. To begin with, Vere's name is a source of ambiguity. "Vere" is related to *veritas*, truth, or *vir*, meaning man; also vereor, a verb meaning to be afraid of. His acquired name "Starry" can mean lofty, theoretic, comprehensive, high-principled; or abstract, remote, unfeeling, cold, undiscriminating. About his bearing as an officer, Melville says that "he had seen much service, been in various engagements, always acquitting himself as an officer mindful of the welfare of his men, but never tolerating an infraction of discipline; thoroughly versed in the science of his profession, and intrepid to the verge of temerity, though never injudiciously so" (*BB*, p. 60). It is impossible to say precisely what Melville means by this description. Do the qualifiers diminish Vere's attributes, or signify a judicious balance of opposed responsibilities in an officer? Both views have been defended.

Vere is said to lack brilliant qualities but shortly after is called an "exceptional character" (*BB*, p. 62). He is a reader of books, but only Montaigne is named: "With nothing of that literary taste which less heeds the thing conveyed than the vehicle, his bias was toward those books to which every serious mind of superior order occupying any active post of authority in the world naturally inclines" (*BB*, p. 62). And what kinds of books are these? "Books, treating of actual men and events no matter of what era — history, biography and unconventional writers like Montaigne . . ." (*BB*, p. 62). Because fiction does not usually treat "actual men and events," it is presumably not part of Vere's reading. Moreover, Vere apparently ignored technique, "which less heeds the thing conveyed than the vehicle," but a full understanding of the novel of which Vere is a part requires precisely an understanding of rhetorical structure. The ironic implication is that Vere would have no interest in the story in which he played a foremost role.

Lastly, the narrator remarks that, despite the philosophical austerity of his spirit, Vere "may yet have indulged in the most secret of all passions, ambition, [but] never attained to the fulness of fame" (*BB*, p. 129).

These observations will serve to illustrate the difficulties in arriving at Melville's intention in the novel. Who speaks for Melville — the narrator? Vere? The surgeon? Unless we are prepared to argue that these difficulties indicate Melville's failure to make up his own mind about his story, we must assume that his ambiguities are part of his intention. We are not free to heed less the *vehicle* than the *thing conveyed* if we mean to understand *Billy Budd*.

II

Melville frequently used what we may call a rhetoric of concealment in his works.[6] His meanings are found beneath the surface narration and often hidden by it. This is the lesson in his review-essay of Hawthorne's collection of short stories, *Mosses from an Old Manse*. The review-essay was written anonymously for the *Literary World* in 1850. The work is important for the insight it offers on how Melville intended his readers to approach his own writings. Near the end of the essay is this important statement: "No man can read a fine author . . . without subsequently fancying to himself some ideal image of the man and his mind. And if you rightly look for it, you will almost always find that the author himself has somewhere furnished you with his own picture."[7]

A close study of the essay reveals that Melville has indeed furnished the reader with a picture of himself as well as of Hawthorne. "It is curious," Melville remarks, "how a man may travel along a country road, and yet miss the grandest, or sweetest of prospects, by reason of an intervening hedge, so like all other hedges, as in no way to hint of the wider landscape beyond. So it has been with me concerning the enchanting landscape in the soul of this Hawthorne, this most excellent man of Mosses" ("Hawthorne and His Mosses," p. 536).

That Melville connects this hidden landscape with the idea of enchantment suggests that there is a dark and menacing side to Hawthorne's thought, which he alludes to later in the essay: ". . . spite of all the Indian-summer sunlight on the hither side of Hawthorne's soul, the other side — like the dark half of the physical sphere — is shrouded in blackness, ten times black" ("Hawthorne and His Mosses," p. 540).

Still later in the essay Hawthorne is compared to Shakespeare. According to Melville, the latter played his "grandest conceits" against an infinitely obscure background. Through the mouths of Hamlet, Timon, Lear, and Iago — his "dark characters" — Shakespeare insinuates truths "that it were all but madness for any good man, *in his own proper person*, to utter, or even hint of them" ("Hawthorne and His Mosses," p. 542, italics added). Shakespeare, like the other masters of "The Great Art of Telling the Truth," was compelled to disclose his meanings "covertly and by snatches."

A number of insights emerge from a study of Melville's review-essay. First, the opening section of the work may itself be viewed as an intervening hedge, which, by its lighthearted tone, partially conceals the meaning of the remainder of the essay. In this respect Melville's method as a reviewer imitates the method he ascribes to Hawthorne as a writer. Second, Melville endorses Hawthorne's unwillingness to disclose openly the basis of his gloomy prospect on life by not disclosing it himself. He suggests that he agrees with Hawthorne's secret by refusing to tell it. This inference is strengthened by an examination of Melville's letters to Hawthorne during this period. In one of them Melville praises Hawthorne as "the man who, like Russia or the British Empire, declares himself a sovereign nature (in himself) amid the powers of heaven, hell and earth. He may perish; but so long as he exists he insists upon treating with all Powers upon an equal basis. If any of those other Powers choose to withhold certain secrets, let them; that does not impair [his] sovereignty" (reprinted in *Moby-Dick*, p. 555). Here is a theme that is crucial to Melville's intention in *Billy Budd*: the powers of heaven, hell, and earth stand opposed to the sovereignty of man. Third, by writing anonymously Melville throws up a hedge to prevent easy identification of these observations with his own works.

Like Hawthorne's his meanings are "hedged"; like Hawthorne's and Shakespeare's, they are revealed covertly and by snatches; like them, he does not speak "in his own proper person." If one's view of the writer's tasks requires concealment, what better way to explain it, while maintaining the concealment, than by attributing the same view to another and imitating the very tactics described?

Consider a statement from chapter 3 of *Billy Budd* to see how this perspective on the review-essay applies. In the chapter the narrator points out the significance of the Great Mutiny for the British navy. He states that concern for national pride and policy induced certain British historians to abridge their accounts of the Mutiny. Then follows this statement by the narrator: "Such events [like the Mutiny] cannot be ignored, but there is *a considerate way* of historically treating them. If a well-constituted individual refrains from blazoning aught amiss or calamitous in his family, a nation in the like circumstances may without reproach be equally discreet" (*BB*, p. 55). It is not clear why this comment is made. It does not further our understanding of the mutiny or conditions in the British navy in 1797. It makes no comment on a political event proper, but on the historical treatment of a political event. Herein lies its importance. It is relevant to the story, it seems to me, only as it suggests to the alert reader that Melville himself may be employing a *considerate way* of treating deeply disturbing events in political life. Plainly told, the story of Billy Budd *as seen from the inside* is profoundly disturbing to the foundations of free political orders. However, Melville's story is *not* plainly told. He gives us an inside narrative, as he promises; the meaning of the work is truly inside the narrative and concealed by it. *Billy Budd* contains the author's view of political life but does not disclose it. This we must do for ourselves.

We have now prepared the ground for our examination of the novel. The remainder of this essay will center on the meaning of *Billy Budd*, beginning with a look at the three principal characters.

III

The singular feature of Billy Budd is his innocence, which leaves him unable to understand and defend himself against evil. We are told that his virtues are "pristine and unadulterate," deriving from a time "prior to Cain's city and citified man" (*BB*, p. 53). His virtues are natural in the sense that they are neither acquired from nor dependent upon the city or social life. In this sense they are prepolitical.

However, it is insufficient to attribute Budd's being to presocial nature. Rather, his particular being is attributable to Nature's God. At one point he is compared to Adam before the Fall, an implication of God's hand. At another Budd is asked details of his birthplace and paternity, but can give no answer: "God knows, Sir!" (*BB*, p. 51). Later, following Budd's killing blow to Claggart, Vere realizes the full import of the event: "Struck dead by an angel of God! Yet the angel must hang!" (*BB*, p. 101).

Emblematic of the foretopman's innocence is a stutter he suffers "under sudden provocation of strong heart-feeling." If we compare the three occasions on which Budd stutters, it is clear that on each he is confronted with an evil he cannot understand but knows he must somehow address. The situations he cannot deal with except by recourse to physical defense are those that the law and political authority are established to mediate. From this we may fairly infer that his vocal defect is a consequence of his inability to make his way among men for whom political responsibilities have replaced natural impulse. Budd is a prepolitical character lost among political men.

Three further points emerge from this discussion. First, Budd has no capacity for political behavior because he cannot grasp by reason or experience the conventional basis of order aboard the *Bellipotent*. The ship is run by rules, whereas Budd is moved by his feelings. Budd's drubbing of Red Whiskers aboard the *Rights-of-Man* foretells that the sailor's feelings and the actions that follow from them will run afoul of the ship's rules. Second, the sailor's lack of awareness makes him defenseless. With no sense of evil in himself, Budd lacks the means for understanding it in others. Moreover, his innocence serves to provoke those in whom evil is more than usually concentrated. Third, because innocence is oblivious to evil, as Budd is oblivious to the wellsprings of Claggart's behavior, it is unwittingly made to serve its ends, as we note in Budd's failure to report the supposed mutiny he is invited to join in chapter 14. In the strict application of the Mutiny Act, Budd's failure to report what he supposes to be a conspiracy is interpreted as complicity in it.

Several matters stand out in the assessment of Claggart's role and character. Charged with hatred for Budd, Claggart nonetheless folds himself in the "mantle of respectability" (*BB*, p. 75). His malady does not partake of the sordid or sensual. He shows every appearance of rectitude. He is never mercenary, never avaricious. He is without "vices or small sins." "Toward the accomplishment of an aim which in wantonness of atrocity would seem to partake of the insane, he will direct a cool judgment sagacious and sound. These men are madmen, and of the most dangerous sort, for their lunacy is not continuous, but occasional, evoked by some special object; it is protectively secret, which is as much as to say it is self-contained, so that when, moreover, most active it is to the average mind not distinguishable from sanity" (*BB*, p. 76). As Budd's innocence is obvious, so Claggart's evil is hidden, and for this reason enjoys a kind of imperviousness to law. For the adequate comprehending of the man, ordinary experience of this world is not sufficient. Recalling a discussion held long ago with an "honest scholar," the narrator says: "I am not certain whether to know the world and to know human nature be not two distinct branches of knowledge. . . . Nay, in an average man of the world, his constant rubbing with it blunts that finer *spiritual insight* indispensable to the understanding of the essential in certain exceptional characters, whether good or evil. . . . Coke and Blackstone hardly shed so much light into obscure spiritual places as the Hebrew prophets. And who were they? Mostly recluses" (*BB*, p. 75; my italics).

We are instructed to look elsewhere than the words of Coke and Blackstone, works of legal and political theorists, to gain insight into exceptional characters like Claggart's and Budd's. We are instructed to look at the bible.

As the chronicle of God's covenant with His chosen people, the Bible is the account of God's intervention in secular history. Is there divine intervention in *Billy Budd?* I have earlier suggested this in attributing Budd's innocence to the hand of God. Claggart's part is also given by God: "With no power to annul the elemental evil in him, though readily enough he could hide it; apprehending the good, but powerless to be it; a nature like Claggart's, surcharged with energy as such natures almost invariably are, what recourse is left to it but to recoil upon itself and, *like the scorpion for which the Creator alone is responsible*, act out to the end the part allotted it" (*BB*, p. 78; my italics).

Great difficulties have arisen over Melville's intention respecting Vere. Many ambiguities surround his role and character. Can we with any confidence establish Melville's intention amidst these ambiguities? I think we can, though it must be admitted that the following interpretation cannot resolve all our questions.

It will be helpful to consider two aspects of Vere's role. First, it is by reliance upon the Mutiny Act, a legal convention, that Vere decides to execute Budd. It is by reliance upon a literary convention that we might better determine Melville's intention regarding Vere. The description of Vere in the novel falls between those of Budd and Claggart. Budd is treated in chapters 2 and 3, Claggart in 8 through 13, and Vere in 6 and 7. Budd and Claggart are so opposed in their natures that they are safe only if separated. Melville implies the same by interposing the description of Vere between the description of the other two. It is only when Vere physically steps aside during the accusation scene that Budd and Claggart are made to confront one another. Had Vere stood between them, the blow from Budd almost surely would not have come. The captain's physical presence, his interposition, becomes a correlate of his political role; his movement away from the two signals the removal of political authority from the confrontation. Political authority, represented in Vere, is given the role of *standing between* innocence and depravity—not to modify them, for this is beyond human agency—but to interpose itself between the two in order to forestall the deadly consequences of their contact.

There is another way in which Melville attributes to political authority the role of standing between. The triad of Budd-Vere-Claggart is most important in the story, but Vere is part of a second triad. Graveling (the captain of the *Rights-of-Man*), Admiral Nelson (whom Melville compares to Vere in chapters 4 and 5), and Vere are each sea captains and each political officers. What kind of rule does each represent? Graveling may be said to represent the rule of the *benevolent father*. There is little or no need for coercive rule aboard the *Rights*. The disorders aboard his ship are trivial and untroubling.

Nelson embodies the rule of the *hero*. He is called by the narrator a "poetic reproach" to the "martial utilitarians" who suggest that the "ornate publication of his person in battle was not only unnecessary, but not military, nay, savored of foolhardiness and vanity" (*BB*, p. 57). The narrator takes the opportunity to criticize the "Benthamites of war" for failing to observe that Nelson's bravado was in fact calculated to move his men to the accomplishment of the great deeds for which they and he have since been immortalized. While a rear admiral, Nelson was commanded to shift his pennant from the *Captain* to the *Theseus*, a ship that had participated in the Great Mutiny, and that the admiralty feared might incite new disturbances: ". . . Danger was apprehended from the temper of the men; and it was thought that an officer like Nelson was the one, not indeed to terrorize the crew into base subjection, but to win them, by force of his mere presence and heroic personality, back to an allegiance if not as enthusiastic as his own yet as true" (*BB*, p. 59).

In these few words Melville provides an account of the nature and function of heroism. The authority of the hero resides in his person rather than his position. This point highlights both the strength and the weakness of the hero. The narrator suggests early in the account of Nelson's death that a country needs heroes, who must of necessity be great men, and who must, when the occasion calls, be sacrificed. Why? Because under conditions of dire threat to the country, that is, during war, heroism helps to forge a disinterested attachment of the citizen-soldier to his country's well-being above his own.

However, although heroism may be indispensable in situations of dire threat, by its nature it is limited to the extraordinary in political life. Because the individual is not inclined by nature to sacrifice self-preservation to the preservation of the whole, the hero must by his own example provide the incentive for the soldier to overcome his passionate interest in life. One incentive, which Melville intimates by quoting Tennyson's praise of Nelson as "the greatest sailor since our world began," is the promise of immortality. One's life is offered on the condition that one's name be immortalized.

But where the prospect of immortality is missing, the hero is out of place. This means that the hero cannot be a ruler in the ordinary sense of the word, because there is no place for heroism in the ordinary affairs of men. In such a situation, allegiance must reside in position — law and contractual authority — not person.

Vere represents the third variety of rule. His falls between the prepolitical rule of the *benevolent father* and the transpolitical rule of the *hero*, and is appropriately described as the *rule of law*, the rule of human authority resting upon what Vere calls "measured forms" (*BB*, p. 128). Because the rule of law seeks to capture a wide range of possibilities in language general enough to contain them all, its "measured forms" inevitably encounter the uncovered instance, the event that cannot be fairly treated by the language or spirit of the law. The rule of law, then, has the disadvantage of being at times insensitive and even pitiless. But it has the advantage of permanence. Unlike heroism, laws are not dependent upon exceptional men for their application. During the battle between the *Bellipotent* and the French ship *Athée*, Vere is badly wounded. Under the senior lieutenant the *Bellipotent* eventually defeats the *Athée*. However able Vere is, command may be passed to a subordinate without grievous consequences. Unlike the hero, those who rule according to law may come and go without impairment to society as a whole. Just as politics occupies a middle ground between depravity and innocence, Vere occupies an ambiguous moral ground between benevolence and heroism.

IV

Billy Budd is a novel that mixes the divine, the demonic, and the human. An adequate explication of this mixture brings us to the trial scene in the novel. Budd's trial poignantly indicates Melville's conception of the gulf between God's will and man's, though the gulf is not stated openly. At his trial Budd is asked three questions: Why did Claggart bear such malice for him? Was he aware of any incipient trouble aboard ship? Why should Claggart lie if there was no malice between them? Let us focus on the first and third questions.

To the first, Budd answers that he cannot explain Claggart's malice. Budd then interjects: "I had to say something, and I could only say it with a blow, God help me!" (*BB*, p. 106). *God help me;* why does Melville give these last words to Budd? Consider the very suggestive coincidence implied in Budd's plea, *God help me.* In chapter 2 the narrator describes the foretopman as lacking "any trace of the wisdom of the serpent, nor yet quite a dove. . . ." The point contains Christ's injunction to the apostles in Matthew 10: to be innocent as doves but wary as serpents. But further: "you will be brought before governors and Kings on my account, so that you can bear witness before them, and before the Gentiles. *Only, when they hand you over thus, do not consider anxiously what you are to say or how you are to say it; words will be given you when the time comes; it is not you who speak, it is the Spirit of your Father"* (Matt. 10:16-20; my italics).

The Spirit of the Father has indeed spoken through Budd with the killing blow to Claggart's forehead. Budd's invocation of God's help is more than rhetorical. He has in fact already been given the help he seeks — he kills his assailant — but not help that will save him.

Turning to the third question: why should Claggart lie if there was no malice between them? "At that question, unintentionally touching on a *spiritual sphere* wholly obscure to Billy's thoughts, he was nonplussed" (*BB*, p. 107; my italics). Vere then intervenes to narrow the inquiry to two points: did Budd strike a superior officer, and did the blow kill? Disturbed by this narrowing of the inquiry, the captain of marines asks if there is anyone "who might shed lateral light . . . upon what remains mysterious in this matter" (*BB*, p. 108). Instead of replying to the suggestion for secondary witnesses, Vere underscores the mysteriousness of the event by calling it a "mystery of iniquity, a matter for psychologic theologians to discuss" (*BB*, p. 108).

Vere's characterization of the affair as a "mystery of iniquity" can have no clear meaning to the judges. What is mysterious to them is simply unknown, not unknowable. The illumination the judges seek has nothing to do with witnesses. Witnesses could not answer their questions. However, Vere's response is not meant for the judges; it is meant for the reader.

The phrase "mystery of iniquity" is taken from Paul's Second Epistle to the Thessalonians in which he warns against the appearance of false prophets: "Let no man deceive you by any means: for that day shall not come, except there come a falling away first, and that man of sin be revealed, the son of perdition; . . . Remember ye not, that, when I was yet with you, I told you these things? And now ye know what withholdeth that he might be revealed in his time. For the mystery of iniquity doth already work" (2 Thessalonians 2: 3-7). Paul's false prophets are not specified, but we can specify a false prophet in Melville's story: Billy Budd himself, the Angel of the Lord, the man whose very innocence provokes evil, the man who poses a threat to the well-being of the *Bellipotent* and the world it defends. Of course he intends no threat. Quite the opposite. But he is a threat nonetheless. His hold upon the compassion of the judges is compelling. But the compassion must be overruled, because at bottom Budd's nature, no less than Claggart's, is impervious to the law and to human reason. The foretopman emerges not only as a prepolitical figure, but also as an antipolitical one who must ultimately contravene the law. Politics is possible only if events can be formalized into regularities of custom and law. To the extent that these regularities are missing or impossible, political life is endangered. In the end, innocence beyond the formalizations of custom and law is as disruptive to society as the profound depravity that "folds itself in the mantle of respectability."

Vere asks rhetorically in his comments to the judges, should not natural justice mitigate the crime? Budd intended no injury to Claggart. These words follow: "It is nature. But do these buttons that we wear attest that our allegiance is to nature? No, to the King. Though the ocean, which is inviolate Nature primeval, *though this be the element where we move and have our being as sailors,* yet as the King's officers lies our duty in a sphere correspondingly natural? So little is that true, that in receiving our commissions we in the most important regards ceased to be natural free agents" (*BB,* p. 110; my italics). In Acts 17, the apostle Paul addresses the Athenians on Mars Hill: "In Him we live, and move, and have our being." And Vere's message? It is not the Divinity but the Secular Prince in whom man moves and has his being. Combining this inference with other hints in the novel, the suggestion is strong that the human order is not only separate from the divine and the demonic, but *opposed* to the divine *no less* than to the demonic. Each emanates from the same source, God Himself. In this view, Budd and Claggart, though mortally opposed in themselves, together comprise the double face of God.

V

Why does Melville conceal his full meaning inside the narrative of *Billy Budd?* The answer to this question brings us to the heart of his perspective on politics. Melville's story is controlled by an intention to speak protectively of the city. Proof of this concern is evident, for example, in his civil war poetry, as well as in the several criticisms in *Billy Budd* itself of the disintegrating effects of the French Revolution. But the need to speak protectively of the city does not require concealment unless openness threatens its well-being. And it is just because the city is founded upon opposition to the demonic and the divine that its well-being is always so tenuous.

What then is the truth about politics that Melville tells covertly and by snatches? His teaching is this: Budd and Claggart, who are the double face of God, threaten the sovereignty of man over his own affairs. They threaten to dissolve the always precarious order we are able to achieve by the rule of law, measured forms. This is so because neither profound evil nor profound innocence can be adequately explained or controlled. Claggart is not only able to use the law to further his own ends, he even advances to the position of chief of police aboard the *Bellipotent.* On the other hand, Budd on several occasions is unable to accommodate his actions to the requirements of naval law and etiquette.[8]

If God comprises both the dove and the serpent, it is vain to expect his patronage. The lesson of *Billy Budd* would seem to be that God has no settled disposition toward mankind. And here lies the necessity for concealment. The dependence upon God's solicitude is the very basis of political order. Without it, the city is unmoored, free to sail in whatever direction force and cunning will carry it. Without this dependence upon

God's care, political moderation is gone. Nor can reason restore it, for Melville was thoroughly antirationalist: *"What though Reason forged your scheme? / Twas Reason dreamed the Utopia's dream. / Tis dream to think that Reason can / Govern the reasoning creature, man."* [9]

Political order requires that the indifference of God not be revealed. Ahab is Melville's Faustian God-hater. The *Pequod* does not survive his command. The *Bellipotent*, the vessel that defeats the *Athée*, survives because it keeps its secret hidden to all but a few. A passage from Melville's *White-Jacket* is appropriate: "Outwardly regarded, our craft is a lie; for all that is outwardly seen of it is the clean swept deck, and oft-painted planks comprised above the waterline; whereas, the vast mass of our fabric, with all its storerooms and secret, forever slides along far under the surface."[10]

Notes

1. Hobbes, *Leviathan*, ed. C. B. Macpherson (Baltimore: Penguin Books, 1968), 81.

2. For an extended treatment of the distinction between modern and ancient political theory, see Leo Strauss, *Natural Right and History* (Chicago: University of Chicago Press, 1953). Strauss provides an elaborate analysis of the tension between nature and convention in the history of western political philosophy. Also important is Strauss's *Persecution and the Art of Writing* (New York: The Free Press, 1952). In this work Strauss argues that there is a conflict between philosophy, the search for truth, and society, which rests upon opinion. Because the search for truth is an attack upon opinion, philosophy is unsettling to society, and even subversive. Believing this, many writers in the tradition of political philosophy have employed a method of writing that contains two teachings, one exoteric, the other esoteric. The esoteric teaching, according to Strauss, is "inside the narrative" and concealed by it. I will argue that this is the method of Melville as well.

3. *Billy Budd, Sailor (An Inside Narrative)*, eds. Harrison Hayford and Merton M. Sealts, Jr. (Chicago: University of Chicago Press, 1962), 63. Subsequent references to *Billy Budd* will be included in the test.

4. See James E. Miller, Jr., *Billy Budd*: The Catastrophe of Innocence," *Modern Language Notes* 73 (March 1958):168–76; Richard Harter Fogle, *Billy Budd* — Acceptance or Irony," *Tulane Studies in English* 8 (1958):107–13; E. L. Grant Watson, "Melville's Testament of Acceptance," *New England Quarterly* 6 (June 1933):319–27; Milton Stern, *The Fine Hammered Steel of Herman Melville* (Urbana: University of Illinois Press, 1957).

5. See Lawrance Thompson, *Melville's Quarrel with God* (Princeton: Princeton University Press, 1952), 355–414; Leonard Casper, "The Case Against Captain Vere," *Perspective* 5 (Summer 1952):146–52; Arthur Sale, "Captain Vere's Reasons," *Cambridge Journal* 5 (October 1951):3–18; Joseph Schiffman, "Melville's Final Stage, Irony: A Reexamination of *Billy Budd* Criticism," *American Literature* 2 (May 1950):128–36; and Phil Withim, "The Case Against Captain Vere," *Modern Language Quarterly* 20 (June 1959):115–27.

6. For a detailed study of Melville's use of concealment, see Thompson, *Melville's Quarrel with God;* also Allen Hayman, "The Real and the Original: Herman Melville's Theory of Prose Fiction," *Modern Fiction Studies* 8 (1962):211–32; Merlin Bowen, "Tactics of Indirection in Melville's *The Confidence-Man*," *Studies in the Novel* 1 (Winter 1969):401–20; and Wilson Carey McWilliams, "Herman Melville," in *The Idea of Fraternity in America* (Berkeley: University of California Press, 1973), 328–71.

7. Reprinted in *Moby-Dick*, ed. Harrison Hayford and Hershel Parker (New York: Norton, 1967), 535–51, under the title "Hawthorne and His Mosses."

8. For example, consider Budd's fight with Red Whiskers and the breach of naval decorum described on pp. 48–49.

9. "A Reasonable Constitution," unpublished poem written in 1860, cited in *The Melville Log*, vol. 2, edited and compiled by Jay Leyda (New York: Gordian Press), 617. The poem is followed by this marginal note: "Observable in Sir Thomas More's "Utopia" are: first, its almost entire reasonableness. Second, its almost entire impracticality. The remark applies more or less to the Utopia's prototype Plato's Republic."

10. *White-Jacket: or, The World in a Man-of-War*, in *The Writings of Herman Melville*, ed. Harrison Hayford, Hershel Parker, and G. Thomas Tanselle, 15 vols. (Evanston and Chicago: Northwestern University Press and the Newberry Library, 1968–), vol. 5, "The End."

Melville's Fist:
The Execution of *Billy Budd*   Barbara Johnson*

The Plot Against the Characters

. . . No consideration of the nature of character in *Billy Budd* . . . can fail to take into account the fact that the fate of each of the characters is the direct reverse of what one is led to expect from his "nature." Billy is sweet, innocent, and harmless, yet he kills. Claggart is evil, perverted, and mendacious, yet he dies a victim. Vere is sagacious and responsible, yet he allows a man whom he feels to be blameless to hang. It is this discrepancy between character and action that gives rise to the critical disagreement over the story: readers tend either to save the plot and condemn Billy ("acceptance," "tragedy," or "necessity"), or to save Billy and condemn the plot ("irony," "injustice," or "social criticism").

In an effort to make sense of this troubling incompatibility between character and plot, many readers are tempted to say of Billy and Claggart, as does W. Y. Tindall, that "each is more important for what he is than what he does. . . . Good and bad, they occupy the region of good and evil."[1] This reading effectively preserves the allegorical values suggested by Melville's opening chapters, but it does so only by denying the importance of the plot. It ends where the plot begins: with the identification of the moral natures of the characters. One may therefore ask whether the allegorical interpretation (good vs. evil) depends as such on this sort of preference for "being" over "doing," and, if so, what effect the incompatibility between character and action may have on the allegorical functioning of *Billy Budd*.

*From *Studies in Romanticism* 18 (1979): 567–599. Reprinted courtesy of the Trustees of Boston University.

Interestingly enough, Melville himself both invites an allegorical reading and subverts the very terms of its consistency when he writes of the murder: "Innocence and guilt personified in Claggart and Budd in effect changed places."[2] Allowing for the existence of personification but reversing the relation between personifier and personified, positioning an opposition between good and evil only to make each term take on the properties of its opposite, Melville thus sets up his plot in the form of a chiasmus:

This story, which is often read as a retelling of the story of Christ, is thus literally a cruci-fiction — a fiction structured in the shape of a cross. At the moment of the reversal, an instant before his fist shoots out, Billy's face seems to mark out the point of crossing, bearing "an expression which was as a crucifixion to behold" (p. 376). Innocence and guilt, criminal and victim, change places through the mute expressiveness of Billy's inability to speak.

If *Billy Budd* is indeed an allegory, it is thus an allegory of the questioning of the traditional conditions of allegorical stability. The fact that Melville's plot requires that the good act out the evil designs of the bad while the bad suffer the unwarranted fate of the good indicates that the real opposition with which Melville is preoccupied here is less the static opposition between evil and good than the dynamic opposition between a man's "nature" and his acts, or, in Tyndall's terms, the relation between human "being" and human "doing."

Curiously enough, it is precisely this question of "being" versus "doing" that is brought up by the only sentence we ever see Claggart directly address to Billy Budd. When Billy accidentally spills his soup across the path of the master-at-arms, Claggart playfully replies, "Handsomely done, my lad! And handsome *is* as handsome *did* it, too!" (p. 350; emphasis mine). The proverbial expression "handsome *is* as handsome *does*," from which this exclamation springs, posits the possibility of a continuous, predictable, transparent relationship between "being" and "doing." It supposes that the inner goodness of Billy Budd is in harmonious accord with his fair appearance, that, as Melville writes of the stereotypical "Handsome Sailor" in the opening pages of the story, "the moral nature" is not "out of keeping with the physical make" (p. 322). But it is precisely this continuity between the physical and the moral, between appearance and action, or between "being" and "doing," that Claggart questions in Billy Budd. He warns Captain Vere not to be taken in by Billy's physical beauty: "You have but noted his fair cheek. A mantrap may be under the ruddy-tipped daisies" (p. 372). Claggart indeed soon finds his suspicions confirmed with a vengeance: when he repeats his accusation in front of Billy, he is struck down dead. It would thus seem that to question the continuity between character and action cannot be done with impunity, that fundamental questions of life and death are always surreptitiously involved.

In an effort to examine what it is that is at stake in Claggart's accusation, it might be helpful to view the opposition between Billy and Claggart as an opposition not between innocence and guilt but between two conceptions of language, or between two types of reading. Billy seemingly represents the perfectly *motivated* sign; that is, his inner self (the signified) is considered transparently readable from the beauty of his outer self (the signifier). His "straightforward simplicity" is the very opposite of the "moral obliquities" or "crookedness of heart" that characterizes "citified" or rhetorically sophisticated man. "To deal in double meanings and insinuations of any sort," writes Melville, "was quite foreign to his nature" (p. 327). In accordance with this "nature," Billy reads everything at face value, never questioning the meaning of appearances. He is dumbfounded at the Dansker's suggestion, "incomprehensible to a novice," that Claggart's very pleasantness can be interpreted as its opposite, as a sign that he is "down on" Billy Budd. To Billy, "the occasional frank air and pleasant word *went for what they purported to be*, the young sailor never having heard as yet of the 'too fair-spoken man' " (pp. 365–66; emphasis mine). As a reader, then, Billy is symbolically as well as factually illiterate. His literal-mindedness is represented by his illiteracy because, in assuming that language can be taken at face value, he excludes the very functioning of *difference* that makes the act of reading both indispensable and undecidable.

Claggart, on the other hand, is the very image of difference and duplicity, both in his appearance and in his character. His face is not ugly, but it hints of something defective or abnormal. He has no vices, yet he incarnates evil. He is an intellectual, but uses reason as "an ambidexter implement for effecting the irrational" (p. 354). Billy inspires in him both "profound antipathy" and a "soft yearning." In the incompatibility of his attitudes, Claggart is thus a personification of ambiguity and ambivalence, of the distance between signifier and signified, of the separation between being and doing: "apprehending the good, but powerless to be it, a nature like Claggart's, . . . what recourse is left to it but to recoil upon itself" (p. 356). As a reader, Claggart has learned to "exercise a distrust keen in proportion to the fairness of the appearance" (p. 364). He is properly an ironic reader, who, assuming the sign to be arbitrary and unmotivated, reverses the value signs of appearances and takes a daisy for a mantrap and an unmotivated accidental spilling of soup for an intentional sly escape of antipathy. Claggart meets his downfall, however, when he attempts to master the arbitrariness of the sign for his own ends, precisely by falsely (that is, arbitrarily) accusing Billy of harboring arbitrariness, of hiding a mutineer beneath the appearance of a baby.

Such a formulation of the Budd/Claggart relationship enables one to take a new look not only at the story itself, but at the criticism as well. For, curiously enough, it is precisely this opposition between the literal reader (Billy) and the ironic reader (Claggart) that is reenacted in the critical readings of *Billy Budd* in the opposition between the "acceptance" school and the "irony" school. Those who see the story as a "testament of acceptance" tend to take Billy's final benediction of Vere at face value; as Lewis Mumford puts it, "As Melville's own end approached, he cried out with Billy Budd: God Bless Captain Vere! In this final affirmation Herman Melville died."[3] In contrast, those who read the tale ironically tend to take Billy's sweet farewell as Melville's bitter curse. Joseph Schiffman writes: "At heart a kind man, Vere, strange to say, makes possible the depraved Claggart's wish—the destruction of Billy. " 'God bless Captain Vere!' Is this not piercing irony? As innocent Billy utters these words, does not the reader gag?" (p. 133) But since the acceptance/irony dichotomy is already contained within the story, since it is obviously one of the things the story is *about*, it is not enough to try to decide which of the readings is correct. What the reader of *Billy Budd* must do is to analyze what is at stake in the very opposition between literality and irony. . . .

Three Readings of Reading

It is no doubt significant that the character around whom the greatest critical dissent has revolved is neither the good one nor the evil one but the one who is explicitly presented as a *reader*, Captain Vere. On some level, readers of *Billy Budd* have always testified to the fact that it is reading, as much as killing, that is at the heart of Melville's story. But how is the act of reading being manifested? . . .

It seems evident that Billy's reading method consists in taking everything at face value, while Claggart's consists in seeing a mantrap under every daisy. Yet in practice, neither of these methods is rigorously upheld. The naive reader is not naive enough to forget to edit out information too troubling to report. The instability of the space between sign and referent, normally denied by the naive reader, is called upon as an *instrument* whenever that same instability threatens to disturb the *content* of meaning itself. Billy takes every sign as transparently readable as long as what he reads is consistent with transparent peace, order, and authority. When this is not so, his reading clouds accordingly. And Claggart, for whom every sign can be read as its opposite, neglects to doubt the transparency of any sign that tends to confirm his own doubts: "the master-at-arms *never suspected the veracity*" (p. 357) of Squeak's reports. The naive believer thus refuses to believe any evidence that subverts the transparency of his beliefs, while the ironic doubter forgets to suspect the reliability of anything confirming his own suspicions.

Naiveté and irony thus stand as symmetrical opposites blinded by their very incapacity to see anything but symmetry. Claggart, in his antipathy, "can really form no conception of an *unreciprocated* malice" (p. 358). And Billy, conscious of his own blamelessness, can see nothing but pleasantness in Claggart's pleasant words: "Had the foretopman been conscious of having done or said anything to provoke the ill-will of the official, it would have been different with him, and his sight might have been purged if not sharpened. As it was, innocence was his blinder" (p. 366). Each character sees the other only through the mirror of his own reflection. Claggart, looking at Billy, mistakes his own twisted face for the face of the enemy, while Billy, recognizing in Claggart the negativity he smothers in himself, strikes out.

The naive and the ironic readers are thus equally destructive, both of themselves and of each other. It is significant that both Billy and Claggart should die. Both readings do violence to the plays of ambiguity and belief by forcing upon the text the applicability of a universal and absolute law. The one, obsessively intent on preserving peace and eliminating equivocation, murders the text; the other, seeing nothing but universal war, becomes the spot on which aberrant premonitions of negativity become truth. . . .

In order to analyze what is at stake in Melville's portrait of Vere, let us first examine the ways in which Vere's reading differs from those of Billy Budd and John Claggart:

1. While the naive/ironic dichotomy was based on a symmetry between *individuals*, Captain Vere's reading takes place within a social *structure:* the rigidly hierarchical structure of a British warship. While the naive reader (Billy) destroys the other in order to defend the self, and while the ironic reader (Claggart) destroys the self by projecting aggression onto the other, the third reader (Vere) subordinates both self and other, and ultimately sacrifices both self and other, for the preservation of a political order.

2. The apparent purpose of both Billy's and Claggart's readings was to determine *character:* to preserve innocence or to prove guilt. Vere, on the other hand, subordinates character to action, being to doing: "A martial court," he tells his officer, "must needs in the present case confine its attention to the *blow's consequence,* which consequence justly is to be deemed not otherwise than as the *striker's deed*" (p. 384).

3. In the opposition between the metaphysical and the psychoanalytical readings of Billy's deed, the deciding question was whether the blow should be considered accidental or (unconsciously) motivated. But in Vere's courtroom reading, both these alternatives are irrelevant: "Budd's intent or non-intent is nothing to the purpose" (p. 389). What matters is not the cause but the consequences of the blow.

4. The naive or literal reader takes language at face value and treats signs as *motivated;* the ironic reader assumes that the relation between

sign and meaning can be *arbitrary* and that appearances are made to be reversed. For Vere, the functions and meanings of signs are neither transparent nor reversible but fixed by socially determined *convention*. Vere's very character is determined not by a relation between his outward appearance and his inner being but by the "buttons" that signify his position in society. While both Billy and Claggart are said to owe their character to "Nature," Vere sees his actions and being as meaningful only within the context of a contractual allegiance:

> Do these buttons that we wear attest that our allegiance is to Nature? No, to the King. Though the ocean, which is inviolate Nature primeval, though this be the element where we move and have our being as sailors, yet as the King's officers lies our duty in a sphere correspondingly natural? So little is that true, that in receiving our commissions we in the most important regards ceased to be natural free agents. When war is declared are we the commissioned fighters previously consulted? We fight at command. If our judgments approve the war, that is but coincidence.
> p. 387)

Judgment is thus for Vere, a function neither of individual conscience nor of absolute justice but of "the rigor of martial law" (p. 387) operating *through* him.

> 5. While Billy and Claggart read spontaneously and directly, Vere's reading often makes use of precedent (historical facts, childhood memories), allusions (to the Bible, to various ancient and modern authors), and analogies (Billy is like Adam, Claggart is like Ananias). Just as both Billy and Claggart have no known past, they read without memory; just as their lives end with their reading, they read without foresight. Vere, on the other hand, interrogates both past and future for interpretative guidance.

> 6. While Budd and Claggart thus oppose each other directly, without regard for circumstance or consequence, Vere reads solely in function of the attending historical situation: the Nore and Spithead mutinies have created an atmosphere "critical to naval authority" (p. 380), and, since an engagement with the enemy fleet is possible at any moment, the *Bellipotent* cannot afford internal unrest.

The fundamental factor that underlies the opposition between the metaphysical Budd/Claggart conflict on the one hand and the reading of Captain Vere on the other can be summed up in a single word: history. While the naive and the ironic readers attempt to impose upon language the functioning of an absolute, timeless, universal law (the sign as *either* motivated *or* arbitrary), the question of *martial* law arises within the story precisely to reveal the law as a *historical* phenomenon, to underscore the element of contextual mutability in the conditions of any act of reading. Arbitrariness and motivation, irony and literality, are parameters between which language constantly fluctuates, but only historical context determines which proportion of each is perceptible to each reader. Melville indeed shows history to be a story not only of events but also of fluctuations in the very functioning of irony and belief:

> The event *converted into irony for a time* those spirited strains of Dibdin. . . .
> (p. 333)

> Everything is *for a term venerated* in navies.
> (p. 408)

The opposing critical judgments of Vere's decision to hang Billy are divided, in the final analysis, according to the place they attribute to history in the process of justification. For the ironists, Vere is misusing history for his own self-preservation or for the preservation of a world safe for aristocracy. For those who accept Vere's verdict as tragic but necessary, it is Melville who has stacked the historical cards in Vere's favor. In both cases, the conception of history as an interpretive instrument remains the same: it is its *use* that is being judged. And the very fact that Billy Budd criticism itself historically moves from acceptance to irony is no doubt itself interpretable in the same historical terms.

Evidence can in fact be found in the text for both pro-Vere and anti-Vere judgments:

> Full of disquietude and misgiving, the surgeon left the cabin. Was Captain Vere suddenly affected in his mind?
> (p. 378)

> Whether Captain Vere, as the surgeon professionally and privately surmised, was really the sudden victim of any degree of aberration, every one must determine for himself by such light as this narrative may afford.
> (p. 379–80)

> That the unhappy event which has been narrated could not have happened at a worse juncture was but too true. For it was close on the heel of the suppressed insurrections, an aftertime very critical to naval authority, demanding from every English sea commander two qualities not readily interfusable — prudence and rigor.
> (p. 380)

> Small wonder then that the *Bellipotent's* captain . . . felt that circumspection not less than promptitude was necessary. . . . Here he may or may not have erred.
> (p. 380)

The effect of these explicit oscillations of judgment within the text is to underline the *importance* of the act of judging while rendering its outcome undecidable. Judgment, however difficult, is clearly the central preoccupation of Melville's text, whether it be the judgment pronounced *by* Vere or *upon* him.

There is still another reason for the uncertainty over Vere's final status, however: the unfinished state of the manuscript at Melville's death. According to editors Hayford and Sealts,[4] it is the "late pencil revisions" that cast the greatest doubt upon Vere; Melville was evidently still fine-tuning the text's attitude toward its third reader when he died. The ultimate irony in the tale is thus that our final judgment of the very reader who takes history into consideration is made problematic precisely by the intervention of history: by the historical accident of the author's death. History here affects interpretation not only within the content of the narration but also within the very production of the narrative. And what remains suspended by this historical accident is nothing less than the exact signifying value of history itself. Clearly, the meaning of "history" as a feature distinguishing Vere's reading from those of Claggart and Budd can in no way be taken for granted.

Judgment as Political Performance

> When a poet takes his seat on the tripod of the Muse, he cannot control his thoughts . . . When he represents men with contrasting characters he is often obliged to contradict himself, and he doesn't know which of the opposing speeches contains the truth. But for the legislator, this is impossible: he must not let his laws say two different things on the same subject.
>
> Plato, *The Laws*

In the final analysis, the question is not: what did Melville really think of Captain Vere? but rather: what is at stake in his way of presenting him? What can we learn from him about the act of judging? Melville seems to be presenting us less with an *object* for judgment than with an *example* of judgment. And the very vehemence with which the critics tend to praise or condemn the justice of Vere's decision indicates that it is judging, not murdering, that Melville is asking us to judge.

And yet Vere's judgment *is* an act of murder. Captain Vere is a reader who kills, not, like Billy, *instead* of speaking, but rather, precisely *by means of* speaking. While Billy kills through verbal impotence, Vere kills through the very potency and sophistication of rhetoric. Judging, in Vere's case, is nothing less than the wielding of the power of life and death through language. In thus occupying the point at which murder and language meet, Captain Vere positions himself precisely astride the "deadly space between." While Billy's performative force occupies the vanishing point of utterance and cognition, and while the validity of Claggart's cognitive perception is realized only through the annihilation of the perceiver, Captain Vere's reading mobilizes both power and knowledge, performance and cognition, error and murder. Judgment is precisely cognition functioning as an act. It is this combination of performance and cognition that defines Vere's reading not merely as historical but as *political*. If politics is defined as the attempt to reconcile action with understanding, then Melville's story offers an exemplary context in which to analyze the interpretive and performative structures that make politics so problematic.

That the alliance between knowledge and action is by no means an easy one is amply demonstrated in Melville's story. Vere indeed has often been seen as the character in the tale who experiences the greatest suffering: his understanding of Billy's character and his military duty are totally at odds. On the one hand, cognitive exactitude requires that "history" be taken into consideration. Yet what constitutes "knowledge of history"? How are "circumstances" to be defined? What sort of causality does "precedent" imply? And what is to be done with overlapping but incompatible "contexts"? Before deciding upon innocence and guilt, Vere must define and limit the frame of reference within which his decision is to be possible. He does so by choosing the "legal" context over the "essential" context: "In a *legal view* the apparent victim of the tragedy was he who had sought to victimize a man blameless; and the indisputable deed of the latter, *navally regarded,* constituted the most heinous of military crimes. Yet more. The *essential right and wrong* involved in the matter, the clearer that might be, so much the worse for the responsibility of a loyal sea commander, inasmuch as he was not authorized to determine the matter on that *primitive* basis," (p. 380). Yet it is precisely this determination of the proper frame of reference that dictates the outcome of the decision: once Vere has defined his context, he has also in fact reached his verdict. The very choice of the *conditions* of judgment itself constitutes a judgment. But what are the conditions of choosing the conditions of judgment?

The alternative, it seems, is between the "naval" and the "primitive," between "Nature" and "the King," between the martial court and what Vere calls the "Last Assizes" (p. 388). But the question arises of exactly what the concept of "Nature" entails in such an opposition. In what way, and with what changes, would it have been possible for Vere's allegiance to be to "Nature"? How can a legal judgment exemplify "primitive" justice?

In spite of his allegiance to martial law and conventional authority, Vere clearly finds the "absolute" criteria equally applicable to Billy's deed, for he responds to each new development with the following exclamations:

"It is the divine judgment of Ananias!"
(p. 378)

"Struck dead by an angel of God! Yet the angel must hang!"
(p. 378)

"Before a court less arbitrary and more merciful than a martial one, that plea would largely extenuate. At the Last Assizes it shall acquit." (p. 388)

"Ay, there is a mystery; but, to use a scriptural phrase, it is a 'mystery of iniquity,' a matter for psychological theologians to discuss." (p. 385)

This last expression, which refers to the source of Claggart's antipathy, has already been mentioned by Melville's narrator and dismissed as being "tinctured with the biblical element": "If that lexicon which is based on Holy Writ were any longer popular, one might with less difficulty define and denominate certain phenomenal men. As it is, one must turn to some authority not liable to the charge of being tinctured with the biblical element" (p. 353). Vere turns to the Bible to designate Claggart's "nature"; Melville turns to a Platonic tautology. But in both cases, the question arises: what does it mean to seal an explanation with a quotation? And what, in Vere's case, does it mean to refer a legal mystery to a religious text?

If Vere names the Absolute — as opposed to the martial — by means of quotations and allusions, does this not suggest that the two alternative frames of reference within which judgment is possible are not Nature and the King, but rather two types of textual authority: the Bible and the Mutiny Act? This is not to say that Vere is "innocently" choosing one text over another, but that the nature of "Nature" in a legal context cannot be taken for granted. Even Thomas Paine, who is referred to by Melville in his function as proponent of "natural" human rights, cannot avoid grounding his concept of nature in Biblical myth. In the very act of rejecting the authority of antiquity, he writes: "The fact is, that portions of antiquity, by proving every thing, establish nothing. It is authority against authority all the way, till we come to the divine origin of the rights of man, at the Creation. Here our inquiries find a resting-place, and our reason a home."[5] The final frame of reference is neither the heart nor the gun, neither Nature nor the King, but the authority of a Sacred Text. Authority seems to be nothing other than the vanishing-point of textuality. And Nature is authority whose textual origins have been forgotten. Even behind the martial order of the world of the man-of-war, there lies a religious referent: the *Bellipotent*'s last battle is with a French ship called the *Athée*.

Judgment, then, would seem to ground itself in a suspension of the opposition between textuality and referentiality, just as politics can be seen as that which makes it impossible to draw the line between "language" and "life." Vere, indeed, is presented precisely as a reader who does not recognize the "frontier" between "remote allusions" and current events:

In illustrating of any point touching the stirring personages and events of the time he would be as apt to cite some historic character or incident

of antiquity as he would be to cite from the moderns. He seemed unmindful of the circumstance that to his bluff company such remote allusions, however pertinent they might really be, were altogether alien to men whose reading was mainly confined to the journals. But considerateness in such matters is not easy to natures constituted like Captain Vere's. Their honesty prescribes to them directness, sometimes far-reaching like that of a migratory fowl that in its flight never heeds when it crosses a frontier.
(p. 341)

Yet is is precisely by inviting Billy Budd and John Claggart to "cross" the "frontier" between their proper territory and their superior's cabin, between the private and the political realms, that Vere unwittingly sets up the conditions for the narrative chiasmus he must judge.

As was noted earlier, Captain Vere's function, according to many critics, is to insert "ambiguity" into the story's "oversimplified" allegorical opposition. Yet at the same time, it is precisely Captain Vere who inspires the most vehement critical oppositions. Captain Vere, in other words, seems to mobilize simultaneously the seemingly contradictory forces of ambiguity and polarity.

In his median position between the Budd/Claggart opposition and the acceptance/irony opposition, Captain Vere functions as a focus for the *conversion* of polarity into ambiguity and back again. Interestingly, he plays exactly the same role in the progress of the plot. It is Vere who brings together the "Innocent" Billy and the "guilty" Claggart in order to test the validity of Claggart's accusations, but he does so in such a way as to effect not a clarification but a reversal of places between guilt and innocence. Vere's fatherly words to Billy are precisely what triggers the ambiguous deed upon which Vere must pronounce a verdict of "condemn *or* let go." Just as Melville's readers, faced with the ambiguity they themselves recognize as being provided by Vere, are quick to pronounce the Captain vicious *or* virtuous, evil *or* just; so, too, Vere, who clearly perceives the "mystery" in the "moral dilemma" confronting him, must nevertheless reduce the situation to a binary opposition.

It would seem, then, that the function of judgment is to convert an ambiguous situation into a decidable one. But it does so by converting a difference *within* (Billy as divided between conscious submissiveness and unconscious hostility, Vere as divided between understanding father and military authority) into a difference *between* (between Claggart and Billy, between Nature and the King, between authority and criminality). A difference *between* opposing forces presupposes that the entities in conflict be knowable. A difference *within* one of the entities in question is precisely what problematizes the very *idea* of an entity in the first place, rendering the "legal point of view" inapplicable. In studying the plays of both ambiguity and binarity, Melville's story situates *its* critical difference neither within nor between, but precisely in the very question of the *relation between the two* as the fundamental question of all human politics. The political context in *Billy Budd* is such that on all levels the differences *within* (mutiny on the warship, the French revolution as a threat to "lasting institutions," Billy's unconscious hostility) are subordinated to differences *between* (the *Bellipotent* vs. the *Athée*, England vs. France, murderer vs. victim). This is why Melville's choice of historical setting is so significant: the war between France and England at the time of the French Revolution is as striking an example of the simultaneous functioning of differences within and between as is the confrontation between Billy and Claggart in relation to their own internal divisions. War, indeed, is the absolute transformation of *all* differences into *binary* differences.

It would seem, then, that the maintenance of political authority requires that the law function as a set of rules for the regular, predictable misreading of the "difference within" as a "difference between." Yet if, as our epigraph from Plato suggests, law is thus defined in terms of its repression of ambiguity, then it is itself an overwhelming example of an entity based on a "difference within." Like Billy, the law, in attempting to eliminate its own "deadly space," can only inscribe itself in a space of deadliness.

In seeking to regulate the violent effects of difference, the political work of cognition is thus an attempt to *situate* that which must be eliminated. Yet in the absence of the possibility of knowing the locus and origin of violence, cognition itself becomes an act of violence. In terms of pure understanding, the drawing of a line *between* opposing entities does violence to the irreducible ambiguities that subvert the very possibility of determining the limits of what an "entity" is:

> Who in the rainbow can draw the line where the violet tint ends and the orange tint begins? Distinctly we see the difference of the colors, but where exactly does the one first blendingly enter into the other? So with sanity and insanity. In pronounced cases there is no question about them. But in some supposed cases, in various degrees supposedly less pronounced, to draw the exact line of demarcation few will undertake, though for a fee becoming considerate some professional experts will. There is nothing nameable but that some men will, or undertake to, do it for pay.
> (p. 379)

As an act, the drawing of a line is not only inexact and violent: it is also that which problematizes the very possibility of situating the "difference between" the judge and what is judged, between the interests of the "expert" and the truth of his expertise. What every act of judgment manifests is not the value of the object but the position of the judge within a structure of exchange. There is, in other words, no position from which to judge that would be outside the lines of force involved in the object judged.

But if judging is always a *partial* reading (in both senses of the word), is there a place for reading beyond politics? Are we, as Melville's readers, outside the arena in which power and fees are exchanged? If law is the forcible transformation of ambiguity into decidability, is it possible to read ambiguity *as such*, without that reading functioning as a political act?

Even about this, Melville has something to say. For there is a fourth reader in *Billy Budd*, the one who "never interferes in aught and never gives advice" (p. 363): the old Dansker. A man of "few words, many wrinkles," and "the complexion of an antique parchment" (p. 347), the Dansker is the very picture of one who understands and emits ambiguous utterances. When asked by Billy for an explanation of his petty troubles, the Dansker says only, "Jemmy Legs [Claggart] is down on you" (p. 349). This interpretation, entirely accurate as a reading of Claggart's ambiguous behaviour, is handed down to Billy without further explanation: "Something less unpleasantly oracular he tried to extract; but the old sea Chiron, thinking perhaps that for the nonce he had sufficiently instructed his young Achilles, pursed his lips, gathered all his wrinkles together, and would commit himself to nothing further," (p. 349). As a reader who understands ambiguity yet refuses to "commit himself," the Dansker thus dramatizes a reading that attempts to be as cognitively accurate and as performatively neutral as possible. Yet however neutral he tries to remain, the Dansker's reading does not take place outside the political realm: it is his very refusal to participate in it, whether by further instruction or by direct intervention, that leads to Billy's exclamation in the soup episode ("There now, who says Jemmy Legs is down on me?"). The transference of knowledge is not any more innocent than the transference of power. For it is precisely through the impossibility of finding a spot from which knowledge could be all-encompassing that the plays of political power proceed.

Just as the attempt to "know" without "doing" can itself function as a deed, the fact that judgment is always explicitly an act adds a further insoluble problem to its cognitive predicament. Since, as Vere points out, no judgment can take place in the *Last* Assizes, no judge can ever pronounce a Last Judgment. in order to reach a verdict, Vere must determine the consequences not only of the fatal blow, but also precisely of his own verdict. Judgment is an act not only because it kills, but because it is in turn open to judgment:

> "Can we not convict and yet mitigate the penalty?" asked the sailing master. . . .
> "Gentlemen, were that clearly lawful for us under the circumstances, consider the consequences of such clemency. . . . To the people the foretopman's deed, however it be worded in the announcement, will be plain homicide committed in a flagrant act of mutiny. What penalty for that should follow, they know. But it does not follow. *Why?* They

will ruminate. You know what sailors are. Will they not revert to the
recent outbreak at the Nore?"
(p. 389)

The danger is not only one of repeating the Nore mutiny, however. It is also
one of forcing Billy, for all his innocence, to repeat his crime. Billy is a
politically charged object from the moment he strikes his superior. He is no
longer, and can never again be, plotless. If he were set free, he himself
would be unable to explain why. As a focus for the questions and intrigues
of the crew, he would be even less capable of defending himself than
before, and would surely strike again. The political reading, as cognition,
attempts to understand the past; as performance, it attempts to eliminate
from the future any necessity for its own recurrence.

What this means is that every judge is in the impossible position of
having to include the effects of his own act of judging within the cognitive
context of his decision. The question of the nature of the type of historical
causality that would govern such effects can neither be decided nor
ignored. Because of his official position, Vere cannot choose to read in such
a way that his reading would not be an act of political authority. But what
Melville shows in *Billy Budd* is that authority consists precisely in the
impossibility of containing the effects of its own application.

As a political allegory, Melville's *Billy Budd* is thus much more than a
study of good and evil, justice and injustice. It is a dramatization of the
twisted relations between knowing and doing, speaking and killing,
reading and judging, which make political understanding and action so
problematic. In the subtle creation of Claggart's "evil" out of a series of
spaces in knowledge, Melville shows that gaps in cognition, far from being
mere absences, take on the performative power of true acts. The *force* of
what is not known is all the more effective for not being perceived as such.
The crew, which does not understand that it does not know, is no less
performative a reader than the Captain, who clearly perceives and
represses the presence of "mystery." The legal order, which attempts to
submit "brute force" to "forms, measured forms," can only eliminate
violence by transforming violence into the final authority. And cognition,
which perhaps begins as a power play against the play of power, can only
increase, through its own elaboration, the range of what it tries to
dominate. The "deadly space" or "difference" that runs through *Billy
Budd* is not located *between* knowledge and action, performance and
cognition: it is that which, within cognition, functions as an act: it is that
which, within action, prevents us from ever knowing whether what we hit
coincides with what we understand. And this is what makes the meaning
of Melville's last work so . . . *striking*.

Notes

1. "The Ceremony of Innocence," in R. M. McIver, ed., *Great Moral Dilemmas in Literature, Past and Present* (New York: Harper & Row, 1956), p. 75.

2. Melville, *Billy Budd*, in *"Billy Budd, Sailor," and Other Stories*, ed. H. Beaver (New York: Penguin Books, 1967), p. 380. Unless otherwise indicated, all references to *Billy Budd* are to this edition, which reprints the Hayford and Sealts Reading Text.

3. *Herman Melville* (New York: Harcourt, Brace & World, Inc., 1929), p. 357.

4. Editors' Introduction, *Billy Budd, Sailor* (Chicago: University of Chicago Press, 1962); see esp. pp. 34–35.

5. Thomas Paine, *The Rights of Man* (Garden City, N.Y.: Anchor Press, 1973), p. 303.

Billy Budd and the Judgment of Silence

Brook Thomas*

> If our judgements approve the war that is but coincidence
> — Melville, *Billy Budd*

A critic would have to be very innocent today to believe in the possibility of an innocent encounter with a text. All readings, it seems certain, have been mediated by interpretive schemas that are conditioned by and help condition the ideologies of a society. There are no innocent readings. One who attempts one is revealing his own ideological assumptions. If his reading does not self-consciously announce its awareness of those assumptions, there will be a critic available to point them out. That critic's reading of a critic reading is in turn subject to another reading that will expose another set of assumptions, and so on. . . .

This essay is about . . . an encounter between a text and its readers, or, more specifically, a particular reader who has studied other readings. The text is *Billy Budd*, a text concerned with innocence, judgment, and possible ways of reading. The reader is Barbara Johnson, who demystifies the possibility of innocent readings by exploring what is involved in an act of judgment. An attempt to ascertain the ideology of Johnson's "Melville's Fist: The Execution of *Billy Budd*"[1] is particularly important because her essay is an excellent example of what has come to be called a "deconstructive" reading, a strategy of reading gaining more and more influence. The text of *Billy Budd* is a good ground to test the self-interestedness of the deconstructive strategy.

In one sense Johnson's reading can be seen as an attempt to place some sort of order on the chaos raging in *Billy Budd* criticism. Controversy

*From *Bucknell Review* 27 (1983):51–78. Reprinted by permission of the editors of *Bucknell Review*.

about the book has tended to focus not on its title character but on Captain Vere. How we read Captain Vere places us on one side of a long-standing critical debate. Should we take Vere as Melville's spokesman and accept Billy's death because innocence cannot survive in the world, or should we view Vere ironically and protest Billy's death as a condemnation of a social order that demands the death of innocence? Is the book Melville's final testament of acceptance or his final testament of re-sistance? Is it the acceptance of tragedy or the tragedy of acceptance?

Johnson accounts for the controversy over Vere by showing that the terms of the dispute, that is, reading Vere literally (as Melville's spokes-man) or ironically, is "one of the things the story is about" (p. 574). The antagonist and protagonist in the story illustrate these two ways of reading. Billy's way of reading is literal. He reads what is on the surface. "To deal in double meanings and insinuations of any sort was quite foreign to his nature" (p. 12). Claggart, on the other hand, distrusts appearances. He reads ironically, always looking for a disparity between a surface meaning and a deeper meaning. Since the critical controversy over how to read the book is something the book is about, "it is not enough to try to decide which of the readings is correct. What the reader of *Billy Budd* must do is analyze what is at stake in the very opposition between literality and irony" (p. 574).

Not surprisingly, Captain Vere, the judge in the drama, offers a third way of reading.

> The naive or literal reader takes language at face value and treats signs as *motivated;* the ironic reader assumes that the relation between sign and meaning can be *arbitrary* and that appearances are made to be reversed. For Vere, the functions and meanings of signs are neither transparent nor reversible but fixed by socially determined *convention.* Vere's very character is determined not by a relation between his outward appearance and his inner being but by the "buttons" that signify his position in society. While both Billy and Claggart are said to owe their character to "Nature," Vere sees his actions and being as meaningful only within the context of a contractual allegiance. . . . Judgment is thus for Vere a function neither of individual conscience nor of absolute justice but of "the rigor of martial law" operating *through* him.
> [Pp. 589–90]

Although Johnson does not call attention to the fact, Vere's way of reading is also represented in *Billy Budd* criticism. It appears in Charles Reich's "The Tragedy of Justice in *Billy Budd*."[2] Anyone familiar with Reich knows that he would not argue that Billy must die, yet he does not condemn Captain Vere for making that judgment. He, like Captain Vere, claims that the law, not the captain, decides Billy's fate. "At the outset, it is vital to note that Melville allows Vere no choice within the terms of the law itself; if the law is obeyed, Billy must hang. . . . We may perhaps criticize the law, but not the officer whose 'vowed responsibility' is to 'adhere to it and administer it' " (p. 369).

What Johnson does by accounting for these three ways of reading is to offer a fourth way of reading: a way of reading that accounts for the different ways of reading *Billy Budd*. Her reading would seem to be a privileged and more enlightened reading, because it avoids the blindness of the other readings. While the first three ways of reading take a definite stand by judging, Johnson's way of reading tries to describe rather than judge. With Captain Vere, "Melville seems to be presenting us less with an *object* for judgment than with an *example* of judgment" (Johnson, p. 592). What this example of judgment shows is that judgment is always "a partial reading (in both senses of the word)" (p. 597).

The partiality of judgment comes from its basic function. "The function of judgment is to convert an ambiguous situation into a decidable one. But it does so by converting a difference *within* . . . into a difference *between*. . . . A difference *between* opposing forces presupposes that the entities in conflict be knowable. A difference *within* one of the entities in question is precisely what problematizes the very *idea* of an entity in the first place, rendering the 'legal point of view' inapplicable. In studying the plays of ambiguity and binarity, Melville's story situates *its* critical difference neither within or between, but precisely in the very question of the *relation between the two* as the fundamental question of all human politics" (p. 596).

The critics who judge Captain Vere succumb to the same partiality. The critical controversy over Vere ignores the inherent ambiguity of Melville's text and tries to transform differences contained *within* the text to differences occurring *outside* the text between critics. The only way to avoid distorting the ambiguity contained within the text seems to be to adopt a strategy typical of deconstruction: the deferred judgment and interpretation.

A deferred interpretation stays "truer" to the text because any interpretation involves a judgment that halts the play of the text's inherently ambiguous language. Opponents of deconstruction might object that, if deconstruction admits that an interpretation can halt the play of language, it must also admit that language does not play by itself and, therefore, is not *inherently* ambiguous. But this notion is undercut when we try to find a fixed ground for judgment, since the ambigutiy of the text's language denies us a grounds by which to judge it. Thus, the advantage of the deferred judgment is that it refuses to construct a false ground from which to judge the text and thereby allows the free play of language that denies a ground of judgment in the first place.

A close look at Johnson's reading of *Billy Budd* shows why traditional students of literature consider this strategy so threatening: it deprives them of their sacred grounds of judgment — the text. While Johnson's reading remains traditional in that it claims to stay consistent with evidence to be found within the text, it is subversive in that it undercuts the notion that staying true to the text will produce a privileged or authorized reading. Unlike a New Critical reading, Johnson's reading shows that the different readings allowed by a text cannot be woven together into an organic unity. "Truth uncompromisingly told will always have its ragged edges; hence the conclusion of such a narration is apt to be less finished than an architectural finial."[3] Since the text of *Billy Budd* can be shown to support consistent readings that are irreconcilable, Johnson shows that it is precisely *because* judgments are based on textual evidence that they lack a solid ground of authority. *Billy Budd* makes her point almost too easy because the text we have is not authorized but patched together from an unfinished manuscript. To make matters worse, the manuscript that exists seems to *support* the subversion of its own authority. As Melville makes "clear," *Billy Budd* is a work of fiction, and "the *might-have-been* is but boggy ground to build on" (*BB*, p. 27). Furthermore, as Johnson very persuasively argues, the text seems to imply that any appeal to a grounds of judgment beyond the text could be traced to another text. At the same time that it denies textual authority, Johnson's reading shows that we are locked into a textual world. To stay true to the text seems to deny that textual evidence can be a ground for judgment, and yet the only evidence we can appeal to is textual.

It goes without saying that Johnson's own reading is included in her critique. Despite its enlightened awareness about the inevitability of blindness, it refuses to grant itself a privileged status. This is shown in Johnson's discussion of the fourth reader in the text, the reader coming closest to her way of reading—the old Dansker. "A man of 'few words, many wrinkles,' and 'the complexion of an antique parchment' [*BB*, p. 50], the Dansker is the very picture of one who understands and emits ambiguous utterances" (p. 597). The Dansker "never interferes in aught and never gives advice" (*BB*, p. 77). But, as Johnson points out, the Dansker's desire to give an accurate reading of events without participating in them has political consequences; it gets Billy into trouble by having him cry out. "There now, who says that Jemmy Legs is down on me!" (*BB*, p. 56). Johnson remarks: "The transfer of knowledge is not any more innocent than the transfer of power. For it is precisely through the impossibility of finding a spot from which knowledge could be all-encompassing that the plays of political power proceed" (p. 598). All readings, even those trying to avoid the political arena, are political.

But to call all ways of reading political still leaves an important question unanswered. Because they risk a judgment, the first three readings clearly reveal their political allegiance. To read Vere literally is to accept the existing system of authority. To read Vere ironically is to undercut it. To claim that the law not Vere is responsible for Billy's death is to accept the authority of the socially accepted code of laws but to admit that laws can be changed. What, however, is the political allegiance of

Johnson's way of reading, a way of reading that rather than judging tries to preserve the ambiguity of the text by ending with these sentences: "The 'deadly space' or 'difference' that runs through *Billy Budd* is not located *between* knowledge and action, performance and cognition: it is that which, within cognition, functions as an act: it is that which, within action, prevents us from ever knowing whether what we hit coincides with what we understand. And this is what makes the meaning of Melville's work so . . . *striking*" (p. 599)?

What I find most striking about Johnson's reading, however, is how her awareness of the problematics of political understanding and action keeps her from risking error by making a judgment. If, as Johnson argues, the text of *Billy Budd* judges those who judge, it should also be added that not to judge is an act of judgment in itself. To examine the ideology of a reading of *Billy Budd* that does not judge, I want to turn from Johnson's reading to *Billy Budd* itself, since, as I suggested earlier, a unique aspect of a literary text seems to be that it judges its readers as much as its readers judge it.

But the sophistication of Johnson's reading draws attention to the difficulties involved in using an encounter with a text to study the ideology of a way of reading. Even though I might argue that the text of *Billy Budd* judges its readers while they judge it, I, no more than earlier readers, can have an immediate encounter with the text. In order to appeal to *Billy Budd* to judge Johnson's way of reading, I have to adopt my own way of reading the text. Thus, to a certain extent, it will always be my way of reading, not the text, that judges her reading. Furthermore, because Johnson has already undercut the authority of any way of reading that relies on the text as a ground for judgment, *merely* to produce another "consistent" reading in opposition to hers is not enough.[4] Instead I need to find a way of reading that can establish a basis for judgment beyond textuality. At the same time, if I hope to stay "true" to the text, I will have to demonstrate that the text itself implies that basis for judgment.

Given these complications, one of the few ways of reading available to us today that can be exposed to a deconstructive reading and not be absorbed by it is one relying on Marxist assumptions. Confronted with deconstruction, a Marxist reading has the advantage that it can agree with deconstruction's two most subversive moves: the denial of textual authority and the deconstruction of the "self."[5] Unlike deconstruction, however, a Marxist reading uses these subversive moves to judge rather than to suspend judgment. My procedure will be first to use the undercutting of textual authority in order to judge Captain Vere and then to use the deconstruction of the autonomy of the self in order to judge Captain Vere's object of judgment, Billy Budd. These two judgments will in turn provide me with a way of judging Johnson's refusal to judge. Before turning to my reading, I want to acknowledge that my judgment of not judging is by no means a judgment that escapes ideology, since, as Giddens remarks, "any type of political discourse, including Marxism, which anticipates an end to ideology, carries thereby the potentiality of becoming itself ideological."[6] In other words, because it would be ideological to claim that my particular Marxist reading at this moment in time is not also a partial reading, I will have to produce a judgment that admits the possibility of its own error while still offering its ground for judgment as the ground by which that error can be judged.

A Marxist reading can go along with and even encourage deconstruction's undercutting of textual authority because, in the political realm, the appeal to textual authority, that is, laws, has been one of the most subtle ways for dominant powers to maintain control. While the defenders of "legal, rational" systems of government place authority in an "impersonal" set of laws,[7] a Marxist can point out that the real power lies in which class writes and administers the laws. Thus, when Johnson shows that the laws Vere appeals to are not grounded in "Nature" but in rhetoric, a Marxist would agree and add the question: What is the nature of the power structure that allows Vere and Vere's way of reading a privileged position to control how those laws are written and interpreted? To answer that question we need to take a closer look at Vere's way of reading.

Johnson claims that in interpreting the law Vere is a historical reader. It would be more accurate, I think, to point out his tendencies toward legal positivism. Niklas Luhmann describes the legal positivist's view: "The law of a society is positivized when the legitimacy of pure legality is recognized, that is, when law is respected because it is made by responsible decision in accordance with definite rules. Thus, in a central question of human co-existence, arbitrariness becomes an institution."[8] The problem with this view is that it can shrink to a belief in mere legality, the parallel in literary studies being a belief in mere textuality.

Jürgen Habermas's summary of the positivist's position shows how similar it is to Vere's. For the positivist,

> the formal rules of procedures suffice as legitimizing premises of decision and require for their part no further legitimation, for they fulfill their function — to absorb uncertainty — in any case. They connect the uncertainty as to *which* decision will come about with the certainty that *some* decision will come about. The abstract imperative validity [*Sollgeltung*] of norms that can do without a material justification beyond the following of correct procedure in their origin and application serves "to stabilize behavioral expectations against disappointment and thereby to guarantee structures."[9]

What is important for Vere is that uncertainty be absorbed and that structure be guaranteed. This is best done by adherence to "formal rules and procedures" or, to use Melville's phrase, "forms and usages," which institutionalize arbitrariness. Questions of "ought" need not be considered in the human realm: when a member of the drumhead court objects that Billy "purposed neither mutiny nor homicide," Vere responds: "Beyond a court less arbitrary and more merciful than a martial one, that plea would largely extenuate. At the Last Assizes it shall acquit" (*BB*, p. 107).

But despite Vere's similarities to a legal positivist, he ultimately betrays an important difference. The legal positivist believes that it is meaningless to search behind the belief in legality for more solid ground of authority. Any claims for an authority beyond the law are "functionally necessary deceptions." Vere, to the contrary, believes that laws can be justified by appealing to the "nature" of human nature. According to Vere the human condition does not change over time.

Relying on T. E. Hulme's definition of the classicist impulse, Milton Stern summarizes Vere's conservative view of human nature as "a belief in the limited nature of human potential and the fallen nature of man and, therefore, in control and decorum and in the illusory quality of change and perfectibility" (*BB*, p. xx). Vere appeals to laws because for him they represent rationality and order and thus control irrationality and chaos. Not at all surprising in a book about reading, Vere finds justification for his beliefs in his reading. The manner in which he does so is a perfect example of a functionally necessary deception.

Vere's normal "bias" is "towards those books to which every serious mind of *superior order* occupying any active post of authority in the world, *naturally* inclines: books treating of actual men and events no matter of what era — history, biography and unconventional writers like Montaigne, who, free from cant and convention, honestly and in the spirit of commonsense philosophize upon realities" (*BB*, p. 36, my italics). Captain Vere wants books that represent the world as it is, not books that fictionalize the world. For Vere the way the world is does not change from era to era; there are timeless truths.

But the next paragraph undermines the sense of reality represented in these books. Vere loves them because they give him "confirmation of his own more reserved thoughts — confirmation which he had vainly sought in social converse" (*BB*, p. 36). Rather than choosing books that reflect a reality outside of himself, a reality confirmed by converse with others, Vere chooses books that reflect his own sense of reality. What Vere considers unconventional is just another convention. Books that seem to have an objective authority turn out to have a subjective authority. Yet it is on the basis of the reality Vere finds confirmed in these books that Vere sentences Billy Budd to death. Similarly, it is the "objective" report of Budd's death in the *News from the Mediterranean* that distorts the facts of the case. Histories and biographies are constructed from such "factual" documents as newspaper reports. Appropriately, Vere's strongest statement defending law and order is supported not by histories and biographies but by a myth. " 'With mankind, . . . forms, measured forms are everything; and that is the import couched in the story of Orpheus with his lyre spellbinding the wild denizens of the wood.' And this he once applied to the disruption of forms going on across the Channel and the consequences thereof" (*BB*, p. 130).

Vere's appeal to the necessity of order through law is a typical strategy of the conservatives of his time. As Douglas Hay writes, "The justice of English law was . . . a powerful ideological weapon in the arsenal of conservatives during the French Revolution." Convincing the lower classes plus itself of the justice of the law allowed the British propertied class that "passed one of the bloodiest penal codes in Europe to congratulate itself on its humanity."[10] People were killed but killed justly. Even the rhetoric Vere uses to condemn Billy to death follows the standard rhetoric eighteenth-century judges used to deliver their death sentences. He adopts both the stance of an impartial agent through whom the law speaks and the role of a paternalistic father folding a position of "natural" authority.

Vere's appeal to the law is successful. It achieves an important aim of the political system he represents: to eliminate ambiguity in judgments by silencing the opposition. It accomplishes its aim subtly because it uses the force of rhetoric not physical force.[11] Vere's strategy of calling the drumhead court is a perfect example of how the rhetoric of the law can be used to enlist the support of those controlled by the law's rhetoric. To call the drumhead court would seem to be precisely the opposite of silencing different points of view. Vere allows the members of the court, including a representative of the crew, to speak while he adopts the role of the impartial witness. But the men speak without a chance of reversing the judgment Vere made at the moment of the murder—" 'Struck dead by an angel of God! Yet the angel must hang!' " (*BB*, p. 95). The moment Vere drops the role of an impartial witness and adopts the role of the prosecutor his "prejudgment" (*BB*, p. 104) of Billy becomes clear. One by one he opposes the scruples of the members of the court and assigns them to a realm of silence. Captain Vere, a member of the class that wrote the laws of the land, takes on the role of witness, prosecutor, and judge. Small wonder that Billy, "a '*King's bargain*' " (*BB*, p. 88), is killed as soon as his existence is no longer seen as an asset.

Once the legal system that Vere defends as impartial is shown to be weighted in favor of the interests of his own class, the foundation for Vere's judgment of Billy collapses. No one is better at exposing Vere's shaky foundation of judgment than Edgar Dryden, who calls attention to those hints in the text which suggest that rather than keeping out the irrational, subversive forces of chaos, Captain Vere's measured forms are the most subtle disguise that the forces of chaos can adopt.

> The appalling truth of *Billy Budd* is not that innocence must be sacrificed to maintain the order of the world, but rather that innocence is destroyed by the forces of chaos and darkness masquerading as "measured forms." The "Bellipotent" is the "Athee" hiding behind the cloak of the impostor chaplain she carries; and the Articles of War

merely cover with an official mask the same irrational forces which are found undisguised "across the Channel." . . . The forces of darkness and chaos achieve their greatest success when they take on and use the forms which men create in order to convince themselves that they live in an ordered world.[12]

Dryden also points out that despite Vere's show of "philosophic austerity," the captain "may yet have indulged in the most secret of all passions, ambition" (*BB*, p. 132). The real motive for Vere's condemnation of Billy Budd may not have been to preserve order, but to gain promotion, "to avoid the possibility of any shadow's being cast on his official reputation" (p. 212). While Dryden admits that we will never know Vere's secret motives, "the mere presence of ambiguity is enough to undermine his world of 'measured forms' " (p. 212). The motives of "reasonable" actions are as difficult to know as the motives of "irrational" ones.

Once Dryden alerts us to the possibility that Captain Vere's orderly world may be controlled by the same force as the formless world the captain so fears, we can reinterpret a number of passages. Most damaging to Captain Vere's position may be the narrator's discussion of insanity. The ship's surgeon, soon after pronouncing Billy dead, questions Captain Vere's mental state. Although fear of being considered insolent or being accused of mutiny keeps him from uttering his doubts, the surgeon considers Vere's "excited exclamations so at variance with his normal manner" (*BB*, p. 96) as a sign of possible mental imbalance. In other words, the surgeon suspects that the captain may be "unhinged" because he deviates from his normal formal behavior.

But earlier we are given an even more frightening possibility to consider. Trying to help us understand Claggart's character, the narrator defines his peculiar madness.

> But the thing which in eminent instances signalizes so exceptional a nature is this: thought the man's even temper and discreet bearing would seem to intimate a mind peculiarly subject to the law of reason, not the less in his heart he would seem to riot in complete exemption from that law, having apparently little to do with reason further than to employ it as an ambidexter implement for effecting the irrational. That is to say: Toward the accomplishment of an aim which in wantonness of atrocity would seem to partake of the insane, he will direct a cool judgement sagacious and sound.
>
> These men are true madmen, and of the most dangerous sort, for their lunacy is not continuous but occasional, evoked by some special object; it is protectively secretive, which is as much as to say it is self-contained, so that when moreover, most active, it is to the average mind not distinguishable from sanity, and for the reason above suggested, that whatever its aims may be — and the aim is never declared — the method and the outward proceeding are always perfectly rational.
> [*BB*, pp. 60–61]

If we use the technique of indirection advocated throughout the book and apply this definition of madness to Vere instead of Claggart, we have an almost perfect fit.[13] Vere's "cool judgement sagacious and sound" to condemn Billy may be the act of a true madman "of the most dangerous sort." The most dangerous madness is not the clinical sort defined by the surgeon as a variance from normal manner but the exceptional sort that retains the appearance of reason and form. Rather than a deviation from normal usage, madness can be adherence to usage. Vere's ordered world can as easily serve the irrational as control it.

Vere's personal madness can be extended to the entire society that he serves. Arguing for Budd's death, Vere eloquently reminds the officers that they owe their allegiance to the king, not to nature. But if we remember our history, we remember who was king at that time, and we remember that King George was mad. Thus we have exactly the type of upside-down world that Dryden suggests. Vere owes his allegiance to a mad king and the irrational forces of war, yet the experts considered capable of detecting insanity — the clergy and men of medicine — are under Vere's command. British rule of law and order serves the very forces of chaos and irrationality that it claims to wage war against, a war fought by either impinging on the rights of nonmilitary sailors or emptying prisons of law-breachers. War itself becomes the master, and it is war's progeny, the Mutiny Act, defended as a product of man's reason through law, which condemns Billy Budd to death. What makes the deceit even more complete is that Captain Vere (along with those readers who support his stand) is probably not aware of the madness of his position. Furthermore, no one, not the chaplain, not Billy's fellow sailors, not even Billy himself, questions this rule by self-interestedness masquerading as impartiality.

If we juxtapose the reading of Vere that I have offered with Johnson's, what is most revealing is that Johnson could accept the possibility of my reading and still refuse to judge Captain Vere. Having recognized the partiality of any judgment, she cannot bring herself to judge. Thus, she adopts the same stance as the members of the crew and Billy — silence. But if my reading has any credibility, we should consider the possibility that within the context of *Billy Budd* the stance of silence, far from being neutral, serves the interests of the system of order that Vere represents. Silence in the face of his judgment is what Vere desires, and silence is what Johnson's reading delivers. . . .

To escape the responsibility of judging by having all foundation for judgment disappear into texts is to risk submitting to the system of authority that controls which passages are included in the reading text we call history. It is to risk accepting a system in which some linguistic possibilities may never be allowed to play because they have been silenced at the level of production. Furthermore, it is to deny an important function of literature, which is not only to represent man's condition in the world as it is but, through providing a glimpse of what might be, to help change man's condition in the world by making us see that our view of "what is" is conditioned by inherited ways of reading. To deny this function of literature is to be like Captain Vere, who carefully selects texts to confirm his convictions, convictions that he could not confirm by turning to society; it is these convictions that act as "a dyke against those invading waters of *novel* opinion, social, political and otherwise"(*BB*, p. 36, my emphasis) coming from France.

Similarly, J. Hillis Miller defends deconstruction's selection of texts from the traditional canon because the texts it selects support deconstruction's conviction that man's "situation in relation to language" or "the human condition generally" will not be affected by a "change in the material base or in the class structure," that, in fact, a determining material base is but "one element in the traditional metaphysical system [deconstruction] wants to put in question."[14]

More sophisticated than Vere, deconstructive critics like Johnson and Miller do not claim directly to know the way it is. Instead they claim that the way it is is that we will never know the way it is. Man's "situation in relation to language" inevitably results in gaps *within* cognition. To be sure, it would be naive to argue that we can eliminate the gaps within cognition and the gaps between action and knowing that, as Johnson shows so convincingly, make politics problematic. At the same time, it is not naive to argue that the action of *Billy Budd* shows that certain political structures contribute to creating more gaps. If Billy's speech defect is a natural condition, his gaps of silence are forced upon him by a repressive political system that exploits his desire to appear innocent. Nor is it naive to point out that rather than working to overcome the problematics of politics, Johnson's way of reading helps to maintain them. Having recognized the inevitability of gaps within cognition and between knowledge and action, Johnson proves her point by adopting a strategy that refuses to risk closing the gap between knowledge and action by judging Captain Vere. Recognition of the way things are leads to a strategy of reading that perpetuates the way things are.

The deconstructive strategy that is so subversive for traditional students of literature turns out to betray a conservative ideology.[15] Although in a society that places so much stock in textual authority deconstruction has a radical potential, that potential is limited because the world deconstruction subverts is limited. The only authority deconstruction undercuts is textual authority. John Brenkman states this point very clearly.

> The deconstructed system remains a purely philosophical one. This indefinite broadening of history into the area of metaphysics, accompanied by the narrowing of the general text, hides the evasion of all historical specificity; such a strategy has a special appeal precisely because it allows the act of radical critique to withdraw from its actual

historical, political, and institutional context. The active neutralization that is so central to deconstructive reading becomes the neutrality of deconstruction itself; the subject who deconstructs is strangely at peace with the work of criticism and negation.[16]

Brenkman might have added that deconstruction can be explained in terms of the historical specificity it seeks to evade. It can be seen as the last-ditch effort of members of a profession, whose role it is to interpret texts, to conserve their position of authority in respect to society. Their method is the ideological one of trying to make their sectional interests appear to be universal ones. More acutely aware than "traditional" humanities that society at large no longer grants the texts they study privileged authority, advocates of deconstruction answer this challenge by demonstrating the groundlessness of all claims to authority. By turning society, history, and nature into texts, they show that their loss of authority is not unique; social, political, and natural authority succumb to the same critique. Having denied all claims to legitimate authority, they are in a position to reclaim the traditional humanist's role in society. Because they are such close readers of texts and because all of civilization is one gigantic text, they, like Captain Vere, claim to be the most sensitive interpreters of man's fate.

It has been my aim in this essay to use the encounter between deconstruction and *Billy Budd* to show that deconstruction's strategy of a closer than close reading is not enough. Rather than giving a more sensitive reading of man's fate, deconstruction works to seal man's fate by confining man to an ahistorical, textual world. Man becomes truly impressed. The ragged edges of *Billy Budd* do not disappear into textuality; they lead outward into history, the realm in which the reader lives and must judge. The text of *Billy Budd* deconstructs the ground of its own textual authority not to render the reader silent but to appeal for a judgment.[17] It is through our acts of judgment that the text of *Billy Budd* in turn judges us. What the encounter of *Billy Budd* with deconstruction shows is that to adopt a judgment of silence is to reveal a conservative ideology, for, as the execution of Billy Budd makes clear, to defer a judgment is ultimately to defer to the existing system of authority.

Notes

1. Barbara Johnson, "Melville's Fist: The Execution of *Billy Budd*," *Studies in Romanticism* 18 (Winter 1979):567–99. Further references to this essay will be cited in the text. This is a special issue entitled *The Rhetoric of Romanticism* edited by Paul de Man. De Man writes of these essays: "Close reading and rhetorical analysis are eminently teachable and it is a common and productive gesture of all of these papers to outdo the closeness of reading that has been held up to them and to show, by reading the close readings more closely, that they were not nearly close enough" (p. 498). Johnson's essay is included in her book *The Critical Difference: Essays in the Contemporary Rhetoric of Reading* (Baltimore, Md.: Johns Hopkins University Press, 1981).

2. Charles A. Reich, "The Tragedy of Justice in *Billy Budd*," *Yale Review* 56 (1967):368–89. Further references to this essay will be cited in the text.

3. Herman Melvile, *Billy Budd*, ed. Milton R. Stern (Indianapolis, Ind.: Bobbs-Merrill, 1975), p. 131. I choose Stern's edition rather than that of Hayford and Sealts because I agree with his editorial decision to be inclusive rather than exclusive. All page references to *Billy Budd* are for this edition, hereafter cited in the text as *BB*.

4. Critics before Johnson seem to ignore the possibility that a text proclaiming that "truth uncompromisingly told will always have its ragged edges" places a critic trying to come up with a consistent reading in an awkward position.

5. See Michael Ryan, "Self-Evidence," *Diacritics* 10 (Summer 1980):2–16, for an attempt to align deconstruction and Marxism.

6. Anthony Giddens, *Central Problems in Social Theory* (Berkeley: University of California Press, 1979), p. 197.

7. See Max Weber, *The Theory of Social and Economic Organization*, trans. A. M. Henderson and Talcott Parsons (New York: Free Press, 1947), p. 328.

8. Quoted by Jürgen Habermas in *Legitimation Crisis*, trans. Thomas McCarthy (Boston: Beacon Press, 1975), p. 97.

9. Habermas, *Legitimation Crisis*, pp. 97–98.

10. Douglas Hay, "Property, Authority and the Criminal Law," in *Albion's Fatal Tree*, ed. Hay et al. (London: Allen Lane, 1975), pp. 37 and 48.

11. See Charles Mitchell, "Melville and the Spurious Truth of Legalism," *Centennial Review* 12 (1968):110–26.

12. Edgar A. Dryden, *Melville's Thematics of Form* (Baltimore, Md.: Johns Hopkins University Press, 1968), p. 215. Further references to this book will be cited in the text.

13. Phil Withim, "*Billy Budd:* Testament of Resistance," *Modern Language Quarterly* 20 (1959):115–27, points out the applicability of this passage on insanity to Vere.

14. J. Hillis Miller, "Theory and Practice: Response to Vincent Leitch," *Critical Inquiry* 6 (Summer 1980):612.

15. Miller admits deconstruction's conservatism in "Theory and Practice." This has been pointed out by Maria Ruegg, "The End(s) of French Style: Structuralism and Post-Structuralism in the American Context," *Criticism* 21 (Summer 1979):189–216; William E. Cain, "Deconstruction in America: The Recent Literary Criticism of J. Hillis Miller," *College English* 41 (December 1979):367–82; Vincent B. Leitch, "The Lateral Dance: The Deconstructive Criticism of J. Hillis Miller," *Critical Inquiry* 6 (Summer 1980):593–608.

16. John Brenkman, "Deconstruction and the Social Text," *Social Text* 1 (Winter 1979):188.

17. See Ruegg's acute comment: "Making value judgments is precisely the *function* of criticism. And if critics continue to write criticism, in spite of a 'crisis' which would logically reduce them to silence, it is because the function of criticism — that is, of making value judgments about some 'reality' (social, historical, literary) — is a necessary function of any society" ("The End[s] of French Style," p. 216).

Melville's Late Poetry and *Billy Budd*: From Nostalgia to Transcendence

Robert Milder*

Shortly after Melville retired from the New York Custom House on December 31, 1885, his wife Lizzie wrote of a "great deal [of] unfinished work at his desk which will give him occupation."[1] A legacy from Lizzie's brother Lemuel Shaw had eased the family situation and placed Melville in the happy predicament he later allegorized in the poem "The Rose Farmer," much as Emily Dickinson had addressed a similar question in "Essential oils — are wrung": whether to cultivate the rose (experience) for its evanescent fullness or laboriously distill and crystallize its attar in a timeless but solitary art. Although "The Rose Farmer" ends inconclusively, a comfortable epicureanism was at most a pleasant fantasy for Melville, who had outlived his male relatives, nearly all of his friends, and his times, but not his chronic demons — metaphysics and the taunting dream of reputation. At home, while generally calmer than before, Melville was still prey to "moods and occasional uncertain tempers,"[2] surfacings of an emotional disquiet that hinted as always with Melville of an intellectual and spiritual disquiet. And though he now wore his obscurity with a silent, protective pride, Melville continued to brood on fame and could guardedly encourage English admirers like James Billson and sea novelist W. Clark Russell whose homage exacted no risks and gave promise of a belated recognition. For almost ten years, since the monumental *Clarel* (1876), Melville's life had been collapsing inward toward a center of private musing, and in the leisure of his retirement Melville gave himself austerely to the art he depended upon for his vindication, privately publishing two books — the verse collections *John Marr and Other Sailors* (1888) and *Timoleon* (1891) — and leaving at his death two incompletely revised manuscripts — the pastoral *Weeds and Wildings*, many of whose poems belong to an earlier period, and *Billy Budd, Sailor (An Inside Narrative)*.

Ever since it first appeared in Raymond Weaver's edition of 1924, *Billy Budd* has impressed readers as a testament of one kind or another, most commonly of Christian acceptance or of irony and political protest. More properly, *Billy Budd* is the product not of a single unified fictive intention but of successive intentions that span the course of Melville's retirement and link the narrative to *John Marr* and *Timoleon*. Begun in or around 1886 as a sailor monologue akin to those in *John Marr, Billy Budd* evolved through three major stages, together with several important

*From *Philological Quarterly* 66 (Fall 1987):493–507. Reprinted with slight revisions by permission.

substages, and was chronologically complete and awaiting final revision when Melville died in 1891. . . .[3] The text we now read, constructed from a genetic analysis of the manuscript, is as close to Melville's final intention as scholars can make it.[4] Even so, *Billy Budd* remains a thematically sequential work whose shifts of interest replicate its compositional history and reflect Melville's inward journey over the last five years of his life.

Though the compositional evidence surrounding *Billy Budd* has been available since 1962, interpreters have rarely drawn upon it to read *Billy Budd* as a work in process. Yet the shape of Melville's 1888 narrative is largely inferable, and by using its themes as a point of reference it is possible to trace the pattern of Melville's late career and at the same time suggest the unfolding logic that governs the final text. In brief, *John Marr* and *Timoleon* show Melville still quarreling with Providence and society, uncertain of the value of his long dedication to art, and divided between a bleak awareness of human tragedy and a fond retrospection. Originating in the nostalgia and despair of *John Marr*, *Billy Budd* developed by 1888 into a last arraignment of God and society—a design that shaped the work, with changing emphasis, until Melville surmounted his anger during the final stages of composition and arrived at the only "testament" he could make, or would ever have wanted to make, a testament to his own spirit.

I

Privately printed in an edition of twenty-five copies, *John Marr* sounds the notes that will dominate Melville's final period: solitude and alienation; a yearning for the color and heroism of wooden ship days; and a gray, unflinching acceptance of life's mischances as they occur against the backdrop of nature's blankness. In the title poem with its long prose headnote, Melville dramatized his isolation through the figure of an aging ex-sailor living miles inland and drawn in his loneliness to memories of his former shipmates. The thematic center of the poem is a contrast between two human communities fronting nature: "staid" landsmen toiling on the oceanic prairie, their social "unresponsiveness . . . of a piece with the apathy of Nature herself," and sailors from a glorified past "Hoisting up the storm-sail cheerly, / *Life is storm—let storm!*"[5] A vision of free-spirited camaraderie amid nature's hardships also informs "Jack Roy," Melville's eulogy to Jack Chase, his messmate from the *United States* and the *beau idéal* of *White-Jacket* (1850) whom Melville would honor again in the dedication to *Billy Budd*. The key virtue in both poems is "geniality," defined in the prologue to "John Marr" as "the flower of life springing from some sense of joy in it, more or less." A hearty fellowship associated with masculine humor and frank, unillusioned talk, geniality had always held a special place among Melville's values and had been crucial to his intellectual and emotional balance. As death shrank his circle of intimates during the 1870s, however, the exuberance Melville once exhibited in family gatherings or evenings with Hawthorne or Evert Duyckinck was channeled into compensatory celebrations of geniality like the unpublished Burgundy Club sketches or poetic jeremiads like "The Age of the Antonines." By the mid 'eighties Melville's geniality had grown rusty from disuse, and in *John Marr* he projected geniality backward into a romanticized past and detached it from its intellectual moorings. Ishmael's "genial, desperado philosophy" — fraternal because clear-eyed about humanity's cosmic plight — became the glamorized recklessness of boy-men courageous toward nature's dangers but insensible of its tragedies.[6]

In "Bridegroom Dick," the rambling monologue of a retired petty officer, nostalgia assumes a political dimension prophetic of *Billy Budd* as Melville revisits the naval world of *White-Jacket* and transforms his midcentury indictment of war and authoritarianism into an *ubi sunt* tribute to past gallantry and a near-Carlylean eulogy of government-by-the-hero — in this case, by the "Kentuckian colossal" Captain Turret, who (unlike Vere) overrides naval statutes and pardons a manly offender slated for punishment. As the actualities of war and class exploitation receded in Melville's memory, the libertarian protest in his work was eclipsed by a skeptical but humane conservatism that grew stronger as he aged. Still, rather than a specifically political or even a philosophical creed, the rose-colored conservatism of *John Marr* — a lame descendant of the tragically-based conservatism of *Battle-Pieces* [1866] and *Clarel* — seems the by-product of a longing for magnanimity that drew Melville backward across the divide he imagined between a poetic and a mechanical age, a divide symbolized in "Bridegroom Dick" by the Civil War engagement in which the wood-and-sail *Cumberland* was sunk by the ironclad *Merrimac*.[7]

In contrast to the sailor poems, the dozen or so "Sea Pieces" that complete *John Marr* are without illusion. Two of the poems ("The Good Craft 'Snow-Bird' " and "To the Master of the 'Meteor' ") are hymns of triumph over the elements, but more typically the poems document shipwrecks and disasters, often amidst the pride of life and usually accomplished through some hidden treachery of reef, iceberg, or oozy, weedchoked floating wreck.[8] The laureates of this world are the window box of "The Aeolian Harp," shrieking its mad plaint for life's victims, and the conch of the closing poem "Pebbles," whispering of an alien, implacable nature with nothing "that give man back man's strain — / The hope of his heart, the dream in his brain." "Pebbles" ends with an accommodation of sorts ("Healed of my hurt, I laud the inhuman Sea"), but its chastened acceptance, amounting virtually to a surrender to amoral power, sits oddly with the devil-may-care spiritedness of "John Marr" and "Jack Roy." Divided structurally between the sailor poems and the "Sea-Pieces," *John Marr* is also divided in vision and tone, consigning heroism to a romanticized past while facing the present neither reconciled to God's universe nor consoled by any victory of the human spirit.

Less deliberately organized than *John Marr*, *Timoleon* is most distinguished for those poems that explore the renunciations and rewards of truth's votaries — the female astronomer in "After the Pleasure Party"; the recluse of "The Garden of Metrodorus"; the artists of "The Weaver," "In a Garret," and "Art"; the insomniac thinker of "The Bench of Boors"; and the light-seeker of "The Enthusiast" — as if Melville, surveying his long career, were trying to persuade himself he had not been a Fool of Truth. As in *John Marr*, the title poem governs the collection. Adapted from Plutarch's story of the Corinthian soldier and statesman (with hints from Balzac's *The Two Brothers*), "Timoleon" is a compendium of Melville themes and a loose allegory of his emotional life: a docile second son overshadowed by his active brother, "the mother's pride and pet"; the son heroically committing himself to virtue (Timoleon slaying his tyrant-brother Timophanes; Melville pursuing truth in his fiction regardless of sales or reputation); and the son, repudiated by his mother and estranged from a weak-hearted populace, exiling himself from the city and railing at the silent gods for their abandonment of "earnest natures." In plot and rhetoric "Timoleon" recalls *Pierre* [1852] when, having sacrificed worldly happiness for truth, Pierre finds himself despised by earth and heaven, mother and divine Father, alike. Yet where Pierre dies scorning the gods, society, and the noblest part of himself, Melville ends "Timoleon" with a vision of triumph in which the hero emerges from retirement to save the state, then — "Absolved and more!" — spurns Corinth's praise and returns to voluntary exile.

The question that frames "Timoleon" is whether glory, belatedly won, is the result of "high Providence, or Chance," a question much on Melville's mind as he pondered his long neglect, too proud or vulnerable to respond to the modest overtures of the New York literati yet scarcely indifferent to posthumous fame. Reading Schopenhauer toward the very end of his life, Melville marked two passages that bear intimately on his situation. The first likens the man of genius to "some noble prisoner of state, condemned to work in the galleys with common criminals" and preserving his integrity by isolation; the second holds that "the more a man belongs to posterity, . . . the more of an alien he is to his contemporaries, since his work is not meant for them as such."[9] In "Timoleon" "high Providence" signified Time correcting life's inequities, as the ages, Melville hoped, would resurrect him. Yet imaged as an absent or withholding father, Providence also represented a voice from without or within justifying the self-doubting hero for his long sacrifice and godlike commitment to truth. Timoleon's most agonized suspicion is that humanity, after all, is made predominantly of clay and for clay, a thought that similarly torments Melville's astronomer awakened to her demanding sexuality

("After the Pleasure Party") and haunts his thought-burdened speaker who muses half-enviously on Teniers' drowsy, beer-soaked peasants ("The Bench of Boors"). The opposing term of this late dialectic is the quenchless aspiration voiced by the speaker of "The Enthusiast" ("Though light forsake thee, never fall / From fealty to light"), so like the motto Melville pasted beside his writing desk: "Keep true to the dreams of thy youth."[10] Nearly forty years after *Pierre* Melville was still fighting the battle of the spirit and the clay and wondering whether his renunciations had been vain. Reputation had been denied him; posthumous fame was uncertain; truth was as elusive as ever; and the gods who might have commended him, if only the metaphoric gods of inward conviction, were silent.

II

Written contemporaneously with *John Marr* and *Timoleon* and drawing its themes partly from the same urgencies, *Billy Budd*, during its long evolution, can be understood as a working through of Melville's bitterness toward a remote Providence and a small-souled, neglectful world.

In its opening eulogy of the 'Handsome Sailor' who flourished in "the less prosaic time" before steamships,[11] *Billy Budd* recalls the nostalgia of "John Marr" and "Jack Roy." What had been sentimentality in the verse, however, is immediately raised to myth as the pre-lapsarian Billy is impressed from the *Rights-of-Man* and introduced to "the ampler and more knowing world of a great warship" (*BB*, p. 50), Melville's symbol, as in *White-Jacket*, for the great world itself. Melville's first intention in opposing Claggart and Billy was probably to illustrate the fate of good-natured innocence amid the mantraps of society, a theme since *Typee* (1846) but one that "John Marr" had focused on the class of sailors — "Barbarians of man's simpler nature, / Unworldly servers of the world." As Melville reworked his manuscript, however, Claggart's motiveless spite became a " 'mystery of iniquity' " that savored of "Holy Writ" (*BB*, p. 76), and *Billy Budd* developed from an exemplary fable to a reenactment of the Christian fall that raised the problem of an omnipotent God's responsibility for evil.

Melville's literary paradigm at this stage of composition was *Paradise Lost*, and echoes of Milton's Satan resound in the expanded portrait of Claggart. Yet lacking the climactic execution scene that some readers interpret as Melville's Christian acceptance, the 1888 *Billy Budd* seems rather an anti-*Paradise Lost* designed to impugn the ways of God. The early narrative concluded with the garbled report of events from "News from the Mediterranean," upon which Melville moralized: "Here ends a story not unwarranted by what sometimes happens in this [one undeciphered word] world of ours — Innocence and infamy, spiritual depravity and fair repute."[12] "Sometimes happens" implies a periodic divine negligence of the sort Ishmael called "an interregnum in Providence" (*MD*, p.

271), and it establishes the injustice done Billy as a recurrent historical fact, complementing the mythic status of the action as a representation of the fall. God is thus arraigned on two counts: his ultimate responsibility for man's temptation and fall — Claggart acts out his part "like the scorpion for which the Creator alone is responsible" (*BB*, p. 78) — and his general *ir*responsibility toward human affairs ever since. Also arraigned are those official versions of events (naval chronicles, Christian apologetics) that play havoc with the truth in order to demonstrate that all goes well. An "inside narrative," in his context, would be one that set the metaphysical record straight and, incidentally, adjusted the wrongs of worldly reputation.

That Melville should chafe against the problem of evil is hardly surprising; he had been doing so since *Mardi* [1849]. The curious fact is that he should press his language and symbols so far in the direction of theological allegory. Melville's sane heroes of thought (Babbalanja in *Mardi*; Ishmael; Rolfe in *Clarel*) retreat from a theistic formulation of evil, first, because they are essentially naturalists in their feeling for how the world operates, and, second, because they are respectful of mysteries not to be adequately propounded, let alone solved, by human reason. It is Melville's mad, or maddened, heroes (Ahab; Mortmain in *Clarel*; Pierre) who become God-hating allegorists by virtue of their native theocentrism and of a cosmic rage that demands a personified antagonist. Melville himself contained both perspectives, and in moments of metaphysical "swearing" (as he characterized it to Hawthorne) he passed between them by a pendulum movement in which an extreme of one mode, skeptical naturalism or fist-shaking supernaturalism, generated a reaction toward the other.[13] *John Marr* shows Melville chilled by a bleak naturalism that allows no closing with life's tragedies save on the ground of stoic resignation. The 1888 *Billy Budd* is Melville's imaginative revolt against the indignity of passive endurance, and its theological idiom serves him much as madness served Ahab; it allows him to personify and pit himself against an otherwise faceless universe in which resistance is impossible. Like his defiant heroes Ahab, Mortmain, Timoleon, and Pierre, Melville in *Billy Budd* reproaches God for not being godly enough, and in so doing he registers his own godlikeness upon the heavens whether or not there is anyone above to acknowledge him.

It may have been the act of recording his protest that freed Melville from its emotional grip, as had happened years earlier with *Moby-Dick*;[14] yet catharsis alone cannot explain the new direction his narrative took. Two magazine articles on the *Somers* incident of 1842, the first appearing in the spring of 1888 as Melville worked on *John Marr*, may have kindled Melville's memories of his cousin Guert Gansevoort, a first lieutenant on the *Somers* when an acting midshipman and two sailors were hanged for conspiracy, and prompted Melville to brood on questions of justice and authority.[15] Whatever the reason, Melville returned to his manuscript and addressed the thinly drawn figure of Vere, a shift of focus that carried the action forward beyond Claggart's death without requiring Melville substantially to recast what he had written. Claggart with his violet eyes and Billy with his welkin-blue had been less — or more — than roundly human characters, but with Claggart's death the fall and its attendant interests became a given and the story descended to the naturalistic world of gray-eyed Vere (comfortably or not, Melville's intellectual home) in which moral and political questions had to be resolved in post-lapsarian terms against "the monotonous blank of the twilight sea" (*BB*, p. 109).

It was the tragedy of governance — a new subject for him — that absorbed Melville now and drew him outward beyond his frustrations, first toward the political world, then toward the psyche, with a humaneness and breadth of comprehension unapproached in the late poetry. In Part 4 of *Clarel* Melville had voiced the negatives of his social thought through the ex-Confederate officer Ungar, on one side a blooded Indian who rails at injustice with the rage of the dispossessed, on the other a lapsed-Catholic reactionary who berates radicals and flabby progressives for their neglect of original sin. *Billy Budd* preserves the terms of Ungar's neither/nor in its harsh portrayal of French Jacobinism and British repression, but it focuses upon the empowered ruler who must act. The long trial scene in Chapter 21 is a masterpiece of ambiguity, with Vere in one reading an anguished but duty-bound representative of the political state, in another a myopic conservative whose narrow and exacting application of a wartime code tyrannical in itself is a double indictment of a martial society that sacrifices justice to order and dehumanizes even its most conscientious men. That both readings are not merely justified but demanded by the text is a sign that Melville requires of us something more than ideological choice or a painless, "literary" tolerance of alternatives. Convinced of the need for social bulwarks against nature's chaos — Vere's "forms, measured forms" (*BB*, p. 128) — Melville knew that any particular forms were likely to be radically flawed. He knew, also, that forms had to be administered by human beings enmeshed in events and compromised by their tendencies, limitations, passions, and interests. We are all familiar with the duck/rabbit figure that seems to defy a simultaneous perception of rival shapes. In *Billy Budd* Melville presents a circumstanced "case" with more perspectives on it — and attitudes toward it — than a mortal consciousness can comfortably entertain, and he challenges us to rise to it as a representation of tragic experience in its irreducible and overwhelming truth.

Manuscript evidence suggests that Melville composed a good part of the trial and execution scenes before he interpolated the character analysis of Chapters 6 and 7 that established Vere as a Burkean conservative of a peculiarly inward sort — bookish, prone to dreamy gazing "at the blank sea" (*BB*, p. 61), and touched with " 'a queer streak of the pedantic' " (*BB*, p. 63).[16] Melville's political themes were in place, that is to say, before he altered his focus yet again and diverted his narrative from an abstract morality play to a study of fallible men living and acting in time. Just as Melville's allegory of the fall led him beyond theology to questions of governance in the fallen world, so his exploration of political and legal judgment shaded naturally into a concern with its psychosocial roots in the minds of the governors.

Pertinent to this late emphasis on character is the history of Melville's digression on Lord Nelson (presently Chapter 4), written in 1888 in the nostalgic spirit of "Bridegroom Dick" and under the direct influence of the British naval histories Melville had begun to consult and of Southey's *Life of Nelson*. In revising his manuscript later that year Melville deleted the chapter, probably because he found it inconsistent with the theological turn his story had taken. At the last, however, he decided to reinsert the leaves, apparently just preceding the newly written chapters on Vere and with additional comments disparaging "Personal prudence" and glorifying Nelson's heroic death.[17] What had originated as an exercise in romantic escapism thus became an implied comment on a man "who whatever his sterling qualities was without any brilliant ones" (*BB*, p. 61). The intent to undercut Vere — not so seriously as to invert the story's political meaning, only to destabilize it — is indicated by the fact that "shortly after revising the Nelson chapter," Melville reworked the crucial scene between Vere and the surgeon.[18] Against Nelson — not a captain "to terrorize a crew into base subjection, but to win them" to allegiance "by force of his mere presence and heroic personality" (*BB*, p. 59) — the rigid Vere (*vir*) emerges as a type of the earnest but flawed humanity that makes us agents of avoidable suffering. Politically, the juxtaposition of the captains reaches beyond the specifics of Billy's case to dramatize Melville's skeptical "contention that man, at any level below that of the hero, is the victim of his own ambiguities and inconsistencies, and of history";[19] psychologically, along with the surgeon's questions about Vere's sanity, it directs us further to the idiosyncrasies of Vere's nature that may have been responsible for Billy's death and to the paradigmatic spectacle of a sympathetic but inwardly compelled ruler acting under the press of circumstances and compounding society's failures by private limitations of his own.

After an initial movement upward from exemplary fable to theological myth, *Billy Budd*, during its long gestation, traveled progressively downward toward the particularized world of human action. Novelists commonly speak of their characters escaping the roles assigned them and generating unforeseen action as if from themselves. The shifts in Melville's novels had always had a different source — the logic of his inward discoveries — but in *Billy Budd* Melville seems genuinely to be responding to the latent possibilities of his story and, at the end, to the forward pull of Vere and Billy themselves. Where the late poetry had lent itself to an allegorized brooding on social and metaphysical injuries, the action of *Billy Budd* gradually lifted Melville out of himself and turned him from the objectification of private trials to an absorbed concern with how tragically doomed individuals might behave.

One looks to an authorial explanation of this kind because nothing in Melville's characterization and themes adequately prepares us for the ending of this narrative. Vere's speech to the drumhead court shows human beings hopelessly entangled in the real or mind-forged manacles of their condition. Yet Billy's trial concluded, the focus of the narrative shifts again as issues of justice and political morality give way to the purely human circumstance of two men meeting the inevitable with generosity and strength. The Vere who had argued for coolness during the trial scene is "melt[ed] back into what remains primeval in our formalized humanity" (*BB*, p. 115) and softened by the weight of a judgment made conscientiously and with full awareness of tragic sacrifice, disastrously wrong as it may be. Billy's role — to feel Vere's pain more than his own — is greater still, but his growth is made visible only at the last when, "spiritualized now through late experiences so poignantly profound" (*BB*, p. 123), he becomes, not a symbol of Christ, but an example of humanity's Christlike capacity for self-transfiguration. Billy's "fortunate fall," reminiscent of Donatello's in *The Marble Faun* but without sin, is a justification neither of God's ways nor of the ways of the state. Billy's triumph is personal and has reference to the moral life alone. The "soft glory" that "chanced" to illuminate "the vapory fleece hanging low in the East" (*BB*, p. 124) seems a version of the divine signet craved by Timoleon and Pierre, but its promise is indistinct and we are immediately recalled to our unsanctified world by the image of Billy swaying lifelessly in the "slow roll" of a "great ship ponderously cannoned" (*BB*, p. 124). By this time, however, the injustices of the human world and the remoteness of the divine have ceased to matter. A mood of hushed contemplation has descended upon the narrative, and along with the witnessing sailors we marvel at the timeless heroism of human beings trapped by circumstances and swayed by the imperatives of their nature yet capable toward the last of an extraordinary gesture of magnanimity.[20]

Like Shakespeare's late romances (as Northrop Frye describes them), *Billy Budd* encloses tragedy within a movement "from a lower world of confusion to an upper world of order" and suggests the "transformation from one kind of life to another"; it "outrag[es] reality and at the same time introduc[es] us to a world of childlike innocence which has always made more sense than reality."[21] In *Billy Budd*, however, this upper world is solely the property of the individual, whose transformation neither regenerates the social world nor is properly understood by it. Thus Melville ends *Billy Budd* by having plodding officialdom garble Billy's story and the crewmen fashion a cult of Billy-as-Christ from a nobility it is theirs to imitate. Such will always be the world's judgments, Melville implies; yet missing from his closing ironies (so distant in tone from the bitter didacticism of the 1888 conclusion) is a concern that the travesties of reputation have any bearing on human apotheosis, which knows itself by the inward sign of spiritual repleteness.

Ultimately, the exaltation to which *Billy Budd* testifies toward the last is neither Billy's nor Vere's but the author's own. It seems especially significant that in describing Vere's communication of the verdict to Billy Melville disclaims the omniscience of narrative report and suspends his governing convention of delivering the truth. The scene is offered as a private speculation, evoked with reverence and rendered in a prose as conscious of its own quiet sublimity as of Billy's and Vere's. Though it is ostensibly the characters who claim our attention, the language of the scene, fraught with hypotheticals, continually recalls us to its origin in the sensibility of the narrator. Eloquent in its reserve, the scene hints of depths that cannot be shared with the reader, though they are plumbed with a priestly awe by the narrator himself: "But there is no telling the sacrament, seldom if in any case revealed to the gadding world, wherever under circumstances at all akin to those here attempted to be set forth two of great Nature's nobler order embrace. There is privacy at the time, inviolable to the survivor; and holy oblivion, the sequel to each diviner magnanimity, providentially covers all at least" (*BB*, p. 115).

To the Melville of *Timoleon* "holy oblivion" would have been a fearful oxymoron signifying at once God's betrayal of human hopes for immortality and the susceptibility of all life and reputation to time. In the present context the words assume an opposite meaning: the sufficiency of time-bound greatness to itself. For Billy and Vere, the "diviner magnanimity" is to have reached a level of compassion and understanding that has not obviated tragedy but risen admirably to face it; for Melville, it is to have imagined such a possibility of behavior and have given it full allegiance. Without accommodating himself to the universe, Melville has come to accept the incongruities of what Auden calls the "human position" of suffering,[22] and though he is unsure there can be any other position, any transcendent justification for the sufferer, he has grown to feel that the spiritual is no less divine for being located entirely within the human soul and going unrecognized by the world. In *Clarel* Melville had portrayed his idealized *alter ego*, Rolfe, as living undramatically at humanity's best without suspecting that this itself is divinity. By the closing scenes of *Billy Budd* Melville seems to have realized what Rolfe did not and to have ventured beyond both the nostalgia and despair of *John Marr* and the self-questioning of *Timoleon*. He has arrived at a certainty of inward worth and, thereby, at a qualified peace.

Notes

1. Elizabeth Melville to Catherine Lansing (10 January 1886), in Jay Leyda, *The Melville Log*, vol. 2 (New York: Harcourt Brace, 1951), p. 796.

2. Frances Cuthbert Thomas Osborne, "Herman Melville Through a Child's Eyes," in Merton M. Sealts, Jr., *The Early Lives of Melville* (U. of Wisconsin Press, 1974), p. 180.

3. See Harrison Hayford and Merton M. Sealts, Jr., Editors' Introduction, *Billy Budd, Sailor (An Inside Narrative)*, ed. Hayford and Sealts (U. of Chicago Press, 1962), pp. 1–12.

4. The Hayford-Sealts text of 1962 will soon be superseded by the Northwestern-Newberry text, but revisions should be minor compared to Hayford and Sealts's correction of the deeply flawed texts of Raymond Weaver (1924) and F. Barron Freeman (1948).

5. All quotations from Melville's poems are drawn from Howard P. Vincent's *Collected Poems of Herman Melville* (Chicago: Packard, 1947).

6. Melville, *Moby-Dick; or The Whale*, ed. Harrison Hayford and Hershel Parker (New York: Norton, 1967), p. 196.

7. Four poems from *Battle-Pieces* — "The Stone Fleet," "The Cumberland," "The Temeraire," and "A Utilitarian View of the Monitor's Fight" — deal nostalgically with the passing of wooden ship days, a theme whose biographical relevance is discussed by Edward Stessel in "Naval Warfare and Herman Melville's War Against Failure," *Essays in Arts and Sciences* 10 (1981):59–77.

8. Dedicated to Melville's brother Thomas and drafted in December 1860, "To the Master of the 'Meteor' " is pertinent to Melville's attitudes in the 'eighties primarily as Melville's later revisions tend to bring a light, celebratory poem into line with the darker view of nature expressed in *John Marr*. The waves over which the "Meteor" sweeps in the early "To Tom" become "monstrous" in the revised version. Similarly, the setting of the poem is shifted from the conventional "torrid deep" to "Off the Cape of Storms," where sailors must keep "vigil."

9. Leyda, *Log*, 2:832–833. While reading Schopenhauer, Melville also found and checked a remark by Tacitus pertinent to the theme of reputation that obsessed him: "The lust of fame is the last that a wise man shakes off." Quoted in Merton M. Sealts, Jr., *The Early Lives of Melville* (University of Wisconsin Press, 1974), p. 80.

10. Eleanor Melville Metcalf, *Herman Melville: Cycle and Epicycle* (Harvard U. Press, 1953), p. 284.

11. Melville, *Billy Budd, Sailor (An Inside Narrative)*, ed. Hayford and Sealts, p. 43. All further references to *Billy Budd* will be included in the text.

12. Hayford and Sealts, Editors' Introduction, p. 8.

13. The most dramatic instance of these pendulum swings occurs in Melville's letter to Hawthorne of 16[?] April[?] 1851. See *The Letters of Herman Melville*, ed. Merrell R. Davis and William H. Gilman (Yale U. Press, 1960), pp. 124–25, and Robert Milder, "*Nemo Contra Deum* . . . : Melville and Goethe's 'Demonic,' " in *Ruined Eden of the Present*, ed. G. R. Thompson and Virgil L. Lokke (Purdue U. Press, 1981), pp. 236–38.

14. "I have written a wicked book and feel spotless as the lamb." Melville to Hawthorne, in *Letters*, p. 142.

15. The two articles on the *Somers* incident, which Melvile may or may not have read, are Lieutenant H. D. Smith, "The Mutiny on the *Somers*," *American Magazine* 8 (June 1888):109–14, and Gail Hamilton, "The Murder of Philip Spencer," *Cosmopolitan* 7 (June, July, August 1889):134–40, 248–55, 345–54. Guert Gansevoort is recalled twice in "Bridegroom Dick," the second time as "Tom Tight, lieutenant in the brig-o'-war famed / When an officer was hung for an arch-mutineer."

16. Hayford and Sealts, Editors' Introduction, pp. 8–9.

17. Hayford and Sealts, eds., Genetic Text of *Billy Budd, Sailor*, in Chicago edition, pp. 306–7.

18. Hayford and Sealts, "Table and Discussions of Foliations," in Chicago edition, p. 246.

19. Ralph W. Willett, "Nelson and Vere: Hero and Victim in *Billy Budd, Sailor*," *PMLA*, 82 (1967):373.

20. Warner Berthoff has written eloquently of this theme of "The motions of magnanimity under the most agonizing worldly duress" — *The Example of Melville* (Princeton U. Press, 1962), p. 200. According to Berthoff, the theme governs *Billy Budd* to the virtual exclusion of questions of theology, metaphysics, and political justice. The implication of the compositional evidence, however, is that Melville discovered the theme only late in the process of writing; it is a vision he achieved, not one he began with.

21. Northrop Frye, *Anatomy of Criticism* (Princeton U. Press, 1957), p. 184.

22. W. H. Auden, "Musée des Beaux Arts," *The Collected Poetry of W. H. Auden* (New York: Random House, 1945), p. 3.

Billy Budd, Sailor: Melville's Last Romance
James McIntosh*

Toward the end of chapter 2 in *Billy Budd, Sailor*, Melville makes a curious allusion to a story by Hawthorne, the American writer who had meant most to him in his youth. The narrator, having praised Billy at generous length, grants that his hero has a weakness: "Though our Handsome Sailor had as much of masculine beauty as one can expect anywhere to see; nevertheless, like the beautiful woman in one of Hawthorne's minor tales, there was just one thing amiss in him."[1] What is amiss in Billy is his tendency to stutter "under sudden provocation of strong heart-feeling," and his infirmity, like the rosy "blemish" on Georgianna's cheek in Hawthorne's story "The Birthmark," is not only a mark of imperfection but also a sign of humanity, of the secret ungovernable power of the human heart. The narrator then winds up the chapter in a whimsical paragraph that has sometimes been read with studious literal-mindedness: "The avowal of such an imperfection in the Handsome Sailor should be evidence not alone that he is not presented as a conventional hero, but also that the story in which he is the main figure is no romance" (53). The juxtaposition of "Hawthorne" and "romance" should put us on our guard. What if we were to say that the tiny hand on Georgianna's cheek is proof that "The Birthmark" is likewise not a romance? On the contrary, what Melville intends us to infer from his narrator's cunning association is that *Billy Budd, Sailor* is itself a romance of a special kind, a development of the romance as Hawthorne idiosyncratically conceived it.[2] True, Melville ponders the story with an awareness that his fiction, like Hawthorne's, transcends generic boundaries as usually understood. *Billy Budd* is in part a mediation on the nature of fiction in which Melville plays with generic terms and narrative procedures. Yet in chapter 2, both his focus on Billy's "heart-feeling" and his narrator's self-display recall

*This essay was written specifically for this volume and is published here for the first time by permission of the author.

Hawthorne's practice as a romancer. For Hawthorne, the essential touch-stone of a romance is that it adhere to "the truth of the human heart."[3] Melville too is intent that his story reveal that mysterious truth. Moreover, his offhand allusion to "The Birthmark" is a clue that *Billy Budd* is his last gesture of homage to his dear friend, whom he had not always treated so kindly in his fiction and poetry.

If, as Robert Milder writes, *Billy Budd* for Melville is "a testament to his own spirit"[4] rather than a testament of acceptance *or* rebellion, a coming to terms with his own spiritual anxieties as he meditated on his approaching death, then it is not surprising that it should contain a veiled acknowledgment of Hawthorne's ultimate importance for him. Signs of Hawthorne's presence are evident both in Melville's later writings and in the record of his later life. In 1876 Melville published his long poem *Clarel*, in which he depicts Hawthorne's refined melancholy and personal reticence in the character of Vine. In 1883 he seems to have been powerfully affected by recollections of Hawthorne called up in an inter-view with Julian Hawthorne. (Julian included several of Melville's letters to Hawthorne and an account of their relationship in *Nathaniel Hawthorne and His Wife*, published in 1884, after which Melville was partly known as "the friend of Hawthorne."[5]) In 1891, the year of his death, Melville indicated the vividness of his memory of Hawthorne by including his moving elegy "Monody" in *Timoleon*, his last work published during his lifetime.[6] *Billy Budd* itself suggests that after the measured antagonism with which he had treated Hawthorne as Vine in *Clarel* he was ready to redress the balance with him as part of his general settling of accounts in his late poems and his last work of fiction.

Hawthorne's central discussion of the romance is the preface to *The House of the Seven Gables*. Though that novel has no particular relevance to *Billy Budd*, the general principles Hawthorne sets forth in its preface are highly relevant. At the risk of violating Hawthorne's tone I will summarize them schematically. First, a romance aims not at "a very minute fidelity . . . to the probable and ordinary course of man's experi-ence" (an aim of the novel), but rather seeks to represent "the truth of the human heart." Second, a romance may even deviate from ordinary experience in that its action may include "the Marvellous" along with the probable, though Hawthorne cautions that the marvelous be used as a "flavor" rather than as a substantial portion of the "dish" to be offered to the public. Third, the writer of a romance may "claim a certain latitude, both as to its fashion and material." He has a right to present the truth of the human heart "under circumstances, to a great extent, of [his] own choosing or creation."[7] In other words the romancer, as he is not so bound by the detail and sequence of events in ordinary experience, may manipu-late his fiction more obviously than the novelist. A corollary is that we as readers are the more aware of the romancer's presence and importance in his own fiction, aware that he continually calls attention to his narrative and expository strategies. The romancer's projection of a fiction-making self may irritate some readers. Emerson, for example, complained in his journal, "Hawthorn invites his readers too much into his study, opens the process before them. As if the confectioner should say to his customers Now let us make the cake."[8] But in *Billy Budd*, as in "The Old Manse" (perhaps the text Emerson had in mind), the whimsy of a cake maker is an inescapable component of the story as we read it.

The preface to *The House of the Seven Gables* suggests an inference one could draw from all of Hawthorne's prefaces as well as from his practice both in his tales and in his longer fiction, that romance for him is a hybrid form, combining the actual and the imaginary, fact and fable, the probable and the marvelous, and the historical and the mysterious. Melville seems to have understood the hybrid character of his own fiction in his mediations on genre in *The Confidence-Man* and *Billy Budd*, the two works of his that most reflect the influence of Hawthorne's prefaces. True, while Melville had called both *Mardi* and *Pierre* "romances" (in different senses) in letters to his English publishers,[9] he brings in the term only obliquely in *The Confidence Man* and *Billy Budd*; yet in both works the narrator's deceptively casual references to Hawthorne suggest Melville's wish to link his own struggle for truth in fiction with that of his mentor.[10]

In *Billy Budd* Melville seeks to represent the truth of the human heart in a narrative that joins factuality and romance, and he remembers Hawthorne as one who also went on this quest, in "The Birthmark" and generally. Of course Melville has many other things in mind along with Hawthornean romance in his late, long-spun yarn, and the narrative he assembles in his last years is finally a work *sui generis*. *Billy Budd* is an old man's conglomerate of different kinds of fiction. Like Hawthorne's and Melville's "novels" written at the height of their careers, it mixes its media;[11] it combines romance with autobiographical reminiscence, pseudodocuments pretending to be true with truthfully fictive ballads, and primarily symbolic figures like Billy and Claggart with a primarily novelistic character like Vere. And all these disparate elements are connected by a narrator who reminds the reader continually of what he is doing, including telling a story that is and is not a romance. As Michael Davitt Bell suggests, Hawthorne and Melville differ from other American romancers in that "while writing romance, they also write *about* romance."[12] Though Bell treats *Billy Budd* only in passing, his remark fits it as well as anything Melville wrote. In the course of his story Melville knowingly broadens the common conception of "romance," laying different meanings of the word before the reader without necessarily resolving them. Moreover, at various points in the work as a whole, he enacts in his own way the ideas Hawthorne proposes in the preface to *The House of the Seven Gables*. As an "inside narrative," *Billy Budd* is a story about the truth of the human heart.[13] Though grounded in history, its plot includes an element of the marvelous (as in Hawthorne this element is not understood by prosaic spectators). Finally, the author through his narrator makes his presence felt continually, and assumes a considerable latitude in the fashioning and distorting of his materials.

Billy Budd contains an elaborate account of historical circumstances as background for its inside narrative. Melville means his story to convey an impression of historical authenticity, not an impression one always gets from romances. The narrator keeps insisting that the story is based on humble facts and is free from the distortions of fantasy. He would not, like a garrulous sailor, "exaggerate or romance" (67) the passions he represents. We can take the narrator at his word that Billy Budd is not a romance in this pejorative sense. Nevertheless, this very concern with the relations between fact and fable is characteristic of the way Melville, like Hawthorne, writes about romance in the act of writing it. Moreover, in the course of his narrative Melville shows that he recognizes a more serious meaning in "romance" even while denying that his story is a romantic falsehood. When the narrator explores the character of John Claggart in chapter 11, he claims that it would be easy to invent "some romantic incident" that would lend plausibility to Claggart's seemingly unmotivated hostility to Billy. "But in fact there was nothing of the sort" (74). "And yet," he continues, "the cause necessarily to be assumed . . . is in its very realism as much charged with the prime element of Radcliffian romance, the mysterious, as any that the ingenuity of the author of The Mysteries of Udolpho could devise. For what can more partake of the mysterious than an antipathy spontaneous and profound such as is evoked in certain exceptional mortals by the mere aspect of some other mortal."

Not only is "the mysterious" a prime element in literary romance, whether Radcliffean or Hawthornean; more to the point, the mystery the narrator calls attention to, "an antipathy spontaneous and profound," is nothing other than a condition of the human heart, whose truth Melville means to represent. Indeed, the general point of this whole chapter, worked out in the later stages of the composition of Billy Budd,[14] is that the mysterious truth of a heart such as Claggart's can be arrived at best by what Melville calls "indirection" (74), by digressions that cast cross lights on shadowy psychological areas, by crafty references to old books, by poetic wonder and inquiry. These are Melvillean developments of the methods of Hawthorne's romance art. In contrast, one is unlikely to find "indirection" in the "realistic" novels fashionable in the 1880s. Such novels are perforce direct in their expositions, since they adhere to "the probable and ordinary course of man's experience." They depend, moreover, on what Melville later in this same chapter calls "knowledge of the world" (74). But, as Melville explains in his disguise as an "honest scholar," "to know the world and to know human nature [may be] two distinct branches of knowledge. . . . In an average man of the world, his constant rubbing with it blunts that finer spiritual insight indispensable to the understanding of the essential in certain exceptional characters, whether evil ones or good. In a matter of some importance I have seen a girl wind an old lawyer about her little finger. Nor was it the dotage of senile love. Nothing of the sort. But he knew law better than he knew the girl's heart. Coke and Blackstone hardly shed so much light into obscure spiritual places as the Hebrew prophets. And who were they? Mostly recluses" (75).

The prophets, then, unlike old lawyers and ordinary novelists, have the wisdom to find their way in the obscure spiritual places of the human heart. These mysteries Melville would also convey, "by indirection" or by any means his latitude allows him. *Billy Budd* is concerned throughout with the necessary mysteriousness of the affections in "exceptional characters," not only Claggart's "mystery of iniquity" (76) — his hatred of Billy — but also the mutual love Billy and Vere feel for each other, their "mystery of magnanimity" as Warner Berthoff calls it.[15] And chapter 11 is an indirect and much labored attempt to justify such romance concerns.

The mystery of the human heart is a theme that links all the principal characters in *Billy Budd*, and for Melville this mystery seems to have been one of his key preoccupations in all the stages of composition except the earliest. It is thus a key subject in the text as a whole that helps bind its disparate parts together. Though the heart cannot be explained systematically and is a sealed book to worldly reason, it may manifest itself spontaneously in moments of crisis, especially in the expression of a man's body or in his unguarded speech. Hence a sympathetic observer may note its manifestations, and conjecturally imagine the inner history of his characters.

Because the heart cannot be known by rational understanding alone, the narrator is habitually cautious in his assertions about what goes on emotionally inside the persons in his story. His syntax is typically conjectural concerning the *Bellipotent*'s sailors' feelings when they echo Billy's blessing of Captain Vere: "And yet . . . Billy alone *must have been* in their hearts, even as in their eyes" (123; my italics); or again concerning Vere's secret career motivations: his "spirit . . . 'spite of its philosophic austerity *may yet have* indulged in the most secret of all passions, ambition" (129; my italics). In Vere's case especially we cannot know what was in his heart; "ambition" may or may not explain certain features of his behavior. The reader, as often, is provoked to puzzle out the mystery in a character.

In key scenes, moreover, Melville suggests the difficulty of knowing his characters not only by hedging his observations syntactically but also by manipulating different modes of narration. Rather than simply telling his story, he makes his narrator's presence obtrusively felt, thereby confirming his own "latitude" as a writer in Hawthorne's school. A signal instance of willfully unusual narration is the scene between Billy and Vere after Billy has been condemned to death by the drumhead court. Melville demands that the reader attend to the conjectural character of his rendering of this exchange of hearts. As the narrator puts it, "what took place at this interview was never known," though "some conjectures may be ventured" (114, 115). After this opening the narrator engages in a virtuoso display of conjectures.

> It would have been in consonance with the spirit of Captain Vere should he on this occasion have concealed nothing from the condemned one. . . . On Billy's side it is not improbable that such a confession would have been received in much the same spirit that prompted it. Not without a sort of joy, indeed, he might have appreciated the brave opinion of him implied in his captain's making such a confidant of him. . . . Captain Vere in end may have developed the passion some-times latent under an exterior stoical or indifferent. He . . . may . . . have caught Billy to his heart, even as Abraham may have caught young Isaac on the brink of resolutely offering him up in obedience to the exacting behest.
> (115)

The double negatives, the unassertive assertions, the stream of subjunctive constructions involving Abraham and Isaac as well as Billy and Vere — all this self-conscious hedging consorts strangely with the simple and power-ful passions enacted in the scene. It is as if the narrator is engaged in thwarting the reader's wish for the direct expression of heightened affection at a climactic moment. But the point of this stylistic ingenuity and indirection is a serious one, which the narrator himself articulates later in the chapter. "There is no telling the sacrament . . . wherever . . . two of great Nature's nobler order embrace. There is privacy at the time" (115). What Hawthorne calls "the inmost Me"[16] remains private. The reader is admonished to remember this even with respect to characters in fiction, for in fiction too one must learn to reverence the heart's magna-nimity in such persons as Billy and Vere.

Through his manipulation of this scene the narrator parades the principle, operative throughout his story, that the deepest spiritual events in the lives of is characters are hidden from an outside observer. "Holy oblivion" (115) covers not only the most heart-felt exchanges between persons, but also the essential changes that go on in a single person. For example, the narrator can only speculate what transpires within Captain Vere while he broods over Claggart's body immediately after Billy's fatal blow: "Captain Vere with one hand covering his face stood to all appearance as impassive as the object at his feet. Was he absorbed in taking in all the bearings of the event . . . ? Slowly he uncovered his face; and the effect was as if the moon emerging from eclipse should reappear with quite another aspect than that which had gone into hiding. The father in him . . . was replaced by the military disciplinarian" (99–100). The narrator evokes Vere's impassive "appearance," and then the transfor-mation of his "aspect," as if to infer the change in him from "the father" to "the military disciplinarian" by interpreting the seeming change in his gestures and features. Moreover, the image by means of which he imagines this change, the moon emerging from eclipse, is quintessentially mysterious. He signals with this image as well as with his questioning, conjecturing style that he guesses the truth about Vere from a distance rather than knowing it from within. In such a scene the truth of the human heart is revealed "by cunning glimpses," to adopt the language of Melville's early review of Hawthorne's *Mosses from an Old Manse*.[17] For just because Melville insists that the heart is a mystery does not mean that one cannot dramatize it. It is a mystery with an ongoing life; and it reveals itself in dramatic and poetic images if not in definitive explanations. Thus a master of the "Art of Telling the Truth"[18] may with luck and industry embody it in an inside narrative.

Often in *Billy Budd*, these images that evoke the heart are images of the human body. Like "The Birthmark" (or *The Scarlet Letter*, or *The House of the Seven Gables*) *Billy Budd* is full of passages in which the heart speaks through the body. Billy's stutter, we recall, is provoked by "strong heart-feeling." But his active goodness of soul also appears in his bodily expression. His face is "lit . . . from within . . . The bonfire in his heart made luminous the rose-tan in his cheek" (77). Later, when Billy lies in irons on the gundeck after the agony of his trial, the narrator observes a change in his face—"the skeleton in the cheekbone at the point of its angle was just beginning delicately to be defined under the warm-tinted skin"—and then comments, "In fervid hearts self-contained, some brief experiences devour our human tissue as secret fire in a ship's hold consumes cotton in the bale" (119). His heart, though spiritual and unknowable, nonetheless shows itself transparently in the wasting away of his physical substance.

Claggart is hardly so transparent a character as Billy. Hypocrite that he is, he habitually conceals the lawless "riot" in his heart beneath a "discreet bearing" (76). Yet his bodily appearance tends to betray him to those less trusting than Billy. In the soup-spilling incident, for example, he wears for the reader and for any messmates who can observe him a "bitter smile, usurping the face from the heart" (73). When he walks away from the mess and is left to his own thoughts the smile becomes a "distorting expression," scaring a drummer-boy who collides with him by chance. The next time we see him he brings his tale of Billy the mutineer to Captain Vere, and Vere immediately suspects him. "Something . . . in [his] aspect . . . provoke[d] vaguely repellent distaste" (91). Then when he accuses Billy before Vere his evil nature is luridly expressed through his eyes, which change color from "rich violet" to "muddy purple," and protrude "like the alien eyes of certain uncatalogued creatures of the deep. The first mesmeristic glance was one of serpent fascination; the last was as the paralyzing lurch of the torpedo fish" (98).

With Claggart as with Billy, then, Melville relies on the body to express the heart, and portrays transformations of character through a painterly display of changing physical images. (Hawthorne likewise uses quick, painterly details as a romancer's shorthand to portray character, for example in "Rappaccini's Daughter" and *The Scarlet Letter*.) Sometimes in *Billy Budd* such images, as in the above passage telling of the changing colors of Claggart's eyes, seem like representations from romance as traditionally understood. For a moment Claggart is an incarnation of evil out of Spenser, multicolored and serpentlike; then he lapses into a torpedo fish, a creature more local to the folklore of Melville's experience as a sailor; before he becomes again the master-at-arms, a man defined more "realistically" through his social role. Billy likewise is often an archetypal figure given interest by the variety of painterly and mythical images with which he is portrayed. Both are characters less "displaced" from romance and myth[19] than Captain Vere, whom Melville conceived later and who appears more thoroughly grounded in his social context. Vere would seem at first a character ill-suited to appear in a romance of any kind. He likes "books treating of actual men and events" and "writers like Montaigne, who . . . honestly and in the spirit of common sense philosophize upon realities" (62). Yet in the story as a whole Vere's essential nature is presented as opaquely and poetically as those of his more "romantic" counterparts.

We have already seen Vere compared to the moon in eclipse and then mysteriously emerging when he seems to decide how he must act toward Billy. In that moment he is "impassive"; like Claggart's, his true feelings are often hidden beneath an official demeanor. Yet sometimes he cannot contain his feelings. He expresses them on occasion in passionate verbal outbursts, for example in the scene when he reacts to the surgeon's confirmation of Claggart's death—"Suddenly, catching the surgeon's arm convulsively, he exclaimed, pointing down to the body, " 'It is the divine judgment on Ananias! Look!' " (100); or in the scene soon afterward before the drumhead court, when he responds to Billy's denial of Claggart's accusation with impulsive agreement—" 'I believe you, my man,' said the witness, his voice indicating a suppressed emotion not otherwise betrayed" (106). Or, more like Billy or Claggart, he occasionally reveals himself not in words but through the particular expression of his body, most graphically and yet enigmatically in the climactic episode of the execution. After Billy blesses him and the crew echoes the blessing, the repressive self-control that Vere imposes on his bearing emerges as a disposition of heart expressed physically. "At the pronounced words and the spontaneous echo that voluminously rebounded them, Captain Vere, either through stoic self-control or a sort of momentary paralysis induced by emotional shock, stood erectly rigid as a musket in the ship-armorer's rack" (123–24). We note the Hawthornean choice of alternative explanations for Vere's rigid bearing. Either he wills this rigidity through self-control, or it results from his being overcome by emotional shock, or some undefined combination of the two. By means of this device Melville, like

Hawthorne, provokes the reader to render his or her own psychological judgment on what is within Captain Vere, thus preserving the text's ambiguous sense of his heart's indeterminacy.

This image of Vere as an enigmatic musket, like the earlier image of Vere's face as the moon in eclipse, suggests that Vere's heart is a mystery like Claggart's or Billy's. Despite his well-defined social pedigree and his abundantly reproduced rational discourse, he remains at key junctures refractory to interpretation. Indeed, in the latest stages of composition Melville seems to have been intent on making Vere still more of a mystery. Late additions in chapters 19 through 21 raise the question, never resolved, of his sanity or insanity in the period after Claggart's death. This question, first attributed to the baffled surgeon, is then adopted by the narrator as his own, with the effect of generalizing Vere's possible malady so that it becomes a potential latent in the human condition: "Who in the rainbow can draw the line where the violet tint ends and the orange tint begins? Distinctly we see the difference of the colors, but where exactly does the one first blendingly enter into the other? So with sanity and insanity" (102). "Some professional experts" may — for a fee — have the effrontery to put doubtful cases of sanity or insanity into definite categories, but these experts, like the lawyers stigmatized in chapter 11, rush in where angels fear to tread. The narrator, in contrast, prefers to keep his distance from such uncertain matters of the heart.

More than Billy or Claggart, Vere is generically mixed as a character. His presence in the story enforces the point that Hawthornean and Melvillean romance is a hybrid. He relishes the actual and the historical as well as appreciating the mysterious. His values are those of common sense as well as of the Bible. He is observed realistically as a socially determined character in a novel, as well as poetically as an enigmatic mediator in an allegory of the heart. Because Vere has both a realistic sense of practical needs and a poetic intuition of human depths, he is the only character who can articulate the problem of the heart's mystery even when his attention is focused on the practical problem of how to maintain military authority. Yet his mixed nature is also tragic. He is forced to make tragic choices between the probable and ordinary course of events as he foresees them and the truth of the human heart as he intuitively perceives it. He chooses not to attend to his intimations of the mysterious insofar as they affect his performance of his duty. This choice, though it goes against the "instincts" (109) of his own heart, is dictated by his fate as an officer of the King. "A " 'mystery of iniquity,' " he says, is "a matter for psychologic theologians to discuss" (108). The malice in Claggart's heart is, with a pun, "hardly material" (107) when a military court must pronounce sentence on a sailor who strikes a master-at-arms. As an instrument of the court, Vere insists that "the heart . . . must here be ruled out" (111) and that the jury must decide the case only on the basis of "the [outward] facts." For this is war and "War looks but to the frontage, the appearance" (112).

By focusing exclusively on the public facts of the case Vere commits himself to an "outside narrative," while his choice causes terrible suffering for his inner man and, one may argue, hastens Billy's tragic death. On the other hand, another choice he makes, to come to Billy with magnanimity of heart in their closeted interview after the judgment of the court, leads to his mysterious expression of affection or peace of mind at the story's end. In another reported, conjectured scene he dies murmuring "Billy Budd, Billy Budd" (129), not with "accents of remorse" but with a feeling no one names. Again, and at the last, the truth of his heart expresses itself in passionate words the reader catches at without benefit of explanation.

In his inside narrative, then, Melville would reveal the truth of the human heart by cunning glimpses into its mysterious tenderness or depravity. Like Hawthorne he means to burrow "into the depths of our common nature"[20] in order to shed light on hidden passions that scarcely show themselves in conventional social intercourse. The better realism of his authentic narrative will perforce be charged with the elements of romance, so that it may be true to the depths of the heart. A merely social or worldly or scientific treatment of men such as Claggart, Billy, and Vere would miss their essence and remain superficial.

A sequence toward the end of the narrative not only reenacts Melville's mockery of mere worldly knowledge with respect to the affairs of the heart, but also shows him adding a flavor of the marvelous to the dish he offers his readers. In his outwardly tactful, yet privately outlandish use of the marvelous he would seem almost to parody Hawthorne's second precept for romance in the *Seven Gables* preface. The texture of moods in the sequence is complex, modulating from the narrator's initial wonder at Billy's spiritual strength to his bemusement at the inability of common-sense men of the world to fathom him. The sequence begins in chapter 25, after Captain Vere is pictured standing "erectly rigid as a musket in the ship-armorer's rack." Then the narrator presents a contrasting image of Billy "ascending" amid "the full rose of the dawn," surrounded by clouds "shot through with a soft glory as of the fleece of the Lamb of God seen in mystical vision." The heightened language prepares the reader for the phenomenal event that follows: "In the pinioned figure arrived at the yard-end, to the wonder of all no motion was apparent, none save that created by the slow roll of the hull in moderate weather, so majestic in a great ship ponderously cannoned" (124). When a moment later the "glorified" clouds vanish, the clear air that remains has a "serenity . . . like smooth white marble" (128). A religious image imposed on the natural setting is thus displaced by an aesthetic one before that too disappears in the texture of ordinary narrative prose. Was the vision of Billy against the rose of the dawn a religious epiphany or a momentary theatrical illusion played out against the blankness of nature? The text vacillates serenely between belief and unbelief in the epiphany. We do not know what happens at death, which is itself a mysterious event in the life of the human heart. Yet Melville apparently wants to leave open the possibility that there may actually be a spiritual presence "out there" that welcomes Billy or that Billy "takes" as he ascends.[21] Even if the impression of Billy's transcendence is an illusion, the poetic awe the narrator expresses may still be a genuine religious emotion, a valid expression of the human will to believe in the spirit when faced with the unknown. The text respects these religious feelings without necessarily endorsing them. Toward the mystery of Billy's death it conveys a stance of reverent agnosticism.

When Billy is hanged, "to the wonder of all" his body betrays no sign of a muscular spasm. This, of course, does not happen in ordinary experience. Normally, a hanged man jerks grotesquely; according to popular folklore at least, he also has an erection. In chapter 26 the purser and the surgeon, two quintessentially average men of the world, discuss this apparent minor miracle. The purser, the more open-minded of the two, strains with English decorousness to find language that will help him understand Billy's state of mind at such a moment; for he is anxious in a confused way to give the event a spiritual rather than a merely mechanical cause. "What testimony to the force lodged in will power" (124), he first exclaims; and after the surgeon dismisses "will power" as an unscientific term the purser asks more meekly, "was the man's death . . . a species of euthanasia?" (125) meaning an easy death free from pain and struggle.[22] "Will power" and "euthanasia," however tentatively used by the purser, are words that describe Billy's inner activity or condition, either his preternatural self-restraint that calms the motions of his body at the hanging, or his utter peace of mind in death, a peace appropriate for one who has blessed his executioner.

The caustic surgeon, however, has no use for this language of the heart. He dismisses the event as unaccountable and negligible; he prefers to go about his business as if it had not happened. He corresponds to the "respectable witness" at the climax of *The Scarlet Letter* who claims never to have seen the letter revealed on Dimmesdale's breast.[23] Like them, he refuses to acknowledge a "ghastly miracle"[24] that symbolizes the secret efforts of a person's will and heart, lest it affect his settled ignorance of man's inner condition. He stands for the modern skeptic in all of us who must be exorcized if we are to read a narrative that focuses on the secret inner life of its characters. In *Billy Budd*, however, his skepticism is a frivolous minority position. The common bluejackets, who represent Hawthorne's "great heart of mankind"[25] in the story, feel instinctively that what happened at Billy's death is somehow miraculous. Their impression of his goodness and innocence is "deepened by the fact that he was gone, and in a measure *mysteriously* gone" (131; my italics).

In his manuscript Melville called the exchange between the purser and the surgeon "a digression"[26] and forcibly wedged it into one of the most affecting scenes he ever wrote, placing it between Billy's hanging and the haunting responsive murmur of the crew a moment later. The effect of this interpolation, so disruptive of a "realistic" illusion, is to remove us from our involvement in the drama and force us to inquire into its meaning, particularly the meaning of "the prodigy of repose in the form suspended in air." As often in Hawthorne, we are drawn away from a "prodigy" — a marvelous event — in order to contemplate it. The purser even provides us with two partially satisfactory alternative explanations for the prodigy (will power and euthanasia), and Melville, in the style of Hawthorne, implicitly invites us to seek for others. By means of his digression Melville promotes a Hawthornean alienation effect in which the reader reflects not only on imperial politics and class divisions but also on the mysterious affections and unspoken struggles of Billy's heart. Finally, another effect of the digression is to call attention to Melville's narrative procedures, to the latitude he enjoys in manipulating his materials. By withdrawing us from the action Melville lets us know, as often in *Billy Budd*, that he exercises the special privilege of the romancer, the privilege of authorial and narrative freedom.

Billy Budd, Sailor, then, not only probes the truth of the heart, not only includes a touch of the marvelous in an otherwise historylike story, but also exhibits the romancer freely playing with his materials in the midst of high drama. This is not the first time Melville follows Hawthorne in claiming "latitude" for the fashions of his fiction. Over and over, both writers play tricks with narrative that Anthony Trollope or William Dean Howells would not allow themselves. They force the reader to focus on the narration as an interest in itself as well as on the story mediated through it, sometimes highlighting the narration at the expense of the story. They exhibit themselves as cake makers, not only because they like to project or stylize their own voices in their fiction — though this *is* a pleasure for them, from "Sights from a Steeple" to *Billy Budd* — but also because they would call attention to the uncertain status of what one can know in fiction. No one knows, for example, what happens in the moment of Billy's execution. Why, in the narrator's cagy language, is "no motion apparent" in "the pinioned figure arrived at the yard-end"? If this "figure" is at peace in its motionlessness, is it still Billy out there, and if so does he beckon to us from the realm of the living or that of the dead?

We are repeatedly made to wonder what we really know in *Billy Budd*. The narrator invites such speculation in his hedging style, his complicating digressions, and his indirect presentation of incidents. Such narrative techniques are suited to one key purpose of this romance: to attract the reader's heartfelt interest to the luminous but mysterious essences of Billy, Claggart, and Vere, and also to keep our wonder labile while we judge or love these phenomenal men. The genial narrator is himself a human mystery. Melville does not allow the reader to get an ideological handle on him — all attempts to give him partisan political convictions, for example, seem to me to diminish the flexibility of his political thinking. (Instead of firm convictions Melville offers intelligent alternatives.) Moreover, Melville makes us question the narrator's existence except as a necessary figment of our readerly imaginations. Once he has told his tale, the narrator moves out of the way and fades into the text in the closing chapters. Melville leaves us not with the narrator's "inside narrative," nor with the false public narrative of Billy's execution in "News from the Mediterranean," but with a poem, "Billy in the Darbies." This ballad, though it displaces the other narratives and presents itself as Billy's own utterance, also is clearly marked as a mediated fiction, the rude fictive utterance of one of Billy's mates on the foretop. It too narrates an imagined sequence of events, not a true history. Its version of events, differing in some details from that of the story proper, is clearly fabulous. Yet the poem is a fiction we can trust for its feeling and tone if not necessarily for its fact. By virtue of its achieved poetic form it moves us closer to what Melville has wanted to approach all along, the truth and mystery of the human heart, in its life and in its bodily death.

Notes

1. Herman Melville, *Billy Budd, Sailor (An Inside Narrative)*, ed. Harrison Hayford and Merton M. Sealts, Jr. (Chicago: University of Chicago Press, 1962), 53. Further references to this edition of *Billy Budd* appear in the text.

2. I agree with Nina Baym that "Hawthorne's distinction between romance and novel . . . was idiosyncratic, his own," and that he meant to supply such a distinction to his own work and not to the rest of American fiction ("The Romance in Hawthorne's America," *Nineteenth-Century Fiction*, 38 [1984]:429–30). This, however, did not keep Melville from paying attention to Hawthorne's *ad hoc* pronouncements. Especially in *The Confidence-Man* and *Billy Budd*, Melville followed Hawthorne in exploring the idea of the romance, though with an awareness that the word "romance" gave a false impression of the things he was attempting.

3. Nathaniel Hawthorne, *The House of the Seven Gables* (Columbus: Ohio State University Press, 1965), 1.

4. Robert Milder, "Melville's Late Poetry and *Billy Budd*: From Nostalgia to Transcendence," *Philological Quarterly* 66 (1987):495.

5. Jay Leyda, ed. *The Melville Log: A Documentary Life of Herman Melville, 1819–1891* (New York: Gordian Press, 1969), 2:803. From excerpts from Julian's several subsequent accounts of his interview with Melville, see *The Melville Log*, 2:782–83.

6. Another piece of evidence that Hawthorne was a key writer as well as a friend for Melville right to the end of his life is the fact that he took the epigraph for *Weeds and Wildings*, the volume of poems he collected after *Timoleon*, from Hawthorne's posthumous *The Dolliver Romance*. The epigraph reads "Youth is the proper, permanent, and genuine condition of mankind." See Lucy M. Freibert, "*Weeds and Wildings*: Herman Melville's Use of the Pastoral Voice," *Essays in Arts and Sciences* 12 (1983):62.

7. *The House of the Seven Gables*, 1.

8. *Emerson in His Journals*, ed. Joel Porte (Cambridge: Harvard University Press, 1982), 356.

9. See *The Letters of Herman Melville*, ed. Merrell R. Davis and William H. Gilman (New Haven: Yale University Press, 1960), 69–72, 150.

10. In *The Confidence-Man*, two of the "authorial" chapters, chapters 14 and 33, seem to me to draw on the preface to *The House of the Seven Gables*. In a passage in chapter 14, the text as printed reads "while to all fiction is allowed some play of invention." In a surviving earlier draft Melville apparently wrote, "while to a fiction is allowed *a certain latitude* of invention," directly echoing Hawthorne (Herman Melville, *The Confidence-Man: His Masquerade*, ed. Elizabeth S. Foster [New York: Hendricks House, 1954], 76, 385; my italics). In chapter 33 the Melvillean narrator's argument for his particular kind of fiction looks like an elaboration of Hawthorne's argument for the romance in the *Seven Gables* preface. It takes as its starting point the supposed objection of ordinary readers to the "unreal" cosmopolitan. The narrator counters that he would appeal to a more open-minded group of readers, who "sit down to a work of amusement tolerantly as they sit at a play. . . . They look that fancy shall evoke scenes different from those of the same old crowd round the custom-house counter. . . . in books of fiction, they look not only for more entertainment, but, at bottom, even for more reality, than real life itself can show. Thus, though they want novelty, they want nature, too; but nature unfettered, exhilarated, in effect transformed," (206–7). The appeal here is similar to Hawthorne's. The narrator would persuade the reader to tolerate authorial latitude ("nature unfettered"), accept the marvelous along with the probable (the unreal cosmopolitan along with the vignettes of American life), and look for a deeper truth than one finds in fiction that only imitates a record of events ("more reality, than real life itself can show"). In addition, the reference to "the same old crowd round the custom-house counter" may well be meant to recall Hawthorne's "Custom-House," thereby surreptitiously acknowledging Hawthorne's influence on the chapter.

Clear evidence that Melville had the *Seven Gables* preface available in his memory during the last years of his career (when he was writing *Billy Budd*) appears in the prefatory remarks to "Rammon," an unfinished prose-and-verse narrative concerned with an alienated son of Solomon and his struggle for belief. In his preface Melville writes:

> In touching upon historical matters the romancer and poet have generously been accorded a certain license, elastic in proportion to the remoteness of the period embraced and consequent incompleteness and incertitude of our knowledge as to events, personages, and dates. It is upon this privilege, assumed for granted, that I have here ventured to proceed.

"A certain license" echoes Hawthorne's "certain latitude," and Melville also seems to recall Hawthorne's "romantic" treatment of history even while introducing a still more remote story of his own devising. Eleanor Tilton assigns a date of 1887–88 to "Rammon," and she views this introductory paragraph as a late addition (Eleanor M. Tilton, "Melville's " 'Rammon': A Text and Commentary," *Harvard Library Bulletin* 13 [1959]:56.

11. See Richard Brodhead, *Hawthorne, Melville and the Novel* (Chicago: University of Chicago Press, 1976), 17–23.

12. Michael Davitt Bell, *The Development of American Romance: The Sacrifice of Relation* (Chicago: University of Chicago Press, 1978), 130.

13. This point has been anticipated in Joel Porte, *The Romance in America: Studies in Cooper, Poe, Hawthorne, Melville, and James* (Middletown: Wesleyan University Press, 1969), 189–91.

14. See the analysis of foliations in Hayford and Sealts's edition, 251–54, and the relevant passages in the Genetic Text, 331–32. The discussion of romance in chapter 11 seems to come from Stage E, the sixth stage in Hayford and Sealts's analysis. It was then partly revised in Stage G, the eighth and penultimate stage. The paragraph in chapter 2 asserting that the story is "no romance" also comes from Stage G, though the reference to "one of Hawthorne's minor tales" is a good deal earlier. (See Hayford and Sealts, 243–44, 297–98.) The upshot is that Melville worked out his play with the idea of "romance" quite late in the

writing of *Billy Budd*. Hence it seems proper to apply the term (or not, as the critic may judge) to the work as a whole.

15. Warner Berthoff, *The Example of Melville* (Princeton: Princeton University Press, 1962), 193.

16. Nathaniel Hawthorne, *The Scarlet Letter* (Columbus: Ohio State University Press, 1962), 4.

17. Herman Melville, "Hawthorne and His Mosses," rpt. in Herman Melville, *Moby-Dick*, ed. Harrison Harford and Hershel Parker (New York: Norton 1967), 542.

18. Melville, "Hawthorne and His Mosses," 542.

19. See Brodhead, *Hawthorne, Melville, and the Novel*, 22.

20. Nathaniel Hawthorne, *The Snow-Image and Uncollected Tales* (Columbus: Ohio State University Press, 1974), 4. From the preface to *The Snow-Image*.

21. Such a possibility is suggested still more explicitly in the earlier version of the epiphany, in which Melville wrote, "Billy ascended; and ascending, took the full shekinah of that grand dawn" (Hayford and Sealts, 412; "shekinah" means "a visible manifestation of the divine presence as described in Jewish theology" [*American Heritage Dictionary*]).

22. Schopenhauer describes euthanasia as "an easy death, not ushered in by disease, and free from all pain and struggle" in his *Counsels and Maxims*, which Melville read in 1891. See Hayford and Sealts, 193.

23. *The Scarlet Letter*, 259. The surgeon's cool verbal dismissal contrasts with the inarticulate passionate response of the crew on beholding Billy, which Hayford and Sealts compare to the "murmur" of the "multitude" following Dimmesdale's death (Hayford and Sealts, 194).

24. *The Scarlet Letter*, 255.

25. *The Scarlet Letter*, 243.

26. Hayford and Sealts, 412.

INDEX